SPACES OF PEACE, SECURITY AND DEVELOPMENT

Series Editors: **John Heathershaw**, University of Exeter, UK, **Shahar Hameiri**, University of Queensland, Australia, **Jana Hönke**, University of Bayreuth, Germany, and **Sara Koopman**, Kent State University, USA

Volumes in this cutting-edge series move away from purely abstract debates about concepts and focus instead on fieldwork-based studies of specific places and peoples to demonstrate how particular spatial histories and geographic configurations can foster or hinder peace, security and development.

Available now

Precarious Urbanism
Displacement, Belonging and the Reconstruction of Somali Cities
By **Jutta Bakonyi** and **Peter Chonka**

Post-Liberal Statebuilding in Central Asia
Imaginaries, Discourses and Practices of Social Ordering
By **Philipp Lottholz**

Doing Fieldwork in Areas of International Intervention
A Guide to Research in Violent and Closed Contexts
Edited by **Berit Bliesemann de Guevara** and **Morten Bøås**

Surviving Everyday Life
The Securityscapes of Threatened People in Kyrgyzstan
Edited by **Marc von Boemcken**, **Nina Bagdasarova**, **Aksana Ismailbekova** and **Conrad Schetter**

Forthcoming

Unarmed Civilian Protection
A New Paradigm for Protection and Human Security
Edited by **Ellen Furnari**, **Randy Janzen** and **Rosemary Kabaki**

Shaping Peacebuilding in Colombia
International Frames and Local Contestations
By **Catalina Montoya Londoño**

For more information about the series and to
find out how to submit a proposal visit
**bristoluniversitypress.co.uk/
spaces-of-peace-security-and-development**

 SPACES OF PEACE, SECURITY AND DEVELOPMENT

Forthcoming

Memory Politics after Mass Violence
Attributing Roles in the Memoryscape
By **Timothy Williams**

Development as Entanglement
An Ethnographic History of Ethiopia's Agrarian Paradox
By **Teferi Abate Adem**

International Advisory Board

Rita Abrahamsen, University of Ottawa, Canada
John Agnew, University of California, Los Angeles, US
Alima Bissenova, Nazarbayev University, Kazakhstan
Annika Björkdahl, Lund University, Sweden
Berit Bliesemann de Guevara, Aberystwyth University, UK
Susanne Buckley-Zistel, Philipps University Marburg, Germany
Toby Carroll, City University of Hong Kong
Mick Dumper, University of Exeter, UK
Azra Hromadžić, Syracuse University, US
Lee Jones, Queen Mary University of London, UK
Louisa Lombard, Yale University, US
Virginie Mamadouh, University of Amsterdam, Netherlands
Nick Megoran, Newcastle University, UK
Markus-Michael Müller, Free University of Berlin, Germany
Daniel Neep, Georgetown University, US
Diana Ojeda, Xavierian University, Colombia
Jenny Peterson, The University of British Columbia, Canada
Madeleine Reeves, The University of Manchester, UK
Conrad Schetter, Bonn International Center for Conflict Studies, Germany
Ricardo Soares de Olivera, University of Oxford, UK
Diana Suhardiman, International Water Management Institute, Laos
Arlene Tickner, Del Rosario University, Colombia
Jacqui True, Monash University, Australia
Sofía Zaragocín, Universidad San Francisco de Quito, Ecuador

For more information about the series and to
find out how to submit a proposal visit
**bristoluniversitypress.co.uk/
spaces-of-peace-security-and-development**

NAVIGATING THE LOCAL

Politics of Peacebuilding in Lebanese Municipalities

Hanna Leonardsson

First published in Great Britain in 2024 by

Bristol University Press
University of Bristol
1-9 Old Park Hill
Bristol
BS2 8BB
UK
t: +44 (0)117 374 6645
e: bup-info@bristol.ac.uk

Details of international sales and distribution partners are available at bristoluniversitypress.co.uk

© Bristol University Press 2024

British Library Cataloguing in Publication Data
A catalogue record for this book is available from the British Library

ISBN 978-1-5292-2426-9 hardcover
ISBN 978-1-5292-2427-6 paperback
ISBN 978-1-5292-2428-3 ePub
ISBN 978-1-5292-2429-0 ePdf

The right of Hanna Leonardsson to be identified as author of this work has been asserted by her in accordance with the Copyright, Designs and Patents Act 1988.

All rights reserved: no part of this publication may be reproduced, stored in a retrieval system, or transmitted in any form or by any means, electronic, mechanical, photocopying, recording, or otherwise without the prior permission of Bristol University Press.

Every reasonable effort has been made to obtain permission to reproduce copyrighted material. If, however, anyone knows of an oversight, please contact the publisher.

The statements and opinions contained within this publication are solely those of the author and not of the University of Bristol or Bristol University Press. The University of Bristol and Bristol University Press disclaim responsibility for any injury to persons or property resulting from any material published in this publication.

Bristol University Press works to counter discrimination on grounds of gender, race, disability, age and sexuality.

Cover design: blu inc, Bristol
Front cover image: Tyre, Lebanon by Hanna Leonardsson

Contents

Acknowledgements		vi
Introduction		1
1	Theorizing Local Peacebuilding	15
2	Lebanese Municipalities, Centralized Peacebuilding and Possibilities for Change	32
3	Service Delivery: Providing for Local Needs	54
4	Local Interactions: Formal and Informal Everyday Interactions	80
5	Vertical Relationships: Connecting the Local to the National and Global	108
Conclusion		134
References		146
Index		162

Acknowledgements

The idea for this book grew from multiple visits to Lebanon, seeing developments on the ground while the news was filled with reports of political stalemate and lack of governance. Getting from idea to book has been an effort over many years and has included the support of numerous persons near and far. The many people who helped me, guided me and cared for me and my loved ones during this time, all share a part in completing this task. To you, I am forever grateful.

And last, but certainly not least, to those of you who shared the story of your municipality with me, your efforts to make me understand the nuances of the Lebanese local space are what made this book possible. Thank you.

Introduction

In post-war contexts, building peace is an obvious, yet troubled task. In contemporary and practical terms, peace is viewed as meaning a world ruled by principle and law, often under the banner of liberal peace, emphasizing democratic values, human rights and market liberalization (Richards, 2005, pp 1–4). However, despite large peacebuilding efforts, the record of peacebuilding is mixed and almost half of all post-conflict countries relapse into conflict within five years (Collier, 2003, p 83; Paris, 2010; Rigual, 2018). Where peace agreements endure, the peace built is frequently centrally controlled, builds on (wartime) elites, reinforces gender roles, lacks local ownership and local legitimacy (Hughes, 2013; Paris and Sisk, 2007, p 3; Rigual, 2018). Lebanon is no stranger to these terms.

While the Lebanese civil war ended in 1989, its post-war developments have included the opening up of political space, economic success and the growth of a Lebanese middle class, a phoenix of coexistence, resilience and joy of life, as well as political stagnation, political assassinations, inter- and intra-state hostilities, fatal political ignorance, massive public protests and economic crisis, to name a few (Harb and Fawaz, 2020; Khalaf, 2012; Majed, 2020; Zahar, 2009). These developments are embedded in Lebanon's political system, which is characterized by sectarian divides. In addition, its geopolitical position triggers internally and externally run developments, conveying both liberal and illiberal agendas. With internal divides and external presures, Lebanon has been described as being in a situation of no war and no peace (Bou Akar, 2018; Burgis-Kasthala and Saouli, 2022; Ghosn and Khoury, 2011; Mac Ginty, 2010b). Despite good intentions, increasing attention and resources directed towards peacebuilding, post-war countries, such as Lebanon, highlight how the peacebuilding agenda has failed to promote a sustainable peace (Mitchell, 2010, p 2; Schneckener, 2016). With the increasing critique against the liberal peacebuilding agenda, a 'local turn in peacebuilding' has emerged (Leonardsson and Rudd, 2015; Mac Ginty and Richmond, 2013). This book is situated at the centre of the local turn debate, empirically exploring local peacebuilding in Lebanon.

The local turn in peacebuilding has its roots in discussions that emerged in the 1990s on the importance of 'the local' for building 'home-grown' peace (Curle, 1994; Lederach, 1997; Nordstrom, 1997; Paffenholz, 2015b). Building on these early works, the local turn in peacebuilding also draws inspiration from debates on participation and decentralized democracy found in development studies (Booth and Cammack, 2013, p 22; Chambers, 1983; Cheema and Rondinelli, 2007b, p 4; Grindle, 2007) as well as post-colonial writings on everyday resistance (Bhabha, 1994; Scott, 1991; Spivak, 1988). With a multitude of influences, the local turn in peacebuilding presents a multitude of responses to current peacebuilding challenges. These responses span along a continuum, on the one hand identified as liberal, orthodox and effective peacebuilding or, on the other hand, post-liberal, critical or emancipatory peacebuilding.[1]

In broad terms, one end of this continuum rests on a liberal peacebuilding logic, where democracy and the rule of law make up the framework for peacebuilding. However, with the flaws of top-down peacebuilding being uncovered, and weak national governments seen as a driver of conflict, some scholars argue for the local implementation of liberal peacebuilding measures to enable greater effectiveness of sub-national governments to build peace (Brinkerhoff, 2011, pp 131–3). These measures give prominence to the inclusion of the local and emphasize closeness to the people and responsiveness to local needs (Hartmann and Crawford, 2008, p 8). For example, such approaches emphasize local participation, proximity of governance and local-level service delivery. In this interpretation, the local turn in peacebuilding feeds well into the ongoing debate among liberal policymakers and peacebuilders in its focus on the role of the individual in a liberalized democracy and economy, making the local a tool for liberal individualism (Hughes et al, 2015, p. 819). Even though such an approach to local peacebuilding may seem like more of the same, localizing liberal peace moves beyond the emphasis on the local as rhetorical and identifies actors and measures for localizing state-building and peacebuilding, and, in essence, peace (Donais, 2012, p 2).

At the more critical end of the continuum of the local turn in peacebuilding, space for local agency to influence peacebuilding is identified as the most important ingredient. Whether liberal or not, this literature argues that peace can never be achieved and sustained if it does not emancipate its subjects from predefined notions of peace. Instead of emphasizing the construction of liberal peace through particular forms of liberal institutions, it stresses the need to leave space for local agency to influence and craft peace on its

---

[1] For discussions of peacebuilding as liberal versus post-liberal, see Debiel and Rinck (2016) and Richmond (2011b). For a discussion of peacebuilding as orthodox versus critical, see Roberts (2011b). And for a discussion of peacebuilding as effective versus emancipatory, see Leonardsson and Rudd (2015).

own terms (Roberts, 2011b, p 421), emphasizing local participation and contestations on the ground. Since the local turn in peacebuilding centres around particularism and local variations, the objective of peacebuilding is to support its subjects rather than define them (Mac Ginty and Richmond, 2013).[2] As such, local critical agency and resistance are given space within peacebuilding, acknowledging that it is a truly localized process where peace finds its legitimacy within its local setting. The emphasis on local legitimacy draws our attention towards the importance of proximity for peacebuilding policies but also policy adaption based on local needs. This highlights how peacebuilding is useful in the local space, thus the function of peacebuilding. However, the local is not regarded as isolated from a bigger whole (Kappler, 2015). Instead, local agencies continuously interact with international peacebuilding agendas, redefining peacebuilding outcomes and creating locally interpreted forms of self-sustaining peace (Mac Ginty, 2010a; Richmond, 2010, 2011a, 2012). Whether this global–local interaction creates new formulations of peace, or merely a hybridization of the liberal peace, it is the space for local agencies to create local variations of peace(s) that enhances peace itself.

The focus on local agency and the changing process of building peace has evolved into new conceptual framings of peace and peacebuilding. Views of peacebuilding as frictional criticize the romanticized picture of the local and the global/local dichotomy, emphasizing the interaction between the two in building peace. As these approaches claim, peacebuilding interventions always occur in relation to locally existing governance structures (Björkdahl and Gusic, 2015; Björkdahl et al, 2016; Kappler, 2013b), contextual power relations (Hameiri et al, 2017) as well as global conflict systems (Millar, 2020). These approaches emphasize the politics of scale as well as the trans-scalarity of peacebuilding (Hameiri et al, 2017; Millar, 2020). Furthermore, conceptualizations of how transformations within peacebuilding occur have prompted more thought on where war and peace take place, providing insights into the dynamics of conflict and processes of peace as situated within, and constitutive of, different spaces and agencies (Björkdahl and Buckley-Zistel, 2016). This has encouraged an emerging spatial turn in peacebuilding that sees processes of transforming post-conflict sites into societies of sustainable peace as occurring through the interlink of the material locality of place and the imagined meaning of a space, in an intertwined and agency driven process of place-making and space-making defining the peace(s) built (Björkdahl and Kappler, 2017; Macaspac and Moore, 2022).

---

[2] In comparison with liberal peacebuilding, which presupposes that subjects individually participate in democratic arenas and the market economy.

As the field has expanded, it has also been subject to increased scrutiny. Rigual (2018) illustrates how the local turn displays an absence of gender perspective, puzzling in relation to its emphasis on emancipation and local realities. According to her, this pertains to the local turn's engagement with solving the flaws of the liberal peace, and thus, simultaneously promoting hybridized (liberal and gender-blind) peacebuilding strategies. The view that local peacebuilding misses the opportunity to provide radical alternatives to current peacebuilding strategies is shared by Bargués-Pedreny and Randazzo (2018) in their argument that hybridizing peacebuilding reasserts the role of the international as an intervener, whose role is either to passively stand by while local agencies build peace, or actively promote hybridized institutions. Randazzo (2016, 2017) further suggests that in a local peacebuilding debate that still emphasizes the 'building' of peace, the local turn is fundamentally tied to the logic of governance, promoting the same understanding of modernity and progress as within the liberal peace (Randazzo, 2017, pp 192, 202). As this critique has surfaced, these authors question how radically different the local turn debate is in its attempt to move the peacebuilding field forward.

Although appreciative of the field of local peacebuilding, Debiel and Rinck (2016), on the other hand, point to the challenges lying ahead for a local turn that has emphasized the dichotomy between the global and the local and promoted a post-liberal peace to challenge the liberal peace. As they argue, the local turn is trapped in a 'methodological reductionism' of empirical studies of the realities on the ground, replacing the top-down and universal approaches to peace found in the liberal agenda with a localism that neglects the broader structures of power and domestic politics. In neglecting the structures of domestic politics, Debiel and Rink argue that the local turn reasserts the international as inevitably liberal, and the local as authentically legitimate, thus promoting an equally one-sided account of peace and peacebuilding. Instead, they argue that research on local peacebuilding needs to bring order and authority back in, focusing on friction and negotiations around building peace, and seeing the local within a particular political order (Debiel and Rinck, 2016, p 247ff). Such critique sets the scene for empirically studying the role of local governments in Lebanese peacebuilding.

While approaches to and critique of the local turn in peacebuilding represent a rough generalization of the field, they illustrate a dilemma within the local peacebuilding debate. On the one hand, the literature presents locally contextualized peacebuilding strategies that say little beyond individual cases and risk becoming insignificant if applied in a different context. On the other hand, the local turn is critiqued for not presenting implementable knowledge in its focus on analytically conceptualizing local acts of agency, presenting analytical frameworks built on concepts such as friction, space and time, and offering few convincing alternatives to peacebuilding practice (Bargués-Pedreny and Randazzo, 2018; Debiel and Rinck, 2016; Millar, 2018; Paris, 2010; Randazzo, 2016). This dilemma captures another critique against the local turn in peacebuilding, namely the detachment between empirical research on local peacebuilding practices and theoretical development (Hughes et al, 2015, p 823; McCandless et al, 2015). This book addresses this gap.

Theoretically, the book identifies three key ideas that capture the scholarly critique towards liberal peacebuilding and the local peacebuilding alternatives proposed. First, as peacebuilding is critiqued for ignoring the local context in the measures it implements, service provision in the local space is put forward as a way to locally ground peace by responding to local needs (see for example Arandel et al, 2015; Krampe, 2016; Roberts, 2011b). Second, as peacebuilding has been argued to alienate the population that lives the peace built, interactions between the local government and its inhabitants are emphasized (see for example Donais, 2012; Jackson, 2013; Kappler, 2012). Third, as peacebuilding tends to be centralized to national elites, interrelations between the local and national or international actors are presented as being important for vertically connecting the local to other levels of peacebuilding (see for example Hancock and Mitchell, 2018; Lederach, 1997; Mitchell and Hancock, 2012). It is from these arguments that the peacebuilding functions of service delivery, local interactions and vertical relationships emerge.

Empirically the book scrutinizes local peacebuilding practices in three Lebanese municipalities: Tyre, Bourj Hammoud and Saida. Analysing local developments through the theoretical lenses of service delivery, local interactions and vertical relationships, the book connects locally contextualized practices to the local peacebuilding debate. While conceptualizations of 'the local' vary within the literature on the local turn in peacebuilding, this book explores local peacebuilding through local governments. Arguing that peace must be locally legitimate and that the state is central to the overall perseverance of peace (Roberts, 2011b; Schneckener, 2016, p 250), the study focuses on local governments that gain legitimacy through local elections and connect the local to the central state through multi-layered governance structures. Analysing Tyre, Bourj Hammoud and Saida through the peacebuilding functions of service delivery, local interactions and vertical relationships, the three represent municipalities large enough to provide functional local governance, characterized by a heterogenous local space but with different sectarian majorities. Adhering to the notion that peace is continuously (re)created through interactions, the study understands local governments as agents, incorporating structures of multi-level governance as well as the agency of actors.

In this book, peacebuilding is defined as 'a range of efforts aimed at political, institutional, social and economic transformations in post-war societies' believed to decrease the risk of violent conflicts and promote development (Björkdahl and Höglund, 2013, p 291). Although not explicitly framed as peacebuilding activities, this understanding enables us to analyse practices that foster state legitimacy, address needs and feelings of insecurity as well as foster trust and positive relationships. Arguing that the foundations of peacebuilding are based in the local, this book analyses waste management and infrastructural developments, as well as local and multi-level governance as issues of relevance for local peacebuilding in Lebanon. While these issues emerged as essential in this study, they represent a temporary snapshot to local peacebuilding in Lebanon. Nevertheless, they illustrate how the peacebuilding functions of service delivery, local interactions and vertical relationships are contextualized into their own variety. Thus, by analysing localized practices of peacebuilding, the book illustrates local peacebuilding as a continuous struggle, performed by multiple actors and their agency in relation to but also going beyond structural forms. In this book, Tyre, Bourj Hammoud and Saida highlight how local governance, local complexities and local agency influence local government practices for peace.

Decentring and increased particularity beyond peacebuilding

While the local turn in peacebuilding is the focus of this book, it has not emerged in a vacuum. Since the 1980s and developments such as globalization and the 'crisis in government' (Rosanvallon, 2011a), modes of governance have found themselves increasingly in need of reform to remain legitimate. In our current world, democratic elections, the will of the majority and an impartial administration no longer provide the basis for legitimate rule because:

> [t]he 'people' are no longer understood as a homogeneous mass but rather as a series of unique histories or a sum of specific situations. Thus, our contemporary societies increasingly understand themselves from the point of view of the minority. (Rosanvallon, 2011b, p 116)

As such, there is an ongoing 'revolution in legitimacy [that] has been an active agent in the global shift of decentring democracy' (Rosanvallon, 2011b, p 118). The paradigm of 'decentring' has been linked to the increasing importance of identity politics and recognition in political life. Surveying the field of political philosophy and discussing emerging challenges for democratic legitimacy, Rosanvallon highlights that attention to particularity has become the hub of political thought, as he claims:

particularity ... has become an essential feature of our discourse about the economy and society. ... What emerges out of this is a new understanding of what is considered legitimate power. In an age defined by the quest for recognition, power is recognized as legitimate if it is attentive to individual situations and makes the language of recognition its own. (Rosanvallon, 2011a, p 179)

From Rosanvallon's perspective, the attention to particularity and the decentring of democracy and legitimacy is as much part of political philosophy as an academic field as it is part of the practicalities of everyday life. As such, it describes a globally changing worldview. In my view, this is also why the move towards the particular has had widespread influence in peacebuilding, which is of interest in this book, but also in academic fields such as democratic theory, governance studies and development studies (Grindle, 2007; Mac Ginty and Richmond, 2013; Rosanvallon, 2011a; Öjendal and Dellnäs, 2013, p 7). The paradigm of decentring democracy fuels increased attention on decentralization, participation and local ownership, as well as the importance of the sub-national as a provider of services and a space for global–local interconnections (Booth and Cammack, 2013; Chambers, 1983; Cheema and Rondinelli, 2007b, p 4ff; Grindle, 2007, p 4ff; Manor, 2007; Öjendal and Dellnäs, 2013, p 6ff).

As the revolution in legitimacy has encouraged more and more decentred democracy, academic writing on post-war legitimacy, key for building peace, has also shifted its focus. While legitimacy, or lack thereof, of external peacebuilding actors in peacebuilding rose as one of the central points for the emerging critique against the liberal peace (Duffield, 2007; Leeuwen et al, 2012; Liden et al, 2009), more recent debate has seen an increased focus on legitimacy as essentially local (Hancock and Mitchell, 2018; Krampe, 2016; Roberts, 2011b; Themnér and Ohlson, 2014).

According to these scholars, internal legitimacy within the post-conflict state becomes the glue that binds the people living in the post-war context to the peace created, enhancing the sustainability of the state's order because, as claimed by Migdal:

legitimacy includes the acceptance of the state's symbolic configuration within which rewards and sanctions are packaged. It indicates people's approval of the state's desired social order through their acceptance of the state's myths. (1988, p 33)

If the people approve the state's social order, the state remains uncontested as the legitimate power, mitigating the risk of conflict. However, the idea of legitimacy as crucial for peace is not new. With the focus on liberal peace, liberal institutions are seen as increasing state legitimacy through democratic elections, which would implement the long since established notion of power emanating from the people (Rosanvallon, 2011a, p 1). However, with the ongoing 'revolution in legitimacy', as claimed by Rosanvallon, the peacebuilding debate has also seen increased attention on local governance structures and local democratic elections to ensure legitimacy (Jackson, 2013; Öjendal and Kim, 2013).

However, with the increased attention to particularity, the attainment of legitimacy is changing, also in peacebuilding literature. What Roberts (2011b), Themnér and Ohlson (2014) and Krampe (2016) emphasize is that legitimacy is not attained through (liberal) institutional structures but through that which is locally defined. What such a focus on legitimacy, or acceptance, of the peace created implies is that it moves beyond institutional structures towards an agency-oriented approach. In focusing on the people who live the peace created, Roberts emphasizes that the everyday priorities of the population must take centre stage in building peace. This does not imply that the state does not matter for the inhabitants, or that it should be dismantled, but as he claims, 'To connect citizenry to the state, public preferences must be fulfilled by the latter' (Roberts, 2011b, p 417). Whether these everyday priorities include access to water, electricity, sanitation, elections or transitional justice is to be defined by each post-conflict context in order to build a locally legitimate peace (Roberts, 2011b). Emphasizing a locally legitimate peace and the everyday priorities that need to be part of that peace in order for it to become legitimate also highlights that peacebuilding performs a function, rather than builds a particular form of peace (Roberts, 2011b).

Exploring 'the local' in peacebuilding

With the increased attention on particularity and evolvement of a local turn in peacebuilding, the local is 'enjoying that particular phase in the life of concepts when it is beloved both by theorists and practitioners alike' (Hughes et al, 2015, p 817). However, as we will see, what the local means greatly varies. Conceptualizations of the local range from using the local as a fixed spatial unit of small scale, to a fluid network of actors and actions (Lambek, 2011). In short, one could describe the conceptualizations as varying along a continuum, where one key aspect is seeing the local as a bounded unit or as agency of actors. The spectrum of definitions allows for varying interpretations of 'the local' in peacebuilding emphasizing institutions or expressions of local agency. Stressing that it is a continuum, I present the two extreme positions and then tease out how this influences the understanding of the local in this book.

At one end of the spectrum, the local is defined as a bounded unit of small scale. It may be a geographical space, level of government or institution. The spatial local has fixed boundaries and as such is placed next to other locals and opposed to the global. In opposition to the global and universal, the local has also been interpreted as the particular. However, in approaches towards the local as spatial, and as a response to modernity and globalization, the particularities of small-scale locals have been downplayed in favour of increased emphasis on equality between the different spatial locals, which allows us to refer to them as the same (Lambek, 2011). Sometimes this spatial, sub-national local is referred to as locality/localities or locale/locales, but for most research and policy work that refers to the local as spatial, such differentiation is rare. In the peacebuilding agenda, tendencies of viewing the local as a unit of small scale can be seen in the increasing emphasis on local democracy and local governments (see for example Jackson, 2013; Sisk and Risley, 2005a; United Nations, 2012; World Bank, 2011). Because it is a unit of smaller scale than the national, local democratic arenas are seen as closer, more accessible, attentive and encouraging greater participation of the people, all essential features of a legitimate state. As such, local governments can be vital for peace agreements (Donais, 2012, p 53; Jackson, 2013, p 354; Sisk and Risley, 2005a, p 37). In this view, to strengthen the local is largely a tool for achieving the outcomes of legitimacy and preventing war. Local governments are often thought to have limited agency; instead, it is their institutional design and formal requirements that are emphasized with 'given' answers to local questions (Donais, 2012, p 145; Sisk, 2009).

At the other end of the spectrum, we find notions of a local that has no physical boundaries. Instead of the local being spatial or institutional units void of agency, the local is defined by agency and actions. The local is de-territorialized and created through human activity, which inhabits a place and as such is an abstract space (Lambek, 2011, p 206; Mac Ginty, 2015). This conceptualization of the local acknowledges mobility, across spaces and across ideas, but denies that the local 'is just there'. The local is constituted as much by the activities of people inhabiting a space as by activities of mutual understanding across space, which, for example, enables the notion of diaspora as local. The local is created by doing and being, by people inhabiting a space, leaving and returning. Thus, the local is formed through actions that engage people and which are understood as internal, even if they may be apparently global (see also Kappler, 2015; Lambek, 2011, p 216). Often, this understanding of the local assumes a romanticized picture of the legitimate local, a local also claimed to be excluded from the peacebuilding agenda. This excluded local, in turn, is a powerful justification for resistance against international (liberal) peacebuilding interventions (Hughes et al, 2015, p 819). However, if the local is understood as practices and actions played out through the agency of actors, such actors may as well belong to local elites with peaceful, or non-peaceful, agendas questioning the romanticized picture and uncritical inclusion of the local (Kappler, 2015; Paffenholz, 2015b; Simangan, 2017).

Within the conceptualization of the local as actions, several terms appear in the peacebuilding literature to illustrate ideas of what the local is or what it does: the subaltern – stemming from postcolonial thinking about those unheard by the hegemon power (Spivak, 1988); local agency – depicting small-scale mobilization of (sometimes, subaltern) agency with the power to shape formal and informal institutions over a longer period of time (Mac Ginty and Richmond, 2013); and everyday life – referring to the multiple ways in which people make use of space and social or political organizations of the society in which they live to manage their existence (de Certeau, 1988, p xiii; Roberts, 2011b, p 411f). In addition, local agency may form a local-local, referring to a unique or indigenous local, sometimes impossible to understand within the liberal or neoliberal rationale of peacebuilding (Debiel and Rinck, 2016, p 248f; Mac Ginty and Richmond, 2013, p 774).

As conceptualization of the local greatly differs, the divergence of what local to include or exclude also defines how local peacebuilding is performed. Through its technocratic approach to peacebuilding, the liberal peacebuilding agenda dismisses everyday practices and local agency in general, but the local-local, in particular, for its inability to fit within formal institutions and liberal peacebuilding measures. Critical peacebuilding scholars see the inability to include a local, which is based on the everyday practices that enable people to survive in their local context, as one of the main explanations for peacebuilding projects being seen as illegitimate by the local population and, thus, being prone to failure (Roberts, 2011b, p 414). Instead of seeing peacebuilding as a toolbox offering suggestions towards which local to include, the perception of the local as shaped by actions argues that peacebuilding must also be shaped by everyday life. When actors involved in building peace also change the norms, institutions and activities of peacebuilding, it is referred to as hybridization and the creation of a hybrid peace (Richmond and Mitchell, 2012, pp 1, 7f). Then, hybridity is what peacebuilding becomes when one idea of peacebuilding is confronted by the everyday life of post-conflict societies. These notions of the local, the everyday and hybridity in peacebuilding are commonly framed within notions of post-liberal peacebuilding, which questions linearity and universal applicability of concepts (Debiel and Rinck, 2016, p 245).

The vast variety of possible conceptualizations of the local allows us to study a great number of actors and activities when researching local peacebuilding. The meaning of the local differs depending on whether we perceive it as a territory or actions, with implications for peacebuilding. In this book, the local government is the key actor. The local government is defined by its geographical space, because the municipality has territorial boundaries as well as boundaries of authority that define its tasks and obligations. However, I do not conceptualize the local government (or municipality) as solely limited by those boundaries, as actors within the municipality can perform actions and express agency. In this, I build on the argument presented by Björkdahl and Kappler (2017) that material place and imaginary space[3] are mutually constitutive; therefore, both are important for peacebuilding.

As such, my understanding of local government includes an understanding of a bounded local, seeing the local government as an elected sub-national authority, with fixed financial duties, in terms of managing budgets and collecting taxes, as well as administrative responsibilities ranging from, for example, waste management and road maintenance to education and public health (Grindle, 2007, p 4ff). In this understanding, local governments gain legitimacy through local elections and improved local governance through proximity (Cheema and Rondinelli, 2007b; Grindle, 2007, p 4ff). Nevertheless, in practice, local governments can have great responsibility and capacity, or be puppets in strongly centralized states (Cheema and Rondinelli, 2007a; Romeo, 2013, p 78). In addition, local governments are not void of agency; rather, local government officials inhabiting them are actors. These actors, for example elected local officials or municipal employees, have agency and shape local government activities in relation to institutionalized structures as well as other interested parties. As such, my conceptualization of local government incorporates an agency-oriented approach (Mac Ginty and Richmond, 2013, p 770; Themnér and Ohlson, 2014). Therefore, the local government is not only a bounded space that represents the central state, but it is also part of a local space where different actors interact and interests play out in relation to the local place. As such, in what I call the 'local space' throughout the book, actions performed through, for example, international interventions, national and sub-national elite capture, legal and customary structures, local stakeholders and everyday life of the population intertwine and relate to the material place (see Paffenholz, 2013, 2015b, 2016). As such, the local government interconnects a bounded territory with the local agency performed. Nevertheless, studying the local through local governments implies studying only part of the existing local expressions of agency. In particular, the actions performed by local government officials represent actions carried out by local powerholders. For example, the local, in this study, is not assessed through 'the people' or 'the subaltern', as this would require its own conceptualization and could potentially provide another view of local peacebuilding. As such, although spatially closer to the everyday lives of the population, local government actions should not be perceived

---

[3] In Björkdahl and Kappler's conceptualization, place is the material locality and physical presence of a territory, whereas space is the imaginary counterpart and the idea of a place (Björkdahl and Kappler, 2017).

as 'the local' by default, but one conceptualization of it. Nevertheless, as locally elected units, local governments do represent what local governance becomes in the Lebanese system of multi-level governance. In addition, the local government is a locus of agencies that offers the potential for locally grounded peacebuilding, while not forgetting that this particular local is a politicized unit of a bigger whole.

By conceptualizing local governments as interconnecting a bounded local and local agency, the study also acknowledges that the state is central to the perseverance of peace. Within the paradigm of decentring, local levels of the state are key in incorporating the particularities of local spaces into (local) state policies, recognizing the broader structures of power and domestic politics at play for legitimizing peacebuilding. Thus, this book argues that there is a need to study local governments, because ignoring the local state in territories where it is present can be detrimental for research as well as peacebuilding goals (Schneckener, 2016, p 250).

A note on methodology

The book builds on interviews with municipal councillors, municipal and state employees, and civil society actors in Bourj Hammoud, Tyre and Saida during 2014 and 2015. The three municipalities capture Lebanon's sectarian diversity and local government potential. Tyre in the Lebanese south has a population that is mainly Shia Muslim with a Christian minority. Bourj Hammoud is a densely populated Beiruti suburb with an Armenian majority and Shia Muslim and Christian minorities. Saida, located between Tyre and Beirut, is a Sunni Muslim town with both Christian and Shia Muslim minorities. Analysing local perceptions and practices of service-delivery, local interactions and vertical relationships in the three municipalities, the empirical chapters emphasize that if we are to understand local peacebuilding, we need to underline how local peacebuilding processes are practised rather than what measures to implement. Adhering to a constructivist approach to research, the book acknowledges the importance of empirical interpretations and the creation of meaning within a particular context in relation to local peacebuilding functions. As such, the book provides knowledge of the everyday reality that surrounds peacebuilding as well as what the interaction between peacebuilding and the local space creates and implies for peace(s). This further emphasizes the importance of local variations and contextual interpretations of peace and peacebuilding.

Outline of the book

Chapter 1 builds and elaborates on the theoretical approach used in the subsequent chapters to analyse the role of Lebanese municipalities in local peacebuilding. The chapter discusses local service delivery, arguing that providing for local needs is central to local legitimacy, which essentially promotes stability and peace. It discusses local interactions, crucial to ground peace in the everyday lives of the population, which make peacebuilding relevant for the population. And it discusses vertical relationships, emphasizing that they matter for peace because they enable other developments, which, in turn, mitigate conflict. Finally, the chapter draws the three peacebuilding functions together arguing that although they are individual functions, none of the three functions stand on their own in building local peace. Chapter 2 examines local governance in Lebanon in relation to Lebanese conflicts and peacebuilding. It discusses past and present developments and their repercussions to enlighten the reader of Lebanese dividing lines, modes of governance and current challenges. In addition, the chapter frames Lebanon and Lebanese municipalities within the local peacebuilding debate, illustrating how a particular regional approach to peacebuilding coexists with Western liberal intervention and a growing interest in municipalities as recipients of aid.

The three consecutive chapters flesh out the empirical findings of the book. Chapter 3, 'Service Delivery: Providing for Local Needs', analyses local governments as service providers in their local setting. The chapter discusses service delivery of waste management and infrastructural developments across all three cases, as well as services provided in relation to the everyday needs of the population. Chapter 4, 'Local Interactions: Formal and Informal Everyday Interactions', discusses local interactions through the constellation of the municipal council, daily interactions with the municipality as the local authority as well as interactions for service delivery. Chapter 5, 'Vertical Relationships: Connecting the Local to the National and Global', analyses relationships between the municipality and national or international actors. In Tyre, Bourj Hammoud and Saida, vertical relationships are discussed within Lebanese multi-level governance and its connections to international actors, and illustrated by tangible local development projects such as infrastructural developments and waste management.

The Conclusion brings together the argument of service-delivery, local interactions and vertical relationships as peacebuilding functions and local governments as actors in long-term local peacebuilding. Picking up on the particularities in the three municipalities, the chapter argues that the municipalities of Tyre, Bourj Hammoud and Saida play different roles and promote different types of peace(s). Tyre, through its close collaboration with national and international actors for local developments, grounds externally decided peacebuilding practices but does not autonomously drive local development. Bourj Hammoud, closely connected to the Armenian local majority, and a representative of the Armenian national minority, is a central actor for local peacebuilding for the Armenian community, while a marginal actor for other local communities. Saida works closely with national and international actors and successfully promotes local peacebuilding through these relationships. However, through its focus on visible projects such as the waste management plant and infrastructural development, Saida is a partial actor in local peacebuilding, demonstrating its engineering skills but leaving social needs to other actors. Through an empirical exploration of local peacebuilding arguments in Lebanese municipalities, the book concludes that while municipalities have a role to play, their role is particular in each case. As this book shows, local government involvement is always contextual and political, performed through structures, activities and relationships, producing particular types of peace(s) on the ground.

1

Theorizing Local Peacebuilding

In this chapter I elaborate on local service delivery, local interactions and vertical relationships and build an analytical framework for studying the role of local governments in local peacebuilding. The chapter is concerned with the notion that liberal peacebuilding has neglected local needs, alienated the population and centralized peacebuilding (Chandler, 2017; Debiel et al, 2016) and that local and decentralized approaches are a locus for legitimacy and locally relevant peace. As such, the chapter discusses local service delivery, arguing that providing for local needs is central to local legitimacy, which essentially promotes stability and peace. It discusses local interactions, crucial to ground peace in the everyday lives of the population, which make peacebuilding relevant for the population. And, it discusses vertical relationships, emphasizing that they matter for peace because they enable other developments, which, in turn, mitigate conflict.

In this book, peacebuilding entails 'a range of efforts aimed at political, institutional, social, and economic transformations in post-war societies engaging a variety of actors ... to reduce the risk of overt violent conflict and to pave the way for durable peace and development' (Björkdahl and Höglund, 2013, p 291). This definition of peacebuilding is intentionally broad to incorporate the interconnectedness between issues that adhere to the fields of security as well as development (Stern and Öjendal, 2010) through a broad range of activities aimed at transforming society. These activities may, or may not, directly aim at preventing violence, and may produce expected and unexpected as well as counterproductive results. This is also at the heart of understanding service delivery, local inclusion and vertical relationships as peacebuilding functions, emphasizing how they perform rather than what form they take. Service delivery, local interactions and vertical relationships may seem mundane at first glance but are indeed relevant to everyday understandings of peacebuilding, through practices, performance and local expectations. This highlights the non-linearity of peacebuilding situated within local understandings of context, institutions and legitimacy, performed through politics.

Service delivery, local interactions and vertical relationships capture core ideas in the effective and emancipatory local peacebuilding debate (see Donais, 2012; Hancock and Mitchell, 2018; Lederach, 1997; Lemay-Hébert, 2019; Leonardsson and Rudd, 2015; Mcloughlin, 2015, 2019; Mitchell and Hancock, 2012). Of course, as a heterogenous scholarly debate, the literature expresses its central concerns through different terms. Such terms include local agency, participation, inclusion, global–local interrelations, multi-level governance, leadership, resource allocation or needs-based approaches. While these terms capture different nuances of local peacebuilding, they tend to lean towards different sides of the emancipatory versus effective local peacebuilding debate. Or formulated differently, engaging with critical or problem-solving approaches to peacebuilding. The peacebuilding functions analysed in this book (service delivery, local interactions and vertical relationships) incorporate ideas found in effective as well as emancipatory approaches to local peacebuilding. As such, the peacebuilding functions bridge the gap between critical and problem-solving research, capturing an empirically grounded analysis of local peacebuilding and potentially moving the field beyond romanticizing the local or localizing the same peacebuilding measures.

In addition, service delivery, local interactions and vertical relationships answer to the often-cited critique of liberal peacebuilding flaws (see Table 1.1). As the liberal peacebuilding agenda has been critiqued for lacking knowledge of the local, and even neglecting the local, peacebuilding is claimed to create

Table 1.1: Liberal peacebuilding flaws addressed by the local turn in peacebuilding and three functions

Liberal peacebuilding flaws	Consequence of liberal peacebuilding flaws	Approaches in local turn literature	Local government function studied
Lack of knowledge of the local	Dissatisfaction with the post-conflict state	Responsiveness to local needs	Local service delivery
Neglect of the local	Adding to grievances		
Alienation of the population living the peace built	Elitist peacebuilding approaches Lack of legitimacy	Participation in local governance Space for local agency in peacebuilding	Local interaction
Centralized Peacebuilding	Locally irrelevant peacebuilding policies	Space to locally define, redefine or promote peacebuilding policies	Vertical relationships

dissatisfaction with the post-conflict state, adding to grievances rather than mitigating them. As such, the local turn in peacebuilding has emphasized a need for peacebuilding to be responsive to local needs. In this book, the function of service delivery, particularly service delivery through local governments, addresses this critique (Hartmann and Crawford, 2008, pp 8, 250; Brinkerhoff, 2011, p 142f; Bland, 2007, p 208f; Romeo, 2013, p 67f).

Furthermore, the liberal peacebuilding agenda is criticized for alienating the population living the peace built. Peacebuilding is therefore seen as emphasizing elitist peacebuilding approaches that suffer from a lack of popular legitimacy. As a response, literature on local peacebuilding claims that participation in local governance as well as space for local agency in peacebuilding are key. In this book, the function of local interaction addresses this critique (Donais, 2012, p 54f; Bland, 2007, p 208f; Jackson, 2013, p 354f; Brinkerhoff, 2011, p 139; Schou and Haug, 2005, p 29).

Finally, liberal peacebuilding is often questioned for being centralized and creating peacebuilding policies that are irrelevant in the local space. Accordingly, the local turn in peacebuilding has claimed the need to leave space to locally define, redefine and promote peacebuilding policies. However, locally defined policies continiously interact with the overarching peacebuilding agenda, to form locally relevant peacebuilding policies. In this book, the function of vertical relationships addresses the need for interactions between local, national and international actors for local peacebuilding (Mitchell and Hancock, 2012, p 2ff; Jackson, 2013, p 354f; Lederach, 1997, pp 41–3; Leonardsson, 2011, p 104f).

In the rest of this chapter, I discuss the peacebuilding functions of service delivery, local interactions and vertical relationships. Having discussed the nuances and possible pitfalls of the peacebuilding functions separately, I then outline how the three functions guide the analysis of local governments as peacebuilding actors. This section highlights the theoretical arguments on how service delivery, local interactions and vertical relationships are assumed to promote peace, emphasizing the analytical construction of the three peacebuilding functions that are at the centre of the empirical exploration of local peacebuilding in Lebanon.

Service delivery

Service delivery as a peacebuilding function draws on the perception that the provision of services strengthens the state through meeting the communities' essential needs, which, in turn, changes the communities' perception of the state. The importance of service delivery is emphasized by scholars who focus on peacebuilding as state-building, with functional institutions delivering services to the public as a basis for state legitimacy. It is argued that when needs are met, people mobilize behind the state, creating a ground for acceptance of tax collection and state policies, which hinders contestation of state agencies and political leadership (Krampe, 2016, pp 53f, 57; Lemay-Hébert, 2009, p 24; Mcloughlin, 2015, p 345; Paris and Sisk, 2009). These ideas echo the notion of peacebuilding as state-building. However, in emancipatory approaches to peacebuilding, the meeting of needs is also considered important. As argued by Roberts (2011b), it is only when peacebuilding takes the locally determined priorities of the everyday into account that peace can be considered legitimate (Mac Ginty, 2013; Mitchell, 2011). Therefore, service deliveries that respond to local needs are key to a locally legitimate and sustainable peace.

However, the relation between service delivery and peace is complex. Research has shown that expectations on and perceptions of services delivered impact the legitimizing capacity of service provision. This includes perceptions of the service itself as well as perceptions of who delivers it. As such, previous experiences, current satisfaction as well as feelings of equal access in comparison to other regions matter (Brinkerhoff et al, 2012). In addition, even if communities benefit from service delivery, if they do not perceive projects as run and financed by state actors, the services provided may still not legitimate the state or, for that matter, change conflict into peace (Krampe, 2016). Therefore, state recognition matters, especially in settings where the state may be perceived as harmful due to past conflicts. However, if the state is missing in the everyday lives of the population, making the state known to the population is a first step in order to commence a process of a positive experience of the state and legitimization through services (Bachmann and Schouten, 2018, p 2; Brinkerhoff et al, 2012, p 279). However, who delivers and who gets attribution is not straightforward. In post-conflict settings state and non-state service provision commonly operate in parallel. Whether such service provision leads to more or less state legitimization is conditional upon the political environment of each context (McLoughlin, 2019). This emphasizes the fact that the way services are delivered matters more than that they are delivered (Bachmann and Schouten, 2018, p 13f), and that there is no blueprint to service delivery. Thus, while service provision is both an everyday manifestation of the social contract, and vital to securing peoples livelihoods and wellbeing, 'the potential for service delivery to enhance state legitimacy depends on the normative value of different services in specific contexts' (Mcloughlin, 2015, p 351f, 2019).

In local peacebuilding approaches, the emphasis on local-level legitimation of the state rests on the idea that local governments exist closer to the population and are therefore better able to cater to the population's needs. Theoretically, localizing service delivery through local governments that regularly interact with the population has better potential for legitimacy gains (Mcloughlin, 2015). However, previous studies of service delivery through informal local governance have also shown this link. These studies suggest that the recognized provider of services gains legitimacy, even if formal institutional structures do not exist, and informal service providers become the locus of legitimacy (Krampe, 2016; Menkhaus, 2006). Thus, as local service delivery is of importance, so too is who provides services in the local space.

How or why local service delivery is beneficial for peace is highly contextual and somewhat of an ideal. However, by bringing together the literature on service provision as a mechanism for peacebuilding, four key notions can be distinguished. First, local service delivery holds peacebuilding potential by delivering services that are responsive. Through its proximity to the users, service delivery at the local level allows for the tailoring of services delivered to specific local needs. As such, local service delivery holds greater potential for being responsive in what, as well as how, services are provided (Brinkerhoff, 2011, p 142f). Services that are responsive in nature then have greater ability to create a needs-based and locally legitimate peace (Roberts, 2011b). Second, knowing the local needs includes hearing the needs of communities that may be a minority in a larger constituency, such as at a national level, but are more prominently present at a local one. Therefore, service provision at the local level may compensate for national unresponsiveness to minority needs, emphasizing the necessity for inclusiveness of local service delivery (Brinkerhoff, 2011, p 142f). When such tailored and needs-based services are provided, ideally in an efficient manner, the theoretical argument then claims that service delivery is key for making the population believe in the local authority, thus making local government legitimate in the eyes of the people. A legitimate (local and/or central) state, would, in turn, counter the conflict driver of public dissatisfaction, fuelling opposition and the public's will to take up arms (Bland, 2007, p 208f; Brinkerhoff, 2011). Third, within this theorized ideal, proponents argue that local service delivery is an opportunity for local governments to focus on local developmental needs. Through service delivery of, for example, infrastructural developments, water and electricity provision or enhancing spaces for increased tourism, locally tailored services are seen as able to improve people's livelihoods and economic opportunities (Bachmann and Schouten, 2018; Brinkerhoff et al, 2012; Causevic and Lynch, 2011; Jackson, 2013, p 355; Krampe, 2016). Although there is little evidence on the link between reduced poverty and conflict mitigation, it is widely believed that a local government that is able to stimulate economic development and, perhaps more importantly, promote the image of themselves as enablers of economic development (Brinkerhoff et al, 2012) increases the legitimacy of the local state (Bland, 2007, p 208f; Brinkerhoff, 2011; Hartmann and Crawford, 2008, pp 8, 250). Again, this claim draws on a positive image of the local state achieved by delivering what is important for local needs.

Finally, local government service delivery highlights the need for viable local governance. The possibility of local governments to promote development and redistribute resources rests on the assumption that they have autonomy and capacities, meaning a combination of the power to take initiatives as well as freedom from control by others (Romeo, 2013, p 67f). Autonomous local governments are crucial but are not possible to achieve without a genuine will from central leaders and authorities to implement decentralization. This combines local room for manoeuvre with local responsibilities and available resources for local governments to work for service delivery and economic development (Cheema and Rondinelli, 2007a, p 9f; Hameiri et al, 2017). This emphasizes the contextual differences that may exist in local government service delivery. If local governments are granted local autonomy, they can play a significant role in assessing local needs and coming up with solutions, enhancing cooperation between international, national and local actors, mobilizing and combining local resources, as well as generating additional support for national development strategies. Whenever local governments lack autonomy, even the implementation of national development plans at a local level risks missing important opportunities for change, and hinders local initiatives for better service delivery. The degree of autonomy enjoyed by the local governments, therefore, directly affects the change that local governments can promote (Romeo, 2013, pp 67, 70–3).

Local interactions

From studies of peace agreements to locally grounded peacebuilding processes, empirical research suggests that the inclusion of actors beyond national elites or governmental actors is beneficial for sustaining peace. Some of these studies argue that the inclusion of civil society actors in peace negotiations makes peace more legitimate and increases its sustainability (John and Kew, 2008; Nilsson, 2012; Zanker, 2014). Other studies claim that through inclusion from the start, civil society is given a role as active agents in the process of building peace (Paffenholz, 2010). Researchers have widely recognized the participation of women as peace negotiators and peacebuilders, arguing that women often promote an understanding of peace that is locally relevant to everyday needs (Gizelis, 2011; Moosa et al, 2013). In some studies, the significance of including the voices of minority groups is emphasized (Schou, 2014), while others emphasize the need to include young men as a particular category in order to prevent armed mobilization (Kent and Barnett, 2012). In addition, the focus on participation and inclusion of local actors through a focus on the everyday is an expanding field (to name a few: Kappler, 2013a; Kappler and Richmond, 2011; Pogodda et al, 2014). In this book, interactions between the local government and the wide variety of local actors have been termed 'local interactions', and include interactions that occur between the municipality and the people and agents who live and/or act within its constituency.

Despite the plethora of academic pieces on the relevant local actors to be included, previous studies also emphasize that 'the mere presence of more actors is not sufficient' (Paffenholz, 2015a, p 85). As such, the appropriation of women's representation in peacebuilding projects has been argued to increase visibility but does little to counter existing gender roles (Hudson, 2012). Furthermore, international actors' engagement in civil society is said to rather reproduce existing power structures than create space for a locally relevant peace (Kappler and Richmond, 2011; Leino and Puumala, 2020). With this in mind, I highlight meaningful inclusion for establishing a process that strengthens political structures for peace (Paffenholz, 2015a, p 85). It is also in line with this thinking that I use the term local interactions to name the peacebuilding function, emphasizing that both participation and influence are part of the whole.

In peacebuilding contexts, increased participation is seen to overcome one of the key problems with post-conflict reconstruction, namely that 'state-level processes remain inaccessible to the vast majority of the population' (Donais, 2012, p 53). Within debates on peacebuilding, the inability of national and international peacebuilding actors to promote democracy and peace has been emphasized, and with it, the focus on local governments' peacebuilding potential increased. This echoes the emphasis on particularity, decentring legitimacy and the local. Through a bottom-up approach, local governments are said to enhance participation and citizen engagement by dealing with issues closer to people's everyday lives, providing better opportunities for local agencies to engage with political elites and to demand accountability, as well as promoting more stable grounds for locally owned peace (Donais, 2012, p 54f). In this sense, it is the proximity of local governments to the population that underpins their peacebuilding potential, providing arenas for local interaction.

By bringing the state closer to the people, sub-national governments provide possibilities for interaction between citizens and the local state. As argued by Bland, this impedes the re-emergence of authoritarian regimes because local state institutions break up the central state's power base and weaken national conflicts by moving the resolution of issues to a local space (Bland, 2007, p 208). In addition, Brinkerhoff (2011) and Brancati (2006) argue that multiple and more localized arenas of state authority enable increased political contestation over resources, where minorities have greater possibilities to influence and address their needs. This possibility to influence the responsiveness of local governments towards local needs is an important element in mitigating conflict, as it counteracts feelings of social exclusion, commonly expressed by minorities that cannot make their voice heard in a national context.

However, what participation, making one's voice heard and thus exercising influence over local government policy means has been debated. Previous research has shown that participating and exercising agency does not necessarily mean resisting existing power structures or ways of life. Whereas agency is commonly perceived as a tool for emancipation, Mahmood and Horst have shown how agents can also choose to use their agency to re-emphasize existing power structures and submission (Horst, 2017; Mahmood, 2001, 2011). As such, even if local interactions assumedly allow for the expression of local needs and contestation of political elites, attention must be paid to how these interactions play out in relation to the power structures at hand.

In addition to allowing for participation and influence, the peacebuilding function of local interactions incorporates the idea of a local government able to influence the local population, particularly through fostering feelings of inclusion, motivation, hope or, to some extent, even happiness (Jackson, 2013, p 354f). Increased opportunities for participation are important in this respect as, it is argued, involvement will build trust between groups that are invited to participate in local institutions (Schou and Haug, 2005, p 29), foster inclusion and citizens' access to authorities as well as allow for the resolution of conflicts through discussion and compromise (Bland, 2007, p 208f).

Propagators of participatory democracy, not only in post-conflict settings, often put forward the idea that participation fosters trust, understanding and consensus. Then, participation is seen as a complement to representative democracy, where meetings, hearings, surveys as well as more direct forms of citizen initiatives, referendums and citizen juries are proposed (Bevir, 2009, p 146f). In the peacebuilding literature, some scholars adhere to the possibility of improving participation through local democratic arenas, arguing that '[m]unicipal councils, as collective decision-making bodies, lend themselves to inclusion and consensus-oriented problem solving' (Sisk and Risley, 2005b, p 37), which counteracts the inaccessibility of the national government and national peacebuilding policies. Inclusion in this sense is often created through the division of seats between different constituent groups (Sisk and Risley, 2005b, p 11), with local governments providing a good choice for including citizens' voices and agency in political processes (Donais, 2012, p 54).

However, as noted previously in relation to inclusion and participation, how practices of interactions play out in local democratic arenas varies between spaces as well as with varying results for the different actors involved. As claimed by Horst (2017), inclusion of the local is rarely straightforward or applicable across the board. Instead, there is a need to contextually understand the workings of power, the population's interactions with power and the different ways in which influence on decision-making occurs, both at a local government level as well as levels higher up in the hierarchy. As such, local interactions as a function of peacebuilding open up multiple possibilities, but do not dictate how participation, influence or trust-building occurs.

Vertical relationships

John Paul Lederach argues that 'relationship is the basis of both the conflict and its long-term solution' (1997, p 26). Traditionally, conflict resolution approached relationships through a focus on third-party intervention to assist conflicting parties on the national level to solve issues between them (Ramsbotham, 2005). However, with the growing emphasis on bottom-up peacebuilding and the capacity for conflict resolution found in conflicting communities themselves, the focus on relationships at all levels, as well as vertically between local, national and international levels, has grown (Lederach, 1997; McCandless et al, 2015; Millar, 2021). In these studies, positive relationships between different actors enhance contacts and lead to a deeper understanding and increased ability to coexist. Also, studies emphasize that relationships hold the key to any other developments that may occur, whether it means prolonged conflict or prolonged peace (Lederach, 1997; Lee, 2015; Leonardsson, 2011, p 104f; Lundqvist and Öjendal, 2018; McCandless et al, 2015; Ramsbotham, 2005, p 51).

Lederach, one of the early advocates for bottom-up peacebuilding, emphasized the importance of middle-range leaders, and the conflict transformation activities that they may undertake, for example, problem-solving workshops (such as interactive conflict resolution), third-party consultation and facilitated dialogues. These approaches promote meetings between non-official representatives of the conflicting parties. Such micro-processes enable the sharing of information, encourage listening and jointly explore future alternatives with the goal of changing relationships between actors (Lederach, 1997; Ramsbotham, 2005, p 48ff). Acknowledging that reconciliation and relationship-building happens across levels[1] and scales,[2] Lederach (1997, p 39) illustrated the leadership of a conflict as a pyramid with many leaders at the grassroots level, fewer at the middle-range level and a few at the top. Although each level has its own tasks in the peacebuilding process, Lederach emphasizes the need for coordination between levels,

---

[1] Understanding level as a horizontal position, particularly in relation to rank and authority (Nationalencyklopedin, n.d.).

[2] Understanding scales as both spatial and temporal, which are used to analyse where processes and activities of a phenomena take place. Whether perceived as socially constructed or an empirical given is a debate of its own, but here it suffices to highlight that it is a concept that serves the purpose of organizing how we make sense of the world (Castree, Kitchin and Rogers, 2013).

from the grassroots to the national. In his writing, the middle-range leaders offer a particular opportunity for connecting the grassroots-level to the top-level leaders in a conflict (Lederach, 1997, pp 39ff, 152). Lederach's focus on relationships across levels allowed for moving beyond 'islands of civility' (Kaldor, 1999, p 110f) or local zones of peace (Mitchell and Hancock, 2012, p 20) which offer refuge to the local population but have little impact on the conflict as a whole (Öjendal et al, 2017, p 36).

In more recent studies, interactions across levels has been emphasized by McCandless et al (2015), who underline vertical integration of peacebuilding and its importance for peacebuilding success, Millar (2020) writing on trans-scalar conceptions of peace, as well as Hameiri and Jones (2017), who focus on the politics of scale in peacebuilding interventions. These perspectives add to Lederach's focus on linkages between the local and national for 'home-grown' peacebuilding by recognizing the need to include the international as part of globalized vertical relationships.

While the distinction between local and international actors is at the core of local peacebuilding and its critique against a top-down imposition of liberal peace (Leeuwen et al, 2012; Mitchell, 2010; Roberts, 2011a), concepts such as vertical integration between local and international actors (McCandless et al, 2015) do not satisfactorily conceptualize this interaction. To conceptualize what I mean by vertical relationships, I borrow from the debates on trans-scalarity and multi-level governance in that they acknowledge the increasing interactions that occur between actors and agencies on different levels and scales (vertical), as well as across levels and scales (horizontal) (Brenner, 1999; Hooghe and Marks, 2002). Both terms emphasize the interconnectivity between local and regional levels of governance and inter-regional, national and international levels, but where multi-level governance focuses on interconnections between and across levels, trans-scalarity emphasizes the holistic and relational in such interconnections (Hooghe and Marks, 2002, p 4; Scholte, 2014, p 14).

However, both the trans-scalar and the multi-level governance terms come with their assumptions of societal organizations. Multi-level governance, in its emphasis on governance, highlights the role of institutions and agencies, in that 'authority ... has come to be shared across global institutions, regional organizations such as the EU, national governments, and subnational governments' (Schakel et al, 2014, p 3). Trans-scalarity, on the other hand, broadens political action to include complex networks that connect state and non-state, formal and informal, local to suprastate actors and agencies in political decision-making (Scholte, 2014, p 4). Although the end goal is still public policy, trans-scalar approaches avoid identifying 'a primary level of political action' and 'rejects the notion of hierarchies among (artificially separated) spaces' (Scholte, 2014, p 14). Instead, decision-making is a 'complex fabric of trans-scalar wheeling and dealing' (Majoor and Salet, 2008, p 95).

In my understanding of vertical relationships, both approaches are useful. The term 'vertical' emphasizes that local governments are part of a layered authority that sometimes has its specific rules and regulations. However, I also understand vertical relationships as incorporating space for interconnections that move more freely across levels and scales. As such, vertical relationships can be vertical and occur within the Lebanese system of multi-level governance, between the municipal, district and national level, and also with regard to international bodies. In addition, interconnections exist across levels to actors outside[3] of the national or international, vertical system of multi-level governance, for example, between Lebanese municipalities and other local governments outside of Lebanon. The trans-scalar term has additionally influenced my thinking on vertical relationships to include interconnections to both formal and informal actors, agencies and bodies. In this way, relationships do not only occur between state actors (on multiple levels). On the contrary, relationships with individual actors or non-state organizations also matter, for example, individuals who hold a position in relation to another (government) level or (spatial) scale, such as national politicians or experts of a field. However, in this book, I differ from trans-scalarity in that I specifically analyse local governments as the primary level of relevance for policies developed. In addition, although I borrow from the conceptualization of multi-level governance, I am not studying sites of multi-level governance per se, but rather how municipal actors make use of vertical interconnections for policy making (Fakhoury, 2018; Hooghe and Marks, 2002).

Although conceptualizing vertical relationships as interconnections between levels and scales opens the box of state hierarchies, a word has to be said on verticality and power. Despite the importance of vertical relationships for developments on the ground, power imbalances between local and national, or international actors cannot be ignored. Even though trans-scalarity is non-hierarchical as an ideal, the trans-scalar approach also reminds us that when decision-making power is dispersed in trans-scalar governance networks, it also 'give[s] power many places to hide' (Hameiri et al, 2017; Scholte, 2014, p 15). In this way, my conceptualization of vertical relationships is not separated from power, and such power can be real or perceived, such as existing within legislation on multi-level governance or a perception of who possesses money, influence or expertise. In addition, hierarchies are not always shunned, as local governments may very well seek them out to promote their aims.

---

[3] Whereas horizontal relationships inside the local space are conceptualized as local interactions in this book.

In this book, such (real or perceived) asymmetries of power are both part of the vertical relationship and the reason why these relationships matter as well as why vertical relationships can be detrimental. As such, vertical relationships are a double-edged sword, solving conflicts or driving them. When the conflict driver is due to the power imbalances within the vertical relationship itself, the cause of the conflict is found in the structure of who the actors are and their mutual relationship (Ramsbotham, 2005, p 21). In these instances, cooperation between actors on different levels is not possible, but rather becomes collaboration on the terms set by the more powerful (Ramsbotham, 2005, p 295). Such vertical relationships can fuel conflict and fragility by favouring the interests and priorities of political and economic actors already in power (McCandless et al, 2015). Conflict resolution is then not about solving issues but rather about changing structures that surround the relationship between the parties. Typically, the hegemonic party will find little interest in changing these structures. However, if the cost of being the oppressor is too high, there might be room for change (Ramsbotham, 2005, p 21). Here, Ramsbotham (2005) and also Curle (1971) refer to asymmetric relationships as the basis for the conflict as a whole. However, asymmetric local–national collaboration may also hinder local cooperation for peace even if conflict drivers are not directly related to the vertical relationship between the local and national actors. As noted by McCandless et al (2015), within vertical relationships, less powerful actors are easily coerced or co-opted by actors higher up in the hierarchy.

However, vertical relationships may also facilitate cooperation. Several scholars writing on local peacebuilding argue that vertical relationships matter because they enable other developments on the ground (Brinkerhoff, 2011; Kälin, 2004; Mitchell and Hancock, 2012). One of the key arguments put forward is that central (national) actors, sub-national actors regionally as well as sub-national actors locally need to see each other as partners for sub-national governance to have a conflict mitigating ability. When the national, regional and local level is working towards the same goal, local governments can enable practices that play a role for peace. This alignment of interests and activities between the local and national is what Mitchell and Hancock refer to as complementarity (Mitchell and Hancock, 2012, pp 34, 175). As such, whether for specific peacebuilding projects or other governance measures that could have a conflict mitigating impact, the acceptance, and/or encouragement from the national level matters for the possibility of local actors to implement measures that could further peace. Both when locally initiated or implemented through a national agenda (Mitchell and Hancock, 2012, p 2ff). As such, it is not only about national–local relationships being complementary, but also about the local gaining enough autonomy and trust from the central level to pursue policies that they see suitable for the local context.

Where a vertical relationship exists, it can counter the isolation of local zones of peace, as well as combine local peacebuilding ambitions into a larger whole. For example, Mouly (2013) demonstrates how peace commissions in Nicaragua made use of vertical, as well as horizontal, connections to transform local initiatives that initially confronted the violence of the civil war in the 1980s into developmental projects and, over time, sustained the peace. Donais (2015) similarly emphasizes that community-based peacebuilding processes in Haiti temporarily calmed local violence but had no transformative role in the broader conflict when disconnected from the larger Haitian state-building process. In a comparative study between rural municipalities in post-conflict Guatemala, Klick (2016) shows that the implementation of pro-poor policies may be heavily distorted if the relationship between the local government and central state agencies is in conflict, but even more so if there is also a conflict between formal and informal, religious and political local actors. These studies show that although vertical relationships matter, the same relationships may also be part of asymmetric power relations and/or hegemonic imposition of national policies, emphasizing that context also matters (McCandless et al, 2015). As the contextual differences illustrate, 'it is difficult to come up with any patterns or even repetitions amid the welter of different details from case to case' (Mitchell and Hancock, 2012, p 2), emphasizing that vertical relationships may be as much of a blessing as a curse for local peacebuilding (Mitchell and Hancock, 2012, p 11). Further problematizing the possibilities and potential pitfalls inherent in vertical relationships as a peacebuilding function, Mitchell and Hancock acknowledge, 'even though complementarity is desirable to a certain extent, it too runs the risk of undermining grassroots ownership and autonomy' (Mitchell and Hancock, 2012, p 176f).

Contextual differences in how vertical relationships perform highlight the agency of actors in local peacebuilding. From this perspective, what actors do as elected representatives and in relation to other actors, agencies and bodies matters, emphasizing that institution-building on the local level is not enough for conflict mitigation (Donais, 2012, p 150). Political posts are not only seats to be filled, but people filling them are agents. Similar to other local and national actors, local governments have the agency to cooperate or resist, accept, adopt, promote or mock larger frameworks of peacebuilding and state-building, as well as initiate alternative processes. By being part of contextual power relations and using their agency within power relations, local governments take part in the politics of scale (Hameiri et al, 2017; Hameiri and Jones, 2017). In this view, central–local, or international–local relationships may be constraining if they are not characterized by complementarity, nor given the local space autonomy to act, but they do not determine every possibility for local leaders (Mac Ginty, 2010a; Richmond and Mitchell, 2012, pp 5, 8, 11, 16). In this book I analyse complementarity, space for autonomy and expressions of agency in vertical relationships as a peacebuilding function.

Analysing the role of local governments in peacebuilding

Having discussed the nuances and possible pitfalls of service delivery, local interactions and vertical relationships as peacebuilding functions, I now outline how the three functions guide the analysis of local governments as peacebuilding actors in Lebanon. This section highlights the theoretical arguments on how service delivery, local interactions and vertical relationships are assumed to promote peace, emphasizing the analytical construction of the three peacebuilding functions (della Porta, 2008, p 206).

Service delivery as a peacebuilding function closely builds on the view that local governments' proximity to the local population offers the best potential for mitigating conflict. First, the proximity of local governments implies that by being part of the local context, they have knowledge of local needs and can tailor service provision according to those needs. Therefore, local governments are *responsive* to local needs. Second, knowing the local needs includes hearing the needs of communities that may be a minority in a larger constituency, such as at a national level, but more prominently present at the local level. Therefore, service provision at the local level may compensate for national unresponsiveness to minority needs, emphasizing the need for *inclusive* local service delivery (Brinkerhoff, 2011, p 142f). With responsive and inclusive services, service delivery legitimizes the local government in the eyes of the population. Assumedly, a legitimate state counters the conflict driver of public dissatisfaction, which fuels opposition and the public's will to revert to violence (Bland, 2007, p 208f; Brinkerhoff, 2011). Third, the *capacity* of local governments to provide services plays a role in the implementation of needs-based, efficient and inclusive service provision that legitimizes peace. As such, autonomous or capable local governments combine local responsibilities and available resources to work for service delivery (Cheema and Rondinelli, 2007a, p 9f). Fourth, local service delivery harbours the *idea of economic development*, modernity and prosperity. This builds on the idea of expectations and perceptions influencing how government services are evaluated, impacting the acceptance of the state (Bland, 2007, p 208f; Brinkerhoff, 2011; Hartmann and Crawford, 2008, pp 8, 250; McLoughlin, 2019). In this book, responsive and inclusive service delivery, service delivery promoting the idea of economic development as well as capable local government, guide the analysis of service delivery as a peacebuilding function.

Local interactions as a peacebuilding function build on the argument of local interaction as important for building local peace through three claims.

First, it builds on the commonly expressed view that without *participation*, peacebuilding is inaccessible, hollow and irrelevant for the population living in the aftermath of conflict. As such, enabling participation is crucial for citizens to gain knowledge over local governance and be able to oversee and control the policies carried out, and hold local power holders accountable for such policies (Donais, 2012, pp 53–5). However, as participation has increased in importance within peacebuilding agendas, it has often become a buzzword with little real implications beyond the word. The second part of the argument for interaction claims that in order to move beyond participation as attendance, citizens need to have *influence* over local issues. Participation and influence allow for a contestation around local issues, enabling for locally adapted solutions that promote peace (Brinkerhoff, 2011, p 139; Brancati, 2006). Third, through local interactions, the local government is claimed to have influence over the population. In particular, practices of participation and influence open up arenas of *fostering trust* in the local government and between local groups and communities (Jackson, 2013, p 354f; Schou and Haug, 2005). In this book I will analyse local interactions as a peacebuilding function through a focus on participation, influence and the fostering of trust.

Vertical relationships as a peacebuilding function build on the argument that vertical relationships enable other developments, which, in turn, mitigate conflict. However, vertical relationships are not necessarily beneficial for local development but hold a rather messy record of accomplishment. Therefore, the conceptualization of vertical relationships as a peacebuilding function requires a discussion of what kinds of vertical relationships are assumed to foster peace. First, *complementarity*, or working towards the same goal, is emphasized as a precondition for aligning interests and coordinating activities between actors at different levels in the society. As such, complementary vertical relationships enable activities that are implemented in relation to the local space, and, thus, appropriate for local conditions (Mitchell and Hancock, 2012, p 175). Second, the importance of vertical relationships depends on the autonomy of local governments. If local governments are *autonomous*, they can pursue policies that they believe are suitable for the local context. On the other hand, if they do not have autonomy to act, acceptance of locally adapted policies from a higher level becomes key (Brinkerhoff, 2011; Kälin, 2004). Third, central–local government relationships are often part of asymmetric power relations, with the central government exercising authority over the local government, which, in turn, impacts on the capacities and autonomy exercised by the local government. Changing asymmetric relations is not easily accomplished (and for some relationships, may require decentralization reform), but scholars in conflict resolution claim that when the price for upholding the asymmetry is too high, change can come about (see for example Ramsbotham, 2005). Adding to the possibility of change, the *agency* of local actors is continuously expressed through, for example, the acceptance, cooperation, resistance, promotion or opposition to the agenda of national or international actors. In this view, even though the asymmetric character of vertical relationships may change when its cost is too high, vertical relationships are continuously challenged and used by local actors, thus emphasizing that expressions of agency are possible even if vertical relationships are constrained (Mac Ginty, 2010a; Richmond and Mitchell, 2012, pp 5, 8, 11, 16). In this book, complementarity, room for autonomy and expressions of agency are the basis on which I analyse vertical relationships as peacebuilding functions.

Although the three peacebuilding functions have been described as separate concepts, they all stem from the debate on local peacebuilding and, thus, they interlink in different ways. As such, the notion of inclusion, expressions of voice and agency as well as the grounding of peace to the local reality underpins all three peacebuilding functions. These interlinkages emphasize that none of the three functions stand on their own in relation to building local peace. In the complexity of post-conflict settings, all three functions are necessary for building local peace, but not in themselves sufficient to achieve that aim.

At this stage, the discussion of analysing peacebuilding functions merits a reflection on what kind of knowledge the analysis will provide for peacebuilding. It might seem tempting to use the conceptualization of local peacebuilding through service delivery, local interactions and vertical relationships as a toolkit or, as best practice, arrived at through a thorough reading of the literature. Although peacebuilding programmes and further research may wish to translate the functions into a method for building local peace or a framework for assessing local peacebuilding, I do not apply such an approach. In emphasizing peacebuilding functions and their respective themes, I do not put forward specific ways to implement or assess them. In my work, the functions and themes describe processes of building peace, but do not dictate how the processes should be constructed or formed. As such, the contextual interpretation, or translation if one prefers, of the functions studied is of great importance in analysing the role of local governments in local peacebuilding. The contextual interpretation also emphasizes that the three functions do not necessarily presuppose the building of a particular version of peace. Thus, the three functions are not to be interpreted as responding to the failures of the liberal peacebuilding agenda by localizing liberal peace or assuming that the liberal peace is being localized and therefore fixed, or, in Paris's words, 'saved' (Paris, 2010). Nor do they assume that the peace formed in the local space is necessarily hybrid, illiberal, or local-local (Mac Ginty and Richmond, 2013), pertaining to different ways of defining peace. Simultaneously, my conceptualization of local peacebuilding does not exclude the possibility of more or less of one of these alternatives or a little of both. In essence, the functions explored in this book do not define a type of peace, but enable a localization of peacebuilding where the kind of peace built is contextually defined.

Conclusion

In this chapter I have outlined an analytical framework for analysing the role of local governments in local peacebuilding. The framework builds on the idea that local service delivery responds to local needs, local interactions create inclusion in the local space and vertical relationships link the national and international to local actors and contexts, thus, countering the ignorance of local needs and voices, as well as centralized or localized peacebuilding as common flaws in liberal peacebuilding approaches. In addition, the chapter conceptualizes service delivery, local interactions and vertical relationships as peacebuilding functions, highlighting that peacebuilding matters based on the function it performs, rather than the form of peace built (Roberts, 2011b). As peacebuilding functions, the analytical focus is on peacebuilding practices, arguing that peacebuilding, and perceptions of peace, develop based on performance and local expectations on outcomes. As such, peacebuilding is non-linear, situated within local understandings of context, institutions and legitimacy, and performed through politics. In the next chapter I introduce local governance in Lebanon, Lebanese conflicts and peacebuilding as well as present developments providing context to how local peace is built in Tyre, Bourj Hammoud and Saida.

2

Lebanese Municipalities, Centralized Peacebuilding and Possibilities for Change

From 1975 to 1989, a violent civil war raged on Lebanese territory, killing 150,000–170,000 people, displacing large portions of the population (with estimates of two-thirds of Lebanese), vastly destroying infrastructure and bringing the Lebanese state close to collapse (Khalaf, 2002, p 232; Leenders, 2012, p 1). As the war came to an end in 1989, the Ta'if Peace Agreement reaffirmed power-sharing between former warring elites and a sectarian influence over Lebanese politics.

While Lebanon's tale is often told through power-sharing arrangements, external influence or reoccurring violence characterized by sectarianism, its post-war development is both a success story and a complete failure, and everything in between. In recent years, Lebanon has seen increased political debates, economic success, the growth of a Lebanese middle class, and a phoenix of coexistence, resilience and a joy of life. At the same time, there have been political assassinations, inter- and intra-state hostilities, fatal political ignorance, massive public protests and economic decline (Harb and Fawaz, 2020; Khalaf, 2012; World Bank, 2021). At the same time, post-war developments are embedded by Lebanon's geopolitical position which encourages international involvement. And, depending on the preference of the interpreter, such involvement is believed to maintain its stability or delay further moves towards peace (Mac Ginty, 2007b; Nagel and Staeheli, 2015).

The Lebanese state may appear weak due to the many ways in which sectarian power intrudes on the sovereignty of the state. However, because of the sectarian divide and the need for individuals to embrace personal links to their sectarian elites in order to claim their share of public resources (wasta), the Lebanese state has implications in people's lives. Thus, as sectarianism is a way of life and influenced by life, sectarianism is constantly reproduced as a political tool, one that the political elite has continuously used to resist reform (Egan and Tabar, 2016; Khalaf, 2002; Nucho, 2016). The past few years have vividly illustrated the obsession with sectarian divides and a political system that focuses on dialogue and unity between elites but overlooks problems associated with the provision of a good life for all Lebanese people (Khalaf, 2012, p 18). The waste crisis in 2015, the increase in taxes that ignited the massive and country-wide demonstration in 2019, the ignorance of the danger posed by storing 2,750 tonnes of ammonium nitrate at the Port of Beirut which blew the city to pieces on August 4, 2020, and the political inability to act on an economy in free fall, are just a few illustrations. The failure of national elites has prompted the focus to move to other actors. In Lebanon, as elsewhere, local governments have become preferred partners for international donors in implementing peacebuilding and development projects (Harb and Atallah, 2015, p 206) and, in some instances, the public's centre of attention when central governance fails (Beirut Report, 2015b). In this chapter I delve into Lebanese local governance, its possibilities and legal restrictions as well as its opportunities for reform over the years. I then discuss past and present developments in Lebanon, focusing on how diversity, disputes and divided consensus has framed Lebanese politics. Finally, I introduce Tyre, Bourj Hammoud and Saida, the three municipalities studied in the empirical chapters, focusing on their relationships to diversity, disputes and conflicts in Lebanon to illustrate how localities have been made and remade.

Local governance in Lebanon

Lebanese local governance dates to the Ottoman period and consists of regions (Muhafazat), districts (Qada) and municipalities (Baladiyyat). While regional officials and district officials are directly appointed by the central government, the municipality holds elections, making it the only autonomous local body according to the law. Nevertheless, municipal autonomy and authority is a site of contestation, promoting development and wellbeing, as well as elite influence and control. In this section I discuss municipal reforms and regulations, decentralization, and increased participation and democratization to describe Lebanese local governance, its restrictions and possibilities.

In 1977 the creation of a new municipal law illustrates how local governance coexists with autonomy and the quest for political gains. Two years after the outbreak of the civil war, political elites, local laypersons and international observers believed that the war was coming to an end. With the warring parties wanting to maintain influence and control over their local constituencies, the law became a tool to end the war, giving municipalities wide jurisdiction over activities with a public character within their territory, for example managing roads and projects to build schools, hospitals and public libraries (Abu-Rish, 2016; Ministry of Interior and Municipalities, 1977/2008). However, as the war continued, the law did not promote a devolution of national powers. Instead, when municipal officials died or moved, the governmentally controlled district (Qada) took control over municipal affairs, or it fell into the hands of local militias or other parties to the war (Harb and Atallah, 2015, p 190f). Furthermore, the war altered the demographic composition of local spaces as people were displaced, and in many instances have not returned (Hanf, 1993, p 342ff; Nucho, 2016, p 21). Displacement during the war and continued urbanization after its end has implications for local constituencies today. As the registry of citizens is based on where your ancestors lived, the inhabitants of a municipal territory are often not the same as the registered voters for the municipal election (Fawaz, 2017; Salamey, 2014, p 118).

As the war came to an end, hopes were that inhabitants would regain some of their lost influence through local elections. However, as the post-war parliamentarians were uninterested, the parliament disregarded municipal elections and extended the mandate for existing municipal councils. In April 1997, the parliament extended the municipal term for a second time. However, Lebanese civil society organizations mobilized, and over a hundred NGOs collected over 60,000 signatures, forcing the government to change its policy (Baroud, 2004, p 7; Harb and Atallah, 2015, p 191f). The first municipal elections were held in 1998 and represented a renewal of decision-making power at the local level, allowing the population a space to engage in politics closer to home (Baroud, 2004, p 8; LCPS, 2012). Since 1998, local elections have been held every six years. Municipal councils are generally less divided along sectarian lines compared to national politics, and to a greater extent integrate different local communities (Salamey, 2014, p 152). Furthermore, Lebanese municipalities have often found themselves taking a hands-on approach to local challenges such as reconstruction after the Israel–Hezbollah war in 2006 or, more recently, in relation to Syrian refugees (Mercy Corps, 2014; Mourad, 2017). As such, Lebanese municipalities offer a potential for grounding a nationally fragile peace.

In 2014, a new decentralization law was proposed reviving the promise of decentralization found in the 1989 Ta'if Agreement. The draft law suggested introducing proportionally elected regional councils with fiscal autonomy and several responsibilities at the district level, improving transparency and civic oversight, facilitating public–private partnerships at the local level, and introducing gender quotas (Carrascal, 2020). However, decentralization reform has not been encouraged by national politicians, partly due to lack of knowledge on decentralization and fear of federalism but also due to the benefits that sectarian elites gain from having weak local governments (Harb and Atallah, 2015, p 192; Salamey, 2014, p 152).

At the same time, a centralized system of governance constrains the municipalities' abilities to act locally, particularly through a lack of funds, personnel, and capacities (Salamey, 2014, p 152). Municipalities work under close control by higher authorities and ultimately the Ministry of Interior and Municipalities and the central government. Most local projects are managed by the central administration, through the Ministry of Interior and Municipalities or government agencies such as the Council for Development and Reconstruction (CDR) (C.A.I.MED., 2004). Local expenses for material costs, projects and events are tightly controlled. For example, expenses over 2,000 USD need to be approved by a chief controller, employed by the municipality but in the larger municipalities appointed by the Council of Ministers. Furthermore, the district level (Qada) approves expenses above 13,000 USD, as well as supervising the municipal budget, while expenses exceeding 53,000 USD must be approved by the region (Muhafazat), Ministry of Interior and Municipalities, or central government (Harb and Atallah, 2015; Ministry of Interior and Municipalities, 1977/2008).

The revenues that the municipality receives come mainly from the collection of fees and tariffs, for example on construction permits and rental values (Harb and Atallah, 2015, p 210). Additional revenues come from taxes collected by other Lebanese public agencies and passed on to the municipality. Finally, municipalities also receive a yearly sum from the Independent Municipal Fund (IMF). However, the municipalities have no control over the amount collected nor when they will receive payments from the Lebanese agencies and the IMF. In particular, the IMF has been severely criticized for delaying payments or for not making payments, and for using the funds for other measures (for example, the vastly over-priced waste deal with Sukleen) (Atallah, 2011; Harb and Atallah, 2015).

In addition to a lack of financial resources, municipalities are also short on human resources. At present, Lebanon has over 1,000 municipalities, and as their size varies, so does the size of the municipal councils. In the smallest municipalities the council has nine councillors while the larger municipalities have 21. It is only in Beirut and Tripoli that municipal councils have 24 members. In addition, the involvement of councillors is on a voluntary basis, and the municipality does not pay them for their time. Most of the municipalities have a small administration team with few employees (Abu-Rish, 2016).

Within the centralized system (and because of a general lack of local capacity), service provision is pursued through individual ministries, with each minister being responsible for the distribution of services within his (commonly his) sector. However, the central state is rarely the direct provider of services, but private companies and civil society actors are the ones who in practice deliver services (Harb and Atallah, 2015, p 197). These civil society actors include a variety of actors such as charities or communitarian organizations with a religious or social character (Haddad, 2017). According to Hamzeh (2001), the ministries' reliance on non-state actors for the provision of services reflects the clientelistic character of the state, where the 'patron' or 'za'im' provides his (again, most commonly his) network with state resources, employment or contracts. As such, services are delivered through organizations with a sectarian alignment and are strategically used to reinforce sectarian belonging. The outsourcing of public services has also been marked by political corruption (Leenders, 2012; Nucho, 2016). However, associations with a sectarian profile do cater to outside groups, sometimes in more generous ways (Cammett and Issar, 2010, p 384).

The services provided by the municipalities themselves mostly relate to rebuilding or the restoration of infrastructure. Mainly, this implies services related to roads inside municipal borders, and sometimes networks for potable water. For most municipalities, central state agencies carry out developmental work, often bypassing the municipality. However, larger and medium-sized municipalities (about 30 per cent of all Lebanese municipalities and all of them located in urban settings) provide some services that are directed towards ameliorating their city. These services may include education or health services, cultural events or initiatives to promote tourism or economic investment. Nevertheless, a lack of financial and human resources restrict what municipalities actually do (Harb and Atallah, 2015, p 199ff). In addition, local governments have strong links to national elites which enable or condition local governance (Ghaddar, 2016; Mourad, 2017; Stel, 2014). Thus, Lebanese local governments both offer a potential for evading national political stalemate and being caught up in the same.

Democratically empowered but financially and administratively constrained, Lebanese municipalities represent a decentralization stopped halfway, common in post-conflict local governance (Romeo, 2013, p 78). Nevertheless, in Lebanon as elsewhere, local governments have become preferred partners for international donors in implementing peacebuilding and development projects as well as becoming the public's centre of attention when central governance fails (Beirut Report, 2015b; Harb and Atallah, 2015, p 206).

Lebanese diversity, disputes and divided consensus

While little of Lebanon's history is re-called as undisputed historical facts, a discussion of past and present developments and the repercussions they are claimed to have had is necessary to understand sustained and changing dividing lines, modes of governance and the issues at stake. Although deciding where to initiate a description of the past always holds risks of ignorance, my focus is on developments since the early 1900s, emphasizing the divisions and disputes that triggered and still influence dividing lines in Lebanese politics and everyday life.

Prior to the First World War, the territories of present-day Lebanon were part of the Ottoman Empire, and the smaller unity of Mount Lebanon was one of its governorates. As the Ottoman Empire fell, Lebanon, as well as other Arab lands, became part of the partition of the Middle East, influenced by the Hussein–MacMahon and Sykes–Picot agreements. In 1922, the League of Nations formally divided the Middle East between Britain and France, with France in control over present-day Lebanon as well as Syria (Rogan, 2013). According to the division, the region of Mount Lebanon expanded to Greater Lebanon, altering the demographic composition of Lebanese territories. Whereas Mount Lebanon had a Christian majority of approximately three quarters, Greater Lebanon incorporated areas with Sunni and Shia Muslim populations. In the new territory, the Shia, as well as the Druze, were content with a minority position among other minorities. However, the Sunni community, which had been part of the majority within the Ottoman Empire, were less satisfied with a minority position within a French Mandate that favoured the Christian Maronite community (Salamey, 2014, p 22ff).

Under the French Mandate, opinions as to what Lebanon should be diverged between the ideas of Arab unity or Lebanese independence. Muslim political circles, as well as some Greek Orthodox notables, supported the notion of Arab unity and the creation of a secular Greater Syria, including present-day Syria, Lebanon and Palestine, drawing on early versions of pan-Arabism. In Maronite circles, as well as among those involved in the political administration of the governorate of Mount Lebanon, the idea of an independent Lebanon was preferred, adhering to Lebanese nationalist ideals. However, proponents were divided. Some preferred a Lebanese state based in Mount Lebanon and Beirut, arguing that a smaller territory with a largely Christian population would best serve their interests. Others argued for a Greater Lebanon based in the territory of present-day Lebanon, claiming that the Christians were strong enough to maintain control. As the French rejected the idea of a Greater Syria, the better-organized propagators of a Greater Lebanon persuaded them to establish the state of Greater Lebanon in 1920 within what came to be perceived as its 'historic' (and present) borders. Although still under a French Mandate, Greater Lebanon held promises of independence, long sought after by Lebanese nationalists (Hanf, 1993, p 64f; Salamey, 2014, p 24f). During the period of the French Mandate, Greater Lebanon institutionalized a parliamentary democracy under a strong president. However, as opposed to secularist France, Lebanese parliamentarianism continued to allocate seats in parliament according to the numerical strength of its communities and allowed considerable sectarian autonomy over matters of family law as well as service provision such as, for example, education (Egan and Tabar, 2016; Hanf, 1993, p 68).

In 1943, the French accepted the Lebanese independence that had been declared in 1941. At the foundation of the new republic was the National Pact, an unwritten agreement between all sectarian elites recognizing diversity. The pact institutionalized sectarian power-sharing according to the population census of 1932 and distributed seats in parliament according to a ratio of six Christians to five Muslims. In addition, the National Pact installed what has been called the Lebanese system of three presidents, with a Maronite Christian president, a Sunni Muslim prime minister, and a Shia Muslim speaker of parliament to (Salamey, 2014, p 30f). This reinforced the communities as political parties (Hanf, 1993, p 68).

The independence in 1943 was achieved after a non-violent struggle situated within a century of calm between 1860 and 1958. However, in 1958, the power-sharing arrangements that the National Pact had put in place were challenged by regional struggles, with domestic repercussions. In the 1950s, and inspired by charismatic Egyptian President Jamal Abdel Nasser, pan-Arab sentiments ushered Muslims in the Middle East to unite for the Palestinian cause, Arab nationalism and the denunciation of foreign interference. In Lebanon, Muslim political leaders questioned the pro-Western alliances and policies performed by the government. Prior to the elections in 1957, peaceful protests and strikes urged the government to step down. However, as the government refused, and elections failed to alter the government, protests spread throughout the country and violence increased in what has been called the 1958 crisis (Khalaf, 2002, p 103ff). Perceived as a communist threat from a socialist and pro-Nasserite opposition, 14,000 US troops intervened in support of President Chamoun. In 1959, tensions between Muslims and Christians eased after an agreement was struck between the pro-Nasserites and Lebanese nationalists, instating a more moderate government under the rule of Fuad Chebab (Salamey, 2014, p 39). Whereas the National Pact had created Lebanon as a country of diversity, the crisis shaped Lebanon as a 'nation of disputants' (Khalaf, 2002, p 143) transformed into communal enmity.

Following the 1958 crisis, Lebanon was characterized by economic prosperity, social transformation and political stability, often described as Lebanon's golden age (Khalaf, 2002, p 151). This period saw an expanding educational system and decreased illiteracy as well as infrastructural projects of electricity, irrigation and roads dispatched to less advantaged peripheral regions, and increased quality of life for all social classes (Hanf, 1993, p 97ff).

However, as the economic situation declined in the 1970s, feelings of relative deprivation between communities increased. The conflict that erupted in 1975 mainly grew out of three domestic and regional issues. First, there were growing demands for economic reforms from the Lebanese working class, consisting mostly of Shia Muslims. This played well into demands for political influence emerging within Muslim groups, mainly from the Sunni Muslims and Druze. This led to dissatisfaction with the power-sharing regime, defended primarily by the Christian Maronite elites (Hanf, 1993, pp 106ff, 130ff). Second, there was the ideological attraction of pan-Arabism uniting Muslims across the region, in Lebanon specifically uniting them against the Maronite alliance with the West. This divided the Lebanese people and elites between Arab nationalists and Lebanese nationalists. Third, there was the effect of the Israel–Palestine conflict and the presence of Palestinians on Lebanese soil. With diverse dividing lines, there were also several igniting factors. One was the assassination of the Nasserite leader Maarouf Saad in Saida, allegedly by the Lebanese army in March 1975. Another was the clashes between Christian Phalangist forces and Palestinian fighters in April 1975. As the war proceeded, it spurred inter- and intra-confessional fighting, which outgrew the issues that had originally caused it.

External interference added to the conflict. Syria entered Lebanese ground in 1976, originally to control the situation but staying on until well after the end of the war. In addition, Israel entered Lebanese territory to fight Palestinian groups in 1978, withdrawing shortly after, only to enter again in 1982 and remaining in the southern parts of Lebanon until 2000 (Milton-Edwards and Hinchcliffe, 2008; Zahar, 2005, p 231ff). However, foreign intervention did not only take place through military intervention. Following the pattern of sustaining close relationships with external actors, different militias maintained close connections with foreign powers. For example, Libya, Israel, Syria and Iran supported the Nasserite group Murabitun, Christian Lebanese Forces, Shi'a Amal and Shi'a Hezbollah. Palestinian groups were allies of foreign powers such as Libya, Syria, Sudan and Iraq. These relationships demonstrate that 'domestic forms of clientelism ... ramify beyond national boundaries [and] serve as a bridgehead for the penetration of foreign patrons or regional interest' (Hamzeh, 2001, p 175). The intervention of foreign interests and actors has prompted some to describe the civil war as a 'war for others' (Haugbolle, 2010; Tueni, 1985).

As the war dragged on, there were also efforts to create peace, and several peace initiatives gathered large support from the population. Trade unions turned their activism towards the war, organizing national strikes and mobilizing against falling wages and economic decline. In addition, peace demonstrations were held in all major cities in Lebanon. However, strikes and demonstrations had little impact and fighting continued. Nevertheless, it enabled the Lebanese to contest the conditions for coexistence set up by war. In addition, the Lebanese population mobilized in civil society associations to respond to the needs created by war and the absence of the state. However, as the war divided Lebanon geographically and by community, most associations adhered to a sectarian character, thus not bridging the dividing lines of the war (Haddad, 2017; Hanf, 1993, p 638ff).

In 1989, a peace agreement was negotiated in Ta'if, Saudi Arabia. The agreement modified the power-sharing regime with an equal division of parliamentary seats between Christians and Muslims, as well as portfolios in the cabinet being equally shared. The agreement reaffirmed the president as Christian Maronite, the prime minister as Sunni Muslim and the speaker of parliament as Shiite Muslim. However, it decreased presidential powers and enhanced the authority of the prime minister and the speaker of parliament, creating three positions with a more equal share of power (Ghosn and Khoury, 2011; Zahar, 2005, p 231ff). The agreement also included elements of a more fundamental change such as the call for the abolishment of sectarianism, decentralization reform and social and economic justice. However, these were formulated as admirable goals in comparison to the hard facts of the division of seats (Khalaf, 2002).

The Ta'if Agreement also legitimized Syrian guardianship for the first two years (Salamey, 2014, p 57). As Syria stayed on, much longer than anticipated, it kept a close watch over Lebanese politics, allowing measures that maintained stability but simultaneously prolonging the sectarian divide, and discouraging deeper democratization and reconciliation (Zahar, 2009, p 293f). In addition, the parliament passed a law of amnesty for all crimes committed against the civilian population during the civil war. Although the law might have been necessary to settle the conflict, it hindered official acknowledgement of the war. With the law in place, former militia leaders turned into parliamentarians and ministers, and the people were urged to forget the war (Ghosn and Khoury, 2011). With no official account of events, history books taught in schools, to this day, still end with Lebanese independence in 1943. Although this conveniently encourages public amnesia, it also implies a recreation of collective memory based on older generations' feelings of fear, anger and lack of trust. As impunity for the ruling elite has continued, so has the narrative of the Lebanese war being in the interest of others, hindering responsibility and action for much needed post-war change (Ghosn and Khoury, 2011; Haugbolle, 2010, p 13; Khalaf, 2002, p 306ff).

Despite the many challenges, the end of the 1990s saw a slight opening of the political debate coupled with the reconstruction of the Lebanese economy and infrastructure. The reconstruction of Lebanon as the liberal economical centre that it had been before the war required extensive support from international actors and, until the early 2000s, Lebanon's economic reconstruction was something of a miracle. Syria did little to object to international financial involvement as it saw Lebanon's liberal economic system as an asset that gave access to resources not available in the Syrian socialist regime. Thus, Syrian interest in economic liberalization in Lebanon simultaneously invited foreign intervention with a different post-war agenda (Zahar, 2005, 2009). This period also saw a wave of massive reconstruction of spaces damaged by the war. Rafiq Hariri, prime minister during 1992–1998 as well as 2000–2004, with close connections to the Saudi royal family, was its master builder. As reconstruction got under way, the historic centre of Beirut's central business district was rebuilt to cater to shops of high-end brands and prestigious offices, inviting global capital and consumerism to historically important local spaces – a development that has also been the subject of severe criticism (Fakhoury, 2009, p 207; Khalaf, 2002). However, the idea of economic development furthering peace was an inspiration for many: 'Rafic Hariri may not be perfect but he's pragmatic. He sees beyond our silly ideologies. And he sincerely wants to rebuild Lebanon. … There will be real peace soon. That means markets and tourism and economic competition' (Miller, 1997, p 246). With intensified infrastructural developments and commercialization, Lebanon, as a 'Merchant Republic', shaped every part of Lebanese life (Khalaf, 2012, p 16).

However, the liberal economic reconstruction and commercialization of the early 2000s also increased tensions between Syrian and western interests in Lebanon, once again highlighting the long-term pro-Arab and pro-West divide. Liberal economic reforms pursued by Western donors, such as privatization, administrative reform and improvement in the investment climate clashed with clientelism and governance practices that had benefited, including but not exclusively, Syrian elites since the end of the war (Leenders, 2012; Zahar, 2009). As Israeli forces withdrew from the south on 24 May 2000, pressure on Syrian troops to do the same increased. However, the Syrian regime intensified its ties to the Lebanese military and security services. In 2004, the UN Security Council adopted Resolution 1559 calling for the respect of Lebanese sovereignty and exclusive authority over Lebanese territory by the Lebanese government, advocating for a Syrian withdrawal. With liberal peacebuilding aimed at establishing 'stable, tolerant, more liberal and democratic regimes' (Zahar, 2009, p 299), Resolution 1559 is seen as the first in a series of liberal peacebuilding interventions in Lebanon (Zahar, 2009).

The assassination of former prime minister Rafiq Hariri in 2005 intensified alliances between foreign and Lebanese actors. With international donors and sections of the Lebanese political elite blaming the Syrian regime, international and Lebanese pressure on Syria to withdraw from Lebanon increased. Massive demonstrations split the Lebanese into two blocs, which today still infiltrate national politics and everyday discussions. One bloc, called March 14, was the movement behind what internationally came to be known as the Cedar Revolution. Consisting of predominantly Christian, Druze and Sunni parties, the movement demanded Syrian withdrawal from Lebanese ground. Currently, March 14 acts within the anti-Syrian, pro-West discourse, collaborating with the Gulf States and with close ties to Saudi Arabia. The other bloc, March 8, gathered mostly Shiite followers who supported the Syrian presence. March 8 takes the position of being pro-Syrian, collaborating with Syria, Iran, sometimes Russia, and in general being perceived as anti-Western or pro-Arab. Both blocs work through regionalized and globalized political dividing lines (Osoegawa, 2013; Safa, 2006, p 31ff; Zahar, 2009). Although alliances have changed from the pro-Western Christians and pro-Arab Muslims that dominated the prelude to the civil war, the blocs signify a continuation of the divide between Western or Arab/regional influence on Lebanese politics and future development.

With the withdrawal of Syrian troops and the 'protector of peace' in April 2005, instability increased in Lebanon. Since then, Lebanon has experienced political stalemate, and repeated periods of no president and no government. Political assassinations and targeted bombings have returned in significant numbers, and recent years have seen increased instability in interconfessional relations with sometimes violent outbreaks (Leenders, 2012, p 2; Zahar, 2009). Liberal intervention intensified with the UN creation of the Independent Investigative Commission (UNIIC) into the death of Rafiq Hariri and the Special Tribunal for Lebanon (STL). STL illustrates a liberal intervention aiming to hold the responsible to account, while its critics questioned it for internationally prosecuting the accused for violating domestic law. Also, the European Union Election Observation Mission for the parliamentary elections in 2005 was yet another measure assuring liberal democratic practice in the first elections after the Syrian withdrawal (Zahar, 2009, p 301f).

In the summer of 2006, the Israel–Hezbollah war severely damaged infrastructure, buildings, mosques and medical centres in the southern parts of Lebanon and the Beirut suburb of Dahiyeh. The war itself cannot be seen as part of a liberal peacebuilding agenda. However, US unwillingness to influence Israel in instigating a quick ceasefire illustrates a reluctance to deal with actors perceived as illiberal and spoilers of a liberal peace. As part of the war on terror and the US plan for the Greater Middle East, illiberal forces in Lebanon – in this case, Hezbollah – 'had to be vanquished' (Zahar, 2009, p 302). Following the war, the UN Interim Force in Lebanon (UNIFIL), present since 1978, increased in number and mandate. Western nations deployed a great part of the increased manpower in 2006, quite unusual for current day UN peace operations (Zahar, 2012, p 81). In addition, the Stockholm Conference for Lebanon's Early Recovery gathered promises from international donors of $900 million for post-conflict reconstruction. Some donations funded the Lebanese government or NGOs, but much reconstruction assistance was channelled through local governments, both from regional donors such as Iran and Saudi Arabia as well as from the

Western donor community (Mac Ginty, 2007a; Ministry of Finance, 2006). Interest in local governments has continued after this acute reconstruction phase through, for example, the United Nations Development Programme (UNDP), individual governments and the EU targeting municipalities and municipal unions for development projects (El-Mikawy and Melim-McLeod, 2010; LCPS, 2012).

The Syrian civil war has further increased tensions within Lebanon, emphasizing the pro- and anti-Syrian/pro-Saudi divide in politics as well as between Lebanese communities. Violent spillovers from the Syrian conflict have occurred on Lebanese territory, and there has been a diversity of Lebanese involvement within Syria, both in the form of Hezbollah militarily supporting the Bashar al-Assad regime and Lebanese territory being used to transfer resources, including weapons and fighters, to Syrian opposition forces. Within Lebanon, over a million Syrian refugees have put pressure on the already fragile country, its infrastructure and service delivery. This has prompted increased international intervention, once again with a focus on the local (Dakroub, 2014a; Mourad, 2017).

Over the past few decades, tensions between pro-Arab March 8 and Pro-Western March 14 have turned hard-negotiated politics into occasional clashes and political stalemate. In 2007, disagreement on, inter alia, Hezbollah as an armed resistance within Lebanon resulted in parliamentarian inability to elect a new president. In May 2008 it escalated into five days of clashes due to the governmental decision to constrain Hezbollah's internal telecommunications network and dismiss supposedly Hezbollah allied Walid Shkair, head of security at Beirut Rafiq Hariri airport (Salamey, 2014, p 69f). According to Hezbollah, these were acts of war taken by the March 14 government, mobilizing a hundred fighters who took over West Beirut (Bou Akar, 2018, p 8). The crisis was solved through intense consultations between Lebanese political parties and sectarian leaders as well as Arab and regional actors such as Saudi Arabia, Turkey, Iran and Syria. The Doha Agreement emphasized the inclusion of foreign powers to solve the crisis in Lebanese politics. It also put a halt to hostilities through a division of ministerial posts and a new electoral law, deepening sectarian divisions and increasing the influence of sectarian elites over Lebanese politics (Salamey, 2014, p 73). The Lebanese cabinet worked under Doha agreed terms until January 2011 when March 8 ministers left the cabinet due to disagreements with the Special Tribunal for Lebanon (STL), thus bringing down the whole government (Salamey, 2014, p 79). Since then, political stalemate has postponed parliamentarian elections in 2013, election of a president in 2014, and government formations in 2018, 2019 and 2020. Political stalemate followed domestic developments with an increasingly dissatisfied Lebanese population and a political elite struggling for power (Aziz, 2015; Dakroub, 2018).

While politics in Lebanon have focused on solving political stalemate, national unity governments and political reforms, less attention has been paid to the quality of life (Khalaf, 2012, p 18). In July 2015, the Naameh landfill site, which had stored garbage from Beirut and surrounding municipalities for 19 years, was closed. With nowhere to put the trash, the private company that collected waste in Greater Beirut stopped its activities. As a result, waste accumulated on the streets, leaving smelly, sometimes burning, mountains of trash (Kraidy, 2016). As the situation dragged on, the inability of the central government to agree on a solution to resume waste collection services sparked public rage against the political elite. Protesters gathered in front of the Lebanese parliament demanding essential services such as waste management, reliable electricity and potable water. Moreover, although violently pushed back by the police, protests continued and demands for government accountability and criticism of the political elite grew (Azzi, 2017; Beirut Report, 2015a, 2015b; Kraidy, 2016). While the demonstrations against the waste crisis ebbed out, conversations about the lack of basic services and an ignorant political elite did not. In October 2019 massive country-wide protests broke out after the political elite proposed raising taxes despite a continuous degradation of services. The rage that shocked the country inspired the population to claim 'Nahna shab wahad' ('We are one people'), emphasizing unity across sectarian divides and peaceful appeals for change. Encouraged by a united population, the October revolution's most repeated slogan 'Killon ya ani killon' ('All of them means all of them') urged the political elites to step down. The revolution was initially victorious, forcing the sitting Hariri government to resign. However, the first euphoric weeks were followed by protests on a smaller scale, as the fury expressed by people of small means faded into their daily struggle to survive.

In 2020, the economic crisis hit Lebanon with full force, helped, but only slightly, by the economic decline following Covid-19 (Synaps, 2020). As if things could not get worse, on August 4th, 2020, 2,750 tonnes of ammonium nitrate stored at the Port of Beirut exploded, shocking the whole city, devastating homes of 300,000 inhabitants, injuring over 7,000 and killing over 200 (Harb and Fawaz, 2020). In 2021, the economic crisis saw staggering inflation rates and income poverty skyrocketing from 25 per cent of the population in 2019, to almost 74 per cent in 2021, coupled with 82 per cent of Lebanese households suffering from multi-dimensional poverty (ESCWA, 2021).[1] The economic decline prompted the World Bank

---

[1] Multi-dimensional poverty considers deprivation in the areas of health care, medicines, services, education, employment, housing and assets. A household is classified as poor if deprived in one area. If a household is deprived in two or more areas, it is classified as suffering from extreme multi-dimensional poverty (ESCWA, 2021).

to classify the Lebanese economic crisis as one of the three worst economic declines in the last 150 years (World Bank, 2021).

Activism and public protests have increasingly mobilized around issues of a non-sectarian and non-political character. This includes civil society initiatives to provide welfare services, mobilization of independent candidates in trade unions and student bodies, as well as numerous spaces for public debate (LCPS, 2020; Majed, 2020). In previous waves of protests, such mobilization has shifted the boundaries of sectarian divides. However, political elites have skilfully coopted protests for their own interests and protests have achieved little in changing the system itself (Clark and Zahar, 2015; Majed, 2020; Siegel, 2021). Thus, while Lebanese mobilization has been massive, it remains to be seen whether the slogan 'All of them means all of them' can continue to bring the Lebanese together.

Three municipalities: Tyre, Bourj Hammoud and Saida

This book looks beyond the national to include the local and everyday practices in Lebanese local peacebuilding. To do so, I analyse local peacebuilding in the municipalities of Tyre, Bourj Hammoud and Saida. While Tyre, Bourj Hammoud and Saida have all endured the Lebanese civil war and are affected by subsequent national disputes, their local particularities and similarities make – and remake – them as local spaces.

Tyre

Tyre is the capital of the most southern district in Lebanon, Caza Tyre, and is often described as lying outside of the immediate attention of central government developmental plans. It has been argued that, in the past, national neglect of the predominantly Shia south spurred the grievances felt by the Shia community towards the state before the outbreak of civil war in 1975. In the 1970s, it was also along the lines of social and economic grievances that the dynamic Shia Imam Musa Sadr initiated the Movement of the Deprived. However, although the movement was peaceful while Sadr was in charge, the wave of militarization sweeping over Lebanon in the 1970s also affected the Shia. In 1975, Sadr announced that he had formed the military wing Amal (in Arabic 'Hope'), trained and equipped by the Palestinians (Hanf, 1993, pp 108, 128). Sadr was a leader with great charisma and the first one to mobilize the Shia by connecting their economic grievances to demands for a political voice. As such, it was a shock for the community when Sadr disappeared without a trace in Libya in 1978. Although having disappeared, the legend of Musa Sadr runs deep. When the Libyan Gaddafi regime fell in 2011, many wanted to find out what had happened. However, the mystery remains, and Sadr continues to be legendary in the Shia community and for Amal in particular (Hanf, 1993, p 190; Rose, 2018).

During the first years of the civil war, south Lebanon stayed out of the power struggles in Beirut, but its events still affected Tyre and the region as a whole. To drive out the Palestinian troops that used the southern Lebanese territory to attack Israel, the Israeli army invaded in March 1978. As systematic bombardment preceded the advancement of the troops, south Lebanon, including Tyre, was severely damaged, and 250,000 Lebanese and Palestinian civilians fled, as did the Palestinian militants. In June 1978, the UN Security Council forced the Israelis to retreat, and the United Nations Interim Force for Southern Lebanon (UNIFIL) was formed. However, as they retreated, they handed over a 10-kilometre-wide strip along the border to the South Lebanese Army, a Christian militia and ally of Israel, headed by Major Haddad. The buffer zone ended just 10 kilometres south of Tyre (Hanf, 1993, p 230).

The continuation of the Palestinian–Israeli war in south Lebanon, together with Sadr's disappearance in 1978 and the Iranian revolution in 1979, spurred Amal's military involvement in the civil war (Chaib, 2009; Rose, 2018). From 1979, Amal fought Palestinian militias in a war that stretched across Lebanon but became a longstanding simmering warfare in the south. In 1980, Nabih Berri, one of the disappeared Sadr's closest confidants, became the military leader of Amal. Under his rule, Amal propagated the idea of a withdrawal of Palestinian guerrillas and a Lebanese republic based on a majority democracy. Today, Nabih Berri is the leader of the Amal political party and has been the speaker of parliament since 1992 (Hanf, 1993, pp 241–6; Rose, 2018).

With the continued Palestinian attacks on Israel, Israel invaded Lebanon for the second time in 1982. This time, Israeli advancements went all the way to the north of Beirut, thus, occupying Tyre, Saida and Bourj Hammoud among many other cities and villages. With the main goal of crushing the Palestine Liberation Organization (PLO), Israeli troops shelled Palestinian camps around Tyre and Saida as they moved north to besiege West Beirut, resulting in the Palestinians and members of the Syrian army being trapped in the area. The siege resulted in an internationally negotiated plan to evacuate the PLO to Tunisia (Hanf, 1993, p 256ff). In the Lebanese south, a few villages welcomed the retreat of the Palestinian militias. However, the evacuation of the PLO did not mean a quick retreat by the Israelis. In 1983, the Israelis withdrew from Beirut to the Awali river, just north of Saida, occupying the south Lebanon and Nabatiye regions (Mohafazaat). In 1985, Israel retreated to a security zone along the border, again controlling it in alliance with the South Lebanese Army.

As Israeli occupation continued, it implied economic restrictions and harsh tactics in the search for weapons, and the population grew angrier by the day. With the Amal movement unwilling to resort to violent means to pressure the Israelis to leave, another player emerged, gathering together disappointed Amal supporters and rebellious citizens. Inspired by the Islamic revolution in Iran, Hezbollah relentlessly fought Israeli occupation in the south and perceived an Islamic Republic of Lebanon as their end goal. As the means and objectives of the two Shia movements of Amal and Hezbollah diverged, their rivalry grew. In 1987, the two movements clashed for the first time, and in 1988 a Shia civil war broke out. Although open fighting ended through Syrian and Iranian mediation by 1989, the rivalry runs deep, dividing family members and still marking a political dividing line in south Lebanon (Chaib, 2009; Hanf, 1993, p 315ff).

With the civil war coming to an end, the first post-war parliamentarian elections in 1992 were a success for both Amal and Hezbollah, increasing their political influence from having no political posts to four and eight, respectively (Khazen, n.d.). As a result, both movements replaced the traditional Shia leaders, and the parliament elected Nabih Berri as the speaker of parliament, a post he still holds today (Hanf, 1993, p 632f). In the parliamentarian elections of 1996, the two parties were allies in an alliance dictated by Syria to counter intra-sectarian divisions (Chaib, 2009). However, at the local level, rivalry between Hezbollah and Amal remained. After the first municipal elections in 1998, Hezbollah controlled 55 municipalities and Amal 86 in south Lebanon. However, in the 2004 elections, it was the reverse with Hezbollah controlling 87 municipal councils and Amal 55. In addition, in 2004, Amal maintained control in only two of the major cities in the province, one of them Tyre (Hamzeh, 2004, p 133).

Even if national and municipal elections were held, the post-war period in Tyre is a mix between war and peace. Although not occupied itself, the continued Israeli occupation of the security zone just south of Tyre marked the period up until the year 2000. During that time, Hezbollah continued its resistance against Israel in the south and considered the Israeli withdrawal in 2000 their victory (Chaib, 2009). In 2006, the 33-day Hezbollah–Israel war caused devastation in Tyre and other Shia areas and many fled. As Israeli aerial bombardments and ground attacks came closer, the Amal-led municipality of Tyre tried to distance itself from the Hezbollah-led war, possibly as a tactic to avoid Israeli shelling and gain support from war-tired Lebanese. However, during the war, Amal's top leader, Nabih Berri, acted as the channel of communication for the Hezbollah leadership that had gone underground (Financial Times, 2006), demonstrating the double-sided coin of Hezbollah–Amal rivalry and cooperation. In addition to human and infrastructural damages, the large devastation of the war caused UNESCO to issue a 'heritage alert' calling for the parties to spare heritage sites in Tyre and other war-affected areas (UNESCO, 2006). With remains from the Roman Empire, Tyre is on UNESCO's world heritage list, one of five world heritage sites in Lebanon (UNESCO, 2017).

After 2006, Tyre has experienced relative calm. As a coastal city with some of the few still publicly available beaches in Lebanon, as well as cultural heritage sites, Tyre has aimed at establishing itself as a touristic site, where different communities live side by side. However, peaceful coexistence does not always seem to be so peaceful. In 2012, several bombings against shops, clubs and restaurants that sell alcohol occurred, marking a tension between Muslim and Christian ways of life (Porter, 2017; Reuters, 2012). As elsewhere in Lebanon, the most prominent consequence of the Syrian civil war is the many Syrian refugees that now live in the city, questioning the sectarian balance when a mostly Shia city receives a large amount of mostly Sunni refugees (Mourad, 2017, p 256). However, the perception of Tyre as a city under the tight grip of the two Shia parties of Amal and Hezbollah was countered in 2019 when the population joined in the nation-wide protests against the country's political elites.

Bourj Hammoud

Compared to Tyre, the municipality of Bourj Hammoud is situated only a few kilometres away from the centre of power in Lebanon. Just east of the Beirut River, Bourj Hammoud neighbours the municipality of Beirut, not far from downtown Beirut which hosts the Lebanese parliament, the prime minister's headquarters (Grand Serail), government agencies and international organizations and embassies. Bourj Hammoud emerged when tens of thousands of Armenian refugees from the Armenian genocide arrived in Lebanon in the 1920s and settled on a patch of land designated to them by the French Mandate administration. Today, it is a densely populated area, with a lively shopping district as well as workshops for shoes and jewellery. For many inhabitants of Beirut, it is known as the 'Armenian quarter', but it is also one of the areas with the lowest rents close to the centre of Beirut, encouraging a mix of inhabitants (Nucho, 2016, p 14ff).

Before the war, Bourj Hammoud was one of the more heterogeneous spaces within Beirut, with Armenian, Maronite as well as Shia and Palestinian communities within its municipal borders. Inter-sectarian affiliations characterized daily life, as the poor inhabitants of Bourj Hammoud met their daily needs in the space where they lived. Nevertheless, sects inhabited different spaces, and the Palestinians and Shia, in particular, were living in the quartier of Nabaa. Political and religious institutions also mattered in peoples' everyday lives. One of the most important is the Armenian party Tashnag, at the centre of Armenian political life but also in control of schools, churches and humanitarian organizations as well as youth and sports clubs. As such, Tashnag was a major force in keeping the Armenians

Armenian, preserving a national Armenian identity and cultural heritage, as well as remembering past suffering and the Armenian genocide (Geukjian, 2014; Joseph, 1975). Thus, despite their Lebanese citizenships and sharing religious practices (Christian Orthodox and Catholic) with many Lebanese, the Armenians have retained their communal identity as yet another sect in Lebanon (Geukjian, 2014).

The civil war further cemented the Armenianess of Bourj Hammoud. As fighting in Beirut divided the city into East and West Beirut, Bourj Hammoud was on the eastern, Christian, side of the green line. Tashnag mobilized the Armenians, and for most of the war Bourj Hammoud became an Armenian controlled area surrounded by fighting among other groups (Nucho, 2016). During the war, the Armenian community, led by the Tashnag party, adopted a policy of positive neutrality. Through this approach, it actively engaged in dialogues with the warring parties, advocating for a peaceful solution to the conflict that would maintain Lebanon as a unitary state with a power-sharing democracy, as it believed their communal rights could only be maintained by such a system. Through its position of neutrality, the Armenian community stayed outside of the warring of other groups, but with violence at its doorstep, the Tashnag party also created an Armenian militia to defend Bourj Hammoud (Geukjian, 2014).

However, the early war years also saw demographic changes within Bourj Hammoud. Starting in January 1976, Christian militias initiated sieges on Palestinian camps, and Shia and Sunni Muslim neighbourhoods inside East Beirut in order to clear the area from enemy groups. Meanwhile, Palestinian militias did the same to Christian areas. As violence played out between opposing parties, imposing or lifting sieges became a strategic tool. In June, the Palestinian and Shia quartier of Nabaa in Bourj Hammoud came under siege by Christian militias. When the inhabitants surrendered in August of the same year, the area was 'ethnically cleansed' by Christian militias. However, Musa Sadr negotiated an evacuation of the Shia population of Nabaa to the south and Beqaa, and the Palestinians left to West Beirut, preventing the forced displacement from becoming yet another massacre in the Lebanese war (Hanf, 1993, pp 223, 327; International Center for Transitional Justice, 2013). The property that was left was taken over by Maronite refugees from other areas in Lebanon as well as Armenians (Nucho, 2016, p 23). For the rest of the war, Bourj Hammoud was further strengthened as an Armenian space. Tashnag's militia of of armed Armenian men, and some women, patrolled the streets. Armenian political and religious organizations supplied basic services to the residents and, as the war dragged on, many Armenian-owned businesses or Armenian-run organizations relocated to Bourj Hammoud. From a public space before the war, Bourj Hammoud became 'a kind of [Armenian] fortress' (Nucho, 2016, p 24).

After the war, many of the displaced residents retained ownership of their properties in Bourj Hammoud. Some of them moved back, while others provided housing for other non-Armenian groups to migrate to Beirut, including Iraqi and Syrian refugees in more recent times. However, the political power has remained concentrated within the Armenian organizations, particularly the Tashnag party, reproducing Armenianess through everyday life (Nucho, 2016).

In the continuation of violent events that have evolved in post-war Lebanon, Bourj Hammoud has been a bystander as well as at the centre of events. Situated in the eastern parts of Greater Beirut, it was outside the immediate scope of the Israeli bombardment of Beirut's southern suburbs in the 2006 war. Close but not directly situated in the city centre, nor being one of the more contested neighbourhoods in Beirut where Lebanese politics or regional involvement of Lebanese actors have had more violent repercussions, Bourj Hammoud has been comparatively calm. However, through the influx of refugees, first, displaced Lebanese in 2006, and more recently Iraqi and Syrian refugees, Bourj Hammoud has felt the effects of domestic and regional events. Some refugees have Armenian roots, but not all. This diversity of new inhabitants has sometimes created conflicts between new and old inhabitants in the local space (Nucho, 2016, p 131). Bourj Hammoud was also one of the municipalities affected by the waste crisis in 2015, creating great dissatisfaction among the public. In the 2016 temporary solution for waste management in Beirut, Bourj Hammoud was at the heart of the solution when it reopened the Bourj Hammoud landfill site, an uncontrolled dumpsite used during the civil war (Massena, 2017). In addition, Bourj Hammoud lies only a few kilometers away from the Port of Beirut, neighbouring Karantina, one of the most severely hit neighbourhoods in the August 4, 2020, Beirut port blast (Fawaz et al, 2012; Harb and Fawaz, 2020).

Saida

Situated along the coast in between Bourj Hammoud and Tyre, Saida is the third largest city in Lebanon. Politically, Saida is the hometown of the Hariri family and its political party the Future Movement. Influential Saidonian representatives include former prime minister Rafiq Hariri, his son Saad Hariri, as well as parliamentarians Bahia Hariri and Fouad Siniora (Ghaddar, 2016). Saida is also hometown to the Saad family and the Popular Nasserist Organization (PNO) founded by Maarouf Saad. In Saida, PNO was a uniting force against the national government during the civil war. Although there have been instances of cooperation between Hariri and Saad, mostly in the later years of the civil war, their two political parties, and allies, make up the main competitors for power for municipal and parliamentarian posts, marking a divide between market-oriented and socialist ideals of development (*The Monthly*, 2016).

Saida is a predominantly Sunni city surrounded by Christian and Shia villages, with the Palestinian camps of Ain al-Hilweh and Nahr al-Bared in its vicinity. During the civil war, the Nasserite militias based in Saida were close allies to the PLO, making Saida and the surrounding camps targets for the Israeli intervention in 1982. As the Israelis withdrew in 1985, Saida was a place for celebration. However, ignited by what the Lebanese Forces saw as unjust allocations of power and economic opportunities happening elsewhere in Lebanon, the celebratory moment turned into one of the darker moments of the civil war. As Lebanese Forces shelled Sunni Muslim suburbs of Saida, Nasserite militias, Sunni army soldiers and the PLO joined forces. As the Palestinians and Sunnis advanced, the clashes resulted in an expulsion of the inhabitants of 50 Christian villages surrounding Saida, villages that were then destroyed, as claimed by Hanf, 'probably for fear of Shi'is moving into the abandoned houses' (1993, p 302). When the war had come to an end, the alliance between the Nasserites and the PLO remained, sharing power over their respective territories in Saida (Hanf, 1993, p 604).

If the war years had seen the prominence of the Nasserites (PNO) led by the Saad family, the post-war years saw the growth of influence by the Hariri family competing for power nationally as well as in Saida. Rafiq Hariri, son of Saida, had spent the years during the war in Saudi Arabia building a fortune in the construction business. After the war, he returned to Lebanon to become a parliamentarian and prime minister from 1992 to 1998 and 2000 to 2004, focusing on rebuilding Lebanon after the civil war. As the power of Rafiq Hariri grew nationally, so did it locally. Today, the sister of Rafiq Hariri, Bahia Hariri, exerts considerable power locally and nationally. A parliamentarian since 1992 and former minister of education (2008–2009), she is at the centre of the political party of the Hariri's, the Future Movement, and the President of the Hariri Foundation, a civil society association founded by Rafiq Hariri and based in Saida (Ghaddar, 2016).

Despite a calm post-war period, Saida has not been exempt from eruptions of violence. With the largest Palestinian refugee camp in Lebanon, Ain al-Hilweh, in its vicinity, Saida has had a ringside seat to reoccurring contestations for power between Palestinian factions in Lebanon and the region as a whole, because 'If you are in control of it [Ain al-Hilweh], you are symbolically in control of the Palestinians in Lebanon' (Mahdawi, 2008). Although the camps' entrances are heavily securitized by the Lebanese army, Palestinian camps, including Ain al-Hilweh, 'have been considered a safe haven for wanted terrorists fleeing arrest' (Zaatari, 2018). In addition, Saida has experienced local clashes pertaining to the war in Syria. In 2012, Sunni Sheikh Ahmed al-Assir and his followers staged sit-ins in Saida, calling for Hezbollah to abandon its arms and support for Syrian President Bashar al Assad. Supporters of al-Assir clashed with supporters of Hezbollah in November 2012, and again in June 2013, with the army intervening to stop fighting (Zaatari, 2012, 2013). Although al-Assir's resort to guns was rejected by Saidonian citizens, he voiced concerns about Shia Hezbollah, which were widely recognized by the Sunni population (Barnard, 2013). As such, the clashes were a local concern but drew on legacies of hostilities between sects from the civil war, as well as the more recent polarization between Sunni and Shia in the Middle East.

Nevertheless, disputes in Saida have less to do with exceptional flashes of violence and more to do with the everyday lives of most Lebanese. In 2019, Saidonian citizens joined the nation-wide protests against the political elite and a country in decline, opening up local spaces for political debates and aspirations. However, with the economic crisis looming over Lebanon, hopes for political change have been replaced by the quest for everyday survival.

Conclusion

In this chapter I have introduced the reader to Lebanese local governance as well as past and present developments and their repercussions for dividing lines, modes of governance and current developments. Based in a broader debate about Lebanese developments, the chapter has introduced the three municipalities of particular interest in the book: Tyre, Bourj Hammoud and Saida. Highlighting the trajectories of the civil war and its aftermath in Tyre, Bourj Hammoud and Saida the chapter has emphasized how the three local spaces have evolved in their own particular way, but still represent part of a common trajectory of Lebanese struggles for diversity and consensus.

Through a discussion of local, national and individual developments in Tyre, Bourj Hammoud and Saida, three themes can be discerned. First, I have considered the polarization in Lebanese politics and its shifts. From the early 1900s to the civil war and its aftermath, alliances between Lebanese actors and Arab powers or Western states have influenced Lebanese politics and development. Present-day politics continue the pattern, divided between the March 8 bloc, as pro-Syria, Iran and Russia (referring to themselves as pro-Arab) and the March 14 bloc, as pro-West and closely collaborating with the Arab states in the Gulf. As the chapter has described, the polarization and its shifts have influenced Lebanese conflicts as well as peacebuilding. While Syria dominated Lebanon's post-war recovery until 2005, later years have seen increasing Western liberal peacebuilding interventions, as well as regional rivalries between Iran and Saudi Arabia playing out through political influence and development assistance to a Lebanese economy in crisis. Second, I have noted the continuous and increased struggle for local and non-political alternatives. The local struggle was visible in the mobilization for peace during the war but has been present ever since. For example, in the civil society mobilization for local elections, international actors turning towards local governments for the delivery of development assistance, as well as civil society mobilization in the aftermath of the waste crisis and Beirut blast. Third, the chapter has highlighted Lebanon as sectarian and clientelistic, but it has also revealed how conflicts and cooperation between sects sustains the political power of elites as well as welfare services and the livelihoods of the Lebanese. In the next three chapters, we turn to exploring local peacebuilding in Tyre, Bourj Hammoud and Saida. As the empirical chapters will show, their differences in sectarian belongings and experiences of events are both particularly local as well as intertwined with Lebanese developments and politics. Thus, studying Lebanese municipalities as cases of local peacebuilding embodies the notion of peacebuilding through local governments, as well as specific circumstances visible only through a closer scrutiny of particular local practices.

3

Service Delivery: Providing for Local Needs

This chapter analyses service delivery as a peacebuilding function. In theory, providing for local needs is central to local legitimacy, which promotes stability and peace. When service delivery provides for local needs, the state is perceived as responsive and therefore, uncontested as a legitimate power (Roberts, 2011b). However, for service delivery to provide a peacebuilding function it should be responsive, inclusive, capable and promote an idea of economic development. Throughout the chapter, the perceptions of municipal councillors, municipal employees and civil society actors in the municipalities of Tyre, Bourj Hammoud and Saida further our understanding of service delivery as part of the municipality's role in local peacebuilding.

The services analysed include waste management, infrastructural developments and the provision for everyday needs. These are not the only services provided by the three municipalities, nor are they solely provided by municipalities. Instead, these are illustrations of the complexities involved in local service delivery and what that means for service delivery as a peacebuilding function. As we will see, services providing waste management may promote an image of the municipality as responsive and capable and therefore, locally legitimate, whereas the lack of management, or inadequate management, spurs discontent. In addition, infrastructural developments serve to illustrate the idea of economic development, or how the belief that changes on the ground improve economic opportunities for the local population, but where responsiveness, inclusiveness and capacity may look different, depending on the context or collaborations enabling infrastructural projects. Furthermore, service delivery related to social needs may be responsive but not necessarily inclusive nor portray an image of a capable local government. The chapter suggests that how service delivery is performed matters for how it is perceived by municipal representatives and local stakeholders, influencing the municipality's engagement with local peacebuilding and the type of peace built.

Tyre

On a daily basis, municipal employees empty refuse bins on the streets and transport the waste to the waste treatment plant in Ain el-Baal, built to treat waste from all 63 towns and villages in the district of Tyre (Tyre Caza). However, the plant, built to treat 120 tonnes of waste daily, cannot treat the 300 tonnes of waste produced daily in the district. As explained by one interviewee: "In Caza of Tyre, we have one place in Ain el-Baal. … But this place was wrong, because we have 63 villages in Caza of Tyre. This can't help, it is too small" (Int. 4, municipal councillor, June 2015). The excess waste is dumped in the landfill site in Ras el-Ain, south of Tyre, or ends up being dumped wherever there is space, also within the urban area of Tyre: "the public garden, it is 16 acres, but now it is used for storing garbage and for parking trucks" (Int. 47, municipal councillor, December 2015). Despite their awareness of the problem, this leaves much to wish for in order to respond to the existing local needs of waste management.

However, at the time of the interviews, the municipality was planning to establish a new waste management plant, together with UN-Habitat. With the project proposal already in place, the municipal councillor described a situation where the "first problem is not money, it is land" (Int. 47, municipal councillor, December 2015). However, as land often belongs to the central state or other nationally influential actors, finding a piece of land suitable for the project had become an issue involving state actors. Another complicating factor was the attainment of an environmental permit from the ministry of environment to build and run the plant, attained only in 2021 through a personal visit to the ministry (Int. 52, municipal councillor, November 2021). With the involvement of UN-Habitat and the Lebanese state, the solution of the waste management problem was no longer a local issue, limiting the municipality's capacity to answer to local needs. The capacity of the municipality to initiate and implement changes for waste management is incorporated in a much larger framework of governmental and local as well as political and personal restrictions, compromising their ability to respond to local needs.

While the issue of waste management remained unsolved, many public spaces in Tyre were undergoing infrastructural developments through the governmentally run and internationally funded project on Cultural Heritage and Urban Development (CHUD). The project had improved the infrastructure of roads, parking areas, pavements and the new vegetable market in the centre of the town. In addition, the project beautified the old town and enhanced the cultural heritage areas of the city, including the restoration of the Beit al-Mamlouk, an old building used by the municipality as a city hall. However, the external ownership and management of the project diminished the role of the municipality to a supportive role, possibly enhancing the efficiency of the project. As one interviewee explained:

'We are shouting and pushing. We are following these projects to ask questions, and to provide them with local help if they need it. These projects should be run by the central government. We are just a buffer, we are asking all parties to accelerate the process to ask if they need any local help that we can provide.' (Int. 1, municipal councillor, December 2014)

The municipality's supportive role was not appreciated by all. Repeating a sentiment I heard from local residents, one interviewee claimed that some of the improvements were meant to put Tyre on the touristic map, but not necessarily meant to make the population feel at home:

'Italian engineers visited the city and found it very beautiful and [thought] that the city should be part of the international tourism. And the mayor ... visited Italy and saw the cities and thought that it should be like that the city; they want Tyre to be like a city in Italy.' (Int. 49, civil society actor, December 2015)

Echoed by another interviewee: "The people see that streets, gardens, etc. are being built. But, there are negative consequences of certain projects. We have broadened the pavements, and we have reduced the roads ... but we are not used to walking" (Int. 50, civil society actor, December 2015). This illustrates the difficulties of creating infrastructural developments that the local population perceive as being for them, without including them. In addition, infrastructural changes create new challenges, as he continued to explain: "Unfortunately, the municipality has not been able to make the municipal police prevent the negative effects of the pavements. For example, you can now find bicycles and motorcycles on the pavements. How can the people walk there if it is like that?" (Int. 50, civil society actor, December 2015).

The civil society actor captures how the created spaces are perceived as unsuitable for the local context but also demonstrates how these new spaces emphasize the municipality's responsibility for them. As such, infrastructural developments are not only concrete changes in the landscape, but they also create new spaces of governance. When the municipality is unable to fulfil this governance role, through policing or convincing the local population to change their habits, the municipality is seen as unable to fulfil its role. Thus, having the capacity to build infrastructure does not necessarily translate to being seen as a capablelocal government.

However, some projects have enhanced public spaces and increased the municipality's ability to manage public places. The construction of a new vegetable market is one such project, as described by an employee at CDR, the governmental agency in charge of the project:

'for this project, we were there next to them. ... We helped them to prepare the resettlement plan, we did it together, and then they submitted it to us. To be sure that they approve it and they are fine with it. And it is also the operation [of the market], for example, the rent based on the yearly maintenance and the usage of infrastructure such as electricity and water, sewages and having people to do the administration of the market to pay him the salary. So, when we do this, it is like giving them the knowhow on how to do for other projects. It is important. Now we know that if they face other projects, they know what points to put and how to go forward.' (Int. 10, government employee, June 2015)

However, moving beyond the material construction of the market as a place, the project also meant something for the imagined meaning of a local space (Björkdahl and Kappler, 2017), in this case, creating a space of reciprocity between the vendors and the municipality, and building trust in the capacity of the local government. As one former municipal councillor explained:

'When I started with them, they [didn't] believe that we will build a new [market]. They thought that we will destroy this one and then we will go home. We started with them; [telling them that] we will build a temporary market, spend money on that [building it]. Now it is better.' (Int. 4, municipal councillor, June 2015)

The inclusive and responsive manner in which the building of the vegetable market was performed promoted an image of a legitimate local government. Although the project was not locally funded and owned, its performance illustrates service delivery as a peacebuilding function. Thus, the infrastructural changes taking place in Tyre both confirm and contradict the theoretical starting points of this chapter. On the one hand, as the CHUD project has evolved since 2004, it has seen the implementation of many projects, such as the building of the new vegetable market, parking areas and pavements. Such visible changes portray a picture of a capable municipality involved in the delivery of services for infrastructural development. In addition, with the municipality as the implementing actor in closest cooperation with the local community, it puts the municipality at the forefront of inclusive and responsive service delivery.

However, the municipality's inclusion in externally run and funded projects also prompted civil society actors to question the ability of the municipality to include and respond to local needs, also revealing the expectation that the municipality should be the actor in charge. This demonstrates that if projects are not responsive or inclusive, the services delivered can become contradictive for the municipality's role in peacebuilding, illustrating how expectations and perceptions of service delivery greatly matter for it as a peacebuilding function (Brinkerhoff et al, 2012). As we have seen, the municipality of Tyre is a beneficiary and participant in infrastructural development projects, but it is not fully in charge and ownership does not belong to the municipality. Through these examples, we start to discern that even if the municipality has the capacity to deliver services in cooperation with other actors, visible progress is not enough, but, also, responsiveness to local circumstances plays an important role in improving legitimacy and creating an uncontested space for the local government. For the municipality's role in peacebuilding, this illustrates that the capacity to provide infrastructural developments is not necessarily the same as the capacity to provide responsive infrastructural developments.

However, service delivery is not only about delivering large infrastructural projects or building a new waste management plant. Through its daily activities, the municipality uses its available capacity, either autonomous or through connections to other central state agencies, to provide services that attend to the population's daily needs. Although these services are diverse, I will here look closer at the role of the municipality in providing for local security and potable water.

Although the army and the national police, called the Internal Security Forces (ISF), are the main actors that monitor the security situation in Lebanon, the municipality employs a municipal police. The main task of the municipal police is to control the public order, normally controlling issues such as traffic, parking and construction permits. However, with the increased number of spillovers from the Syrian civil war and an increased number of Syrian refugees, public safety has become a local issue in Lebanese municipalities. Some municipalities have implemented curfews for Syrians, sometimes as a response to disturbances of the public order, but more often perceived as a precaution to prevent possible disturbances or conflicts, even if they were not common at the time (Taslakian, 2016). According to one municipal councillor, Tyre had not experienced increased tensions due to the influx of Syrian refugees, even if this was dependent on international organizations providing for their basic needs. Nevertheless, the municipal councillor did perceive the increased number of Syrians as demanding a municipal response to increase public order, mirroring developments in other Lebanese municipalities and emphasizing that perceptions of needs and expectations of services are important in assessing responsive service delivery (Mcloughlin, 2015; Taslakian, 2016). As he continued to explain, the municipality had two choices for controlling public order: either implement a curfew or increase the presence of municipal police. In Tyre, the second choice had been selected, as he explained:

'Because we have the capacity to do this, we decided to increase our number of policemen, and that needs an approval from the ministry of interior. We got it, and we increased our patrols in the city. With cooperation with the other security institutions, the Lebanese army, Talaab [the office for official documents and registers] and ISF. Even if it cost us more money. But, we cannot ask Syrians not to move at the same time [when] Palestinians can move, Sudanese can move, etc.' (Int. 1, municipal councillor, December 2014)

Although exercising their capacity to adapt policing services for the local needs was not an autonomous decision in this case, the municipality was able to make the necessary arrangements to be able to respond to emerging needs. This illustrates the interconnectedness of local capacity with the regulations involved in Lebanese multi-level governance.

Another example of how the municipality was able to make the necessary arrangements to address local needs was something I witnessed during an interview with one municipal councillor. Receiving and making multiple phone calls during our interview, the interviewee described that the central state is the foremost body responsible for potable water. However, that does not mean that the municipality stands by and watches when problems occur. As he explained:

'The water authority is responsible for potable water, but they aren't providing diesel for the pumps to work. So, the municipality has two options – provide diesel or leave people without water. [municipal councillor makes a phone call to redirect diesel from the municipality to the water plant]. It comes from the municipality's budget.' (Int. 47, municipal councillor, December 2015)

The municipality, although restrained in its autonomy and resources, does have the ability to assist when governmental capacity is insufficient. The need to sometimes take over responsibilities belonging to the central state, and doing so despite it implying that already scarce resources are redirected towards that need, is not unique to the municipality of Tyre. As will be discussed, the municipality of Bourj Hammoud had no other option than to take over non-municipal tasks as the waste crisis evolved in 2015. In Tyre, the response of the municipality illustrates that proximity and knowledge of local needs do influence the services provided. At the same time, the municipality's involvement in the national authority's affairs demonstrates a grey zone of administrative decentralization where the boundaries of local and national responsibility are blurred. Acknowledging that in this case the municipality is taking over the government's job, the municipal councillor emphasized: "it is legal to do it" (Int. 47, municipal councillor, December 2015). While decentralization is a still unfulfilled undertaking of the Ta'if Peace Agreement, municipalities do seem to be able to create room for manoeuvre to provide for local needs. By providing diesel to the water plant and managing the security in times of an increased refugee population, the municipality uses its available resources, or attracts needed resources, to provide services according to daily needs, thus, navigating their capacity, existing regulations and emerging local needs to provide services.

Service delivery and peacebuilding in Tyre

For the peacebuilding role played by the municipality of Tyre, the ability to respond to local needs is clearly dependent on capacity and autonomy over projects, but also the municipal councillors' knowledge of the population's situation and inclusiveness towards those most in need. At the same time, it is not apparent that a delivery of services that responds to these needs increases the legitimacy of the municipality in the eyes of the population, as they are not always visible to the public but occur through informal decisions or are put in place to prevent a need from occurring. This emphasizes the many difficulties of assessing service delivery as a peacebuilding function, as services may be important but not necessarily seen by the public or perceived as delivered by the municipality (Brinkerhoff et al, 2012; Mcloughlin, 2015).

In Tyre, service delivery as a peacebuilding function is an ongoing process with many twists and turns. As argued, the perception of capacity, responsiveness and inclusiveness, as well as the idea of economic development envisioned, matters for what meaning service delivery has for the municipality's role in local peacebuilding (Mcloughlin, 2015). In a few instances, the municipality of Tyre has addressed local needs within its own capacity. However, as their autonomous service delivery is small in comparison and practically invisible in comparison to ongoing infrastructural projects, their dependence on outside actors for service delivery overshadows autonomous service provision. Therefore, service delivery rather portrays the municipality as a puppet. As expressed by the interviewees, instances of puppetry have given civil society actors the impression that service delivery in the municipality of Tyre is internationally run. If service delivery is internationally run, then it has little possibility of becoming a peacebuilding function through being responsive, inclusive and demonstrating the capacity of the local government, since the importance of proximity is lost (Brinkerhoff, 2011).

However, the different sides of service delivery in Tyre portrayed here, also show that there is an interconnectedness between the instances of capacity and puppetry, as local capacity to respond and include has grown through the nationally run CHUD project. However, even if infrastructural developments were sometimes negatively perceived, service delivery opened spaces of contestation, where the municipality became visible. As such, local service delivery enabled a possibility of increased local legitimacy, thus, performing a peacebuilding function. However, legitimacy through service delivery is not something you have or lack; rather, it is created, and lost, through a constant process of interaction, negotiation and discussion.

Bourj Hammoud

In the 1990s, the Lebanese government outsourced waste management in Greater Beirut, including the municipality of Bourj Hammoud, to the private company Sukleen. This removed waste management from the responsibilities of the municipalities and, as one municipal councillor explained, simultaneously removed an important source of income:

> 'Instead of alleviating the burden of the municipality, it turned it worse because it was a pretext to cancel these taxes or take the taxes away from the municipalities. And the central government would make the contract with the company of its own choosing, not at a very cheap cost, and it would deduct that sum from the money that it should have passed on to the municipality.' (Int. 15, municipal councillor, June 2015)

However, in 2015, the privatized waste collection for Greater Beirut came to a halt. As the Naameh landfill site was closed, Sukleen stopped collecting waste. With waste piling up on the streets, protests mobilized against the state. However, as the central government was unable to agree on, and implement, another solution for waste management, the limelight fell on the municipalities of the affected areas (Dakroub and Lakiss, 2015; Massena, 2017). With the waste piling up on the streets of Bourj Hammoud, the population mobilized towards their nearest authority, the municipality:

> 'Unfortunately, the public knows only that the one responsible for his local affairs is the municipality. Therefore, the one who is to blame for any problems in the locality is the municipality, and people are not interested in finding the root causes of the problems. They see the garbage right beside them and they demand to have that problem solved.' (Int. 29, municipal councillor, November 2015)

Despite the municipality's responsibility for waste being long gone, the lack of service provision caused a reaction against the local government and placed demands on them to provide the service. In interviews conducted in Bourj Hammoud prior to the waste crisis, such demands were largely absent, suggesting that when daily needs were met, how the service was delivered was not questioned. However, the sudden halt in services usually taken for granted demonstrates the link between public expectations and local legitimacy (Mcloughlin, 2015). Although the public did not care much for how services were delivered, they did expect the municipality to govern the local space to ensure that the service was delivered. Thus, the link between service provision and attribution is blurred (Mcloughlin, 2015), and so is the link between lack of provision and accountability.

However, as the crisis dragged on, the municipality did respond:

> 'All of a sudden, we have to rent trucks to pick up the garbage; we have to hire employees, workers to do garbage collection and all of this is happening suddenly. For 18 years, the municipality did not have the equipment, not the human resources to deal with garbage issues. Nor did they have time to do the necessary preparations, nor did they have the necessary sums ... our budget is very strained because of it. But we are doing it. But we are cutting back on other things, other projects that were already in process. But we have to because we have no other option.' (Int. 29, municipal councillor, November 2015)

When the national government failed to find a solution, the municipality had no other option but to step in. However, it came with environmental effects on the local space. With the closing of the Naameh landfill site, each municipality was left on its own to figure out a solution for disposing the waste. For Bourj Hammoud, a dense urban area, the question of space was an additional challenge:

> 'So, we found a small parcel of land and started removing the garbage from the streets ... and put them on this very small plot of land. And, when the crisis went on for days and days, we have almost 150 tonnes of garbage per day, which is a huge quantity, so we started to bring heavy machinery to press down the garbage to be able to bring in more quantities. And, even that is almost at its end. So, I don't know what will happen because it is everyone for himself now, all of a sudden.' (Int. 29, municipal councillor, November 2015)

The feeling of inadequacy of the solution was shared by civil society actors, as one young woman described: "till now, there is still the problem, so it wasn't solved. We should recycle or do something" (Int. 26, civil society actor, November 2015). While waste was no longer on the streets, the interviewee questioned the effectiveness of the response. Thus, while the municipality acted on the acute need, they did not fulfil her expectations for environmentally sound developments. As she perceived the municipality as having missed the opportunity to promote a different route for local development, her unfulfilled expectations tinted her perception of the municipality as a capable and legitimate local actor.

The discussion of waste management in Bourj Hammoud illustrates the connection between expectations and delivery of basic services and the perceived legitimacy of the local state. However, it also highlights the complex interaction of legislation with municipal capacity and popular legitimacy, which allows or restricts the municipality to promote responsive services as well as proactive developments (Mcloughlin, 2015; Romeo, 2013).

In comparison with the issue of waste management, where the crisis that emerged demanded that the municipality acted, infrastructural developments in Bourj Hammoud happened at a much slower pace. With few open spaces within the municipal territory, private and public building projects were in general scarce. However, the lack of space did not mean that infrastructural developments were not on the municipality's agenda. Explaining that the municipality of Bourj Hammoud had built affordable apartments, or social housing, already in the 1950s, one municipal councillor expressed:

> 'A little less than a decade ago, the municipal council of Bourj Hammoud decided to build a new set of houses within the framework of the social housing. It is about 200 apartments, 70 shops to stimulate the economic growth, and also a multi-level car park to solve the problem of parking in the area.' (Int. 12, municipal councillor, May 2015)

Several municipal councillors mentioned the importance of the social housing project for the residents of Bourj Hammoud, especially for making housing more affordable for the young population (Int. 12, 30, 31). This addressed the existing needs expressed by many of the interviewees, from municipal councillors and municipal employees to civil society actors with differing sectarian belonging: that poverty and overcrowding were two of Bourj Hammoud's greatest challenges (Int. 13, 17, 27, 30, 31). Describing the influx of Iraqi and Syrian refugees as well as the rising prices of housing, one civil society actor described Bourj Hammoud as "becoming a more crowded place [and] people are getting poorer" (Int. 27, civil society actor, November 2015). The building of 200 apartments, with the ambition of selling them to the residents at a price equivalent to their construction cost could therefore be of great importance for responding to the growing needs of Bourj Hammoudi citizens. As claimed by one municipal councillor: "the young, and the ones who are registered in Bourj Hammoud, can buy, they have the privilege" (Int. 30, municipal councillor, November 2015).

However, a social housing project like this comes with particular caveats in Lebanese local governance, related to the registry of citizens. In Lebanon, citizens are registered in the municipality of their forefathers, and, where they live matters less than where they are registered for their right to vote and receive municipal services (Salamey, 2014). The project would deliver social housing to the constituency of registered residents in Bourj Hammoud because: "There are government decrees that say that you cannot provide aid to anyone within your district if he or she is not a registered voter in your district" (Int. 12, municipal councillor, May 2015). As such, the inclusiveness of service delivery is stipulated by law.

However, in a time of demographic change, who is included also tells us something about the meaning of Bourj Hammoud. Although the social housing project was highly regarded by Armenian as well as Christian Maronite municipal councillors and civil society actors, the Armenians and Christian Maronites seemed to be endorsing it for slightly different reasons. One interviewee who works with the Christian Maronites emphasized the need for affordable housing, saying that: "When Syrian and Iraqi refugees came to Bourj Hammoud, things started to become more expensive, especially renting an apartment. … So, Lebanese people started to quit this area, to live in other areas" (Int. 27, civil society actor, November 2015). While not disregarding the need for affordable housing, interviewees with an Armenian heritage emphasized the demographic changes that had been going on for a long time: "In 1975, we were more than 250,000. Now, we are no longer [that many], 50,000–60,000 only. Even if the war is over. If they have moved, they are not coming back" (Int. 30, municipal councilor, November 2015).

In a time of demographic change, the inclusiveness in the social housing project caters to the 'original population' rather than supporting newly arrived inhabitants. The quest for preserving the original constellation of the municipality was ongoing for all local communities. However, as 'a kind of [Armenian] fortress' (Nucho, 2016, p 24), and one of only two constituencies that enable Lebanese Armenians to have some, albeit small, national influence, preserving the Armenianess of Bourj Hammoud was crucial. As one interviewee claimed: "the Armenian parties are pushing the Armenian community to stay in Bourj Hammoud or in Anjar, which are the two Armenian municipalities in Lebanon" (Int. 31, municipal councillor, November 2015). In such a context, infrastructural developments can be seen as a way of preserving the Armenianess of Bourj Hammoud, that is preserving the little influence a locality with an Armenian majority can have. Infrastructural developments, through social housing, became one way of preserving the local space.

In Bourj Hammoud, the civil society actively played a role in the provision of health care and education as well as other social services, mirroring the developments in most parts of Lebanon (Cammett and Issar, 2010). Some interviewees perceived this as a division of tasks between the municipality and civil society organizations. As claimed by one civil society actor: "the municipality is about legal issues, papers and things. We have other associations [for cultural and publication activities as well as healthcare, etc.] Each one of them has its fields" (Int. 26, civil society actor, November 2015). However, despite the division of tasks, the municipality was not only actively involved in supporting the service provisions of civil society actors, but also in raising issues and planning for the delivery of projects. According to municipal councillors, the municipality worked "through the civil society" (Int. 12, municipal councillor, May 2015). In 2015, one municipal councillor identified drug abuse as an example:

> 'We contact an NGO that works with youths and one that works on the drug issue, and we schedule a meeting, and tell them that as a municipality we want to work on the drug problem. So please, let us put together a project or several projects and we will support you financially, logistically. We will provide you everything. And we work with and through the civil society. It is very seldom that we do something as a municipality ourselves.' (Int. 12, municipal councillor, May 2015)

This picture was mirrored in interviews with civil society actors. One interviewee emphasized the collaboration in a project on medical check-ups in schools, saying that: "The municipality helps the NGOs and the NGOs help the municipality to do this project. It's not owned by the municipality; it is a cooperation and communication" (Int. 16, civil society actor, June 2015). Several civil society organizations emphasized the cooperation, but also the essential support the municipality provided for the NGOs to be able to attend to local needs such as health care, education, poverty relief or cultural and sporting events. Thus, the cooperation between the municipality and NGOs is a strategy with mutual benefits. For the municipality, active involvement with the civil society to identify, plan and deliver services allows the municipality to be part of the response to local needs. The responsiveness to needs is crucial for building a locally legitimate peace, demonstrating local service delivery as a peacebuilding function.

However, the close collaboration with civil society also raises the question of who is perceived as the provider of services, and thus who makes legitimacy gains (Krampe, 2016; Menkhaus, 2006). In interviews with municipal councillors and civil society actors, the interconnection between the two became apparent for the delivery of services. Nevertheless, even if civil society organizations see the municipality as a crucial partner in service delivery, it is not apparent that the image is shared by the public at large. As McLoughlin (2019) reminds us, who delivers services and who receives praise for the delivery of services is dependent on the political environment of each specific case. In Lebanon, where sectarian divides characterize the political environment of local spaces, the question of inclusion in service delivery becomes key.

The provision of services for all is important in the storyline of the municipality of Bourj Hammoud (Int. 12, 14, 29, 30). Given the presence of sectarianism in Lebanon, the equal provision of services and aid was something that the municipality took extra care to point out:

> 'When we decide on support to local communities and NGOs, we decide to be extremely fair and give all equal chances. The only additional thing that some of them receive is when they cooperate with the municipality on certain projects ... they get additional aid, but not to the NGO but to the project itself.' (Int. 29, municipal councillor, November 2015)

However, through the body language and assertiveness of one municipal councillor when he claimed, "we are very meticulous about being fair and granting all the components of our community equal aid, support and chances. That is very important to us" (Int. 29, municipal councillor, November 2015), I believe I am not the first to ask about equality and inclusion in service provision (see for example Cammett and Issar, 2010; Egan and Tabar, 2016; Joseph, 1975; Nucho, 2016).

Interviewees from the Christian Maronite community raised the issue and expressed a feeling of exclusion. One municipal councillor from the Maronite community agreed with the municipal councillor that the Maronite religious communities as well as local associations also received support from the municipality, emphasizing a good relationship between the communities. However, there was a touch of grievance in his statements as he described a situation where the municipality was supporting the main activities of the Maronite community because of their constant struggle for support. He claimed:

> 'There are 34 committees in the [Maronite] church, and the municipality supports the main activities. We are pushing the municipality to support them. We need to push to get support. The Armenians don't need to push, but the Maronite community needs to do that.' (Int. 31, municipal councillor, November 2015)

The importance of municipal support for religious needs was explained by the lack of civil family law in Lebanon, making religious communities principal actors in service delivery. As one interviewee explained:

> 'There is no civil law in Lebanon so everything is religious. So, we serve the people in everything. When they need us for marriage, divorce, for everything. On the other hand, as a church, we have many social works, like helping the poor, providing education for children, and also after-school activities for children, for youth, for ladies to help

them find work or learn how to work or manage their own business.' (Int. 27, local association, November 2015)

Although some municipal support was channelled through the church to the main activities provided, interviewees from the Maronite community did not perceive service provision as equal. When asked about the picture painted by Armenian municipal councillors on equality between communities, the interviewee chuckled, saying:

> 'It is typical Lebanese [interviewee chuckles]. … They are nice, they are not evil [interviewee chuckles], but sometimes, because the [mayor] of the municipality, when he is someone who is from the community, because he is Armenian and everyone around him is Armenian, it is normal for them to serve their people before they serve other people, ok. It's normal, I don't see that it's something bad. But we always try to ask for more group work and sharing.' (Int. 27, civil society actor, November 2015)

He continued to explain that the congregation itself had connections to influential actors outside of Bourj Hammoud and in this way attracted aid and resources for the congregation. As he explained, "we have people from the ministry of social work; they are here in our community, they help us to serve the people" (Int. 27, civil society actor, November 2015). In this way, the Maronite community of Bourj Hammoud took advantage of their position as a national majority when responding to local needs. This resembles the pattern of welfare provision through sectarian divides as illustrated by Cammett and Issar (2010) (see also Nucho, 2016). The Armeninan community, a local majority but national minority, did not express the same feelings about the support from national actors.

The feelings of unequal inclusion expressed by the Maronite community are a matter of concern for local trust. However, when analysing local service delivery as a peacebuilding function we need to consider the leverage of each community. As responsiveness to local needs matters, so does the local government's ability to answer to the needs of communities that have little influence nationally. Here, the idea of local inclusiveness is that if local government is able to promote an image of locally available services, then the lack of national response to the needs of that community decreases in importance, enabling overall national stability and peace (Brinkerhoff, 2011). What Bourj Hammoud illustrates is that the municipality is perceived as promoting a feeling of Armenian inclusion locally. However, because local spaces are rarely homogenous, it also illustrates that it is not a zero-sum game as it may create a feeling of grievance and local exclusion by other communities, even if they have a larger influence nationally.

Service delivery and peacebuilding in Bourj Hammoud

Service delivery in Bourj Hammoud is characterized by responsiveness to the needs that emerge, such as waste management after the waste crisis in 2015. At the same time, the municipality lacks resources to perform service delivery and is dependent on slow governmental processes for approval of larger projects. This made visionary projects slow, and sometimes unattainable, when delivered by the municipality itself. To compensate for a lack of resources and capacity, the municipality implements service delivery through collaboration with civil society actors. These co-produced services illustrate that service delivery is not a one way flow from the municipality to the communities. At the same time, this collaboration does not necessarily mean that the municipality is less legitimate, as legitimacy is judged in relation to expectations on service delivery rather than who delivers it (McLoughlin, 2019).

At the same time, while the municipality aims at responding to local needs, local and national sectarian allegiances created the lens through which these services were delivered and interpreted by local actors. By analysing local service delivery as a peacebuilding function, the case of Bourj Hammoud teaches us two things. First, local governments can compensate for national ignorance of the needs of a local majority. However, the local is not a homogenous space, which risks creating a feeling of disadvantage among other local communities. This creates a dilemma between local and national peacebuilding, questioning whose peace is built through local service delivery. Second, the national disadvantage of a local majority implies a disadvantaged channelling of resources to the local level. This, in turn, means that the municipality is even less capable of delivering services and even more dependent on its close connections with the local community, creating a circle of dependence between the municipality and the ones with whom it interacts. The close interaction with civil society actors is both what closely connects the municipality to the local community and enables inclusive service delivery, and also what, according to some, implies that the municipality does not equally respond to local needs.

Saida

Since the mid-1970s, Saida and its neighbouring municipalities managed waste by piling it up in a waste dump close to the shore in Saida. After 40 years of use, the 'Jabal al-Zbeleh', the garbage mountain, reached 58 metres high, blocked the sea view of the inhabitants and left a heavy smell in the air. During the summer, fires erupted due to the methane gas generated by decomposing waste, covering the city in toxic fumes. Over the years, the garbage mountain became a notorious landmark of Saida, known for polluting the Mediterranean Sea and risking the health of the inhabitants (Maroun, 2017).

The garbage mountain had been debated for decades in Saida, and in the municipal elections of 2010, closing the dump was one of the promises made by the winning coalition list. According to one councillor: "one of our first priorities, which we had raised in our campaign, was to remove the 'garbage mountain' that is polluting the entire Mediterranean" (Int. 34, municipal councillor, November 2015). Indeed, by 2015 the municipality had established a waste management plant to treat waste from the municipality as well as 16 surrounding municipalities. Although the project also had its controversies, the municipality perceived the project as a success. With the waste crisis that developed in Beirut during the summer of 2015 still fresh, one municipal councillor commented that:

> 'In Lebanon, there are a lot of problems with rubbish, and we don't have this problem because we worked for it. We have a lot of problems with the ministry, but we are strong enough to get what we need. We are proud of what we have done during this time.' (Int. 35, municipal councillor, November 2015)

In addition, several municipal councillors pointed out that removing the garbage mountain transformed a nuisance into an opportunity, and: "by the end of this year, we will have a fabulous garden" (Int. 46, municipal councillor, November 2015). The 35,000 square metre garden that was to be built on part of the land previously occupied by garbage was another source of pride. As one municipal councillor exclaimed: "finally the people of Saida will have a garden with a view of the sea" (Int. 34, municipal councillor, November 2015). Municipal councillors perceived the public garden as enhancing the quality of life for the inhabitants of Saida. Thus, the building of the waste management plant not only mattered in addressing the nuisance of waste, but also allowed the municipal council to promote a picture of a municipality working for an environmentally and people-friendly city.

Civil society actors shared the municipality's enthusiasm towards the waste project. As one actor claimed:

> 'we used to have the garbage problem, the Garbage Mountain, which was smelly and caused health problems. They [the municipality] were able to fix this problem and to install the plant that treats the garbage. … Instead of the mountain, now we have a big garden.' (Int. 42, civil society actor, November 2015)

Responding to the garbage issue, with its hazardous impact on health and the environment, the municipality of Saida addressed one of the greatest needs of the population. But the then present municipal council was not the first one to plan for better waste management in Saida. The plan had been pushed also by the municipality before 2010, headed by Abdul Rahman El-Bizri, but stopped because of rivalry between the locally influential Bizri family and national actors such as the Future Movement. As one interviewee explained:

> '[The garbage plant] was stopped for at least, seven, eight, twelve years. Maybe it was stopped just before approving because the two parties weren't [cooperating]. I don't know who is right and who is wrong, but what we know as the people of Saida is that if they come together, they will serve the city much better.' (Int. 43, civil society actor, November 2015)

The focus on cooperation, and the provision of services through that cooperation matters for the delivery of local services, and thus our understanding of service delivery as a peacebuilding function. In Saida, even those actors critical of the credit assumed by the municipal council acknowledged the importance of the project. As one interviewee pointed out: "now the factory is working. It is an essential project" (Int. 38, civil society actor, November 2015). As the municipality demonstrated a capacity to deliver services, it shows that if needs are met, there are less grounds for contesting the local government (Mcloughlin, 2015). Thus, the waste management plant promotes the picture of a functioning local state. This provides potential for enhancing the municipality's legitimacy, part and parcel of service delivery as a peacebuilding function (Mcloughlin, 2015; Paris and Sisk, 2009).

Through the interviews, it became obvious that the municipal council voted in in 2010 came to office with great ambitions of changing things on the ground. According to one interviewee, they had a list of 48 development projects to accomplish during their six-year term (Int. 34, municipal councillor, November 2015). By November 2015, the municipality had removed the garbage mountain, commissioned a sewage water plant as well as created gardens and enhanced the beach by adding new sand, to name a few examples. In 2015, a European Union funded project was renovating the old town in Saida, bringing to the fore traces of the city's long history. Interviewees explained that the old town represented a space of heritage and nostalgia, but it was also one of the poorest areas in the city (Int. 33, 39, 41, 42, 45). In this project, the inclusion of local NGOs as well as stakeholders was key in initiating and implementing the project, as one municipal employee explained:

> 'They [the municipal council] chose this one because they saw that this was the necessary one, based on the view of the NGOs. [There

were] committees within the project with all stakeholders [that] made the decisions on what to focus on, headed by experts from the AUB [American University of Beirut].' (Int. 33, municipal employee, November 2015)

The old town with its carpentry workshops, producers of traditional sweets and pastries as well as other crafts, represents a continuation of past traditions. However, it also fits well into the municipality's vision of a future Saida, as the interviewee continued to describe:

'[The project] reformed [the old shops] and made a branding of their products. The project taught them how to brand their product. It connected the old Saida with the new Saida.' (Int. 33, municipal employee, November 2015)

The connection of the old Saida with the new Saida meant that the old parts were incorporated into economic developments, with a focus on the consumer-based economy that has evolved in the city at large. The emphasis on promoting economic activities illustrates that infrastructural renovations are seen as promoting an idea of economic development. By specifically addressing the beneficiaries' needs through their own knowledge and economic activities, the project incorporated this part of the city into a vision of a progressive and modern city. This vision of a modern city incorporates consumerism and the individualization of one's own fate, typical of the consumer culture that characterizes present-day Lebanon (Khalaf, 2012, p 15f). However, this also puts focus on individuals as consumers of beautiful spaces and the belief in tourism as a generator of economic development. As one municipal councillor explained:

'The old town of Saida is an old Ottoman town, but now [it is] not in a good shape, it needs to be restored. … It is important for boosting tourism in Saida. To keep the face of the old town like a nostalgia for the whole city.' (Int. 36, municipal councillor, November 2015)

Furthermore, the municipality perceived infrastructural developments as key in moving Lebanon away from a chaotic past and towards a future of development and economic growth; as one municipal councillor explained:

'we should enhance the infrastructure in all of Lebanon, after years of chaos and carelessness, where there were chaotic scenes such as of electricity and phone cables installed randomly to houses. Now we are taking the infrastructure seriously, with the support of donor states, The Arab Fund, with which we not only renovate the infrastructure of the city itself but also to the surrounding areas, which had old infrastructure that is not suitable for the growth of these areas throughout the years.' (Int. 34, municipal councillor, November 2015)

Nevertheless, the role of the municipality is not to deliver infrastructural developments. Instead, the municipality acts by bringing together external actors with resources and/or greater decision-making power to address the needs of Saida and promote economic development. The mayor of Saida was perceived as playing a crucial role:

'With his wisdom, [the mayor] could bring together all conflicted parties and put forward the people's interest above any other considerations. We succeeded in the last 5 years to achieve things that the former municipal councils fell short on. We could, with the leadership of the mayor and his connections with the different political powers, activate the projects that were frozen for years.' (Int. 34, municipal councillor, November 2015)

According to the municipal councillors interviewed, infrastructural developments promoted a picture of a functional state by governing public spaces to enhance economic development. In this way, the municipal council embraced infrastructural developments to demonstrate local government capacity and to aim at increasing local legitimacy. Nevertheless, the service provision of such infrastructural developments was possible only through collaboration with local as well as national and international actors. Thus, despite the focus of the municipality on infrastructural developments on the ground, such developments were dependent on outside support.

Nevertheless, a few interviewees questioned whether infrastructure should be the priority of the municipality. One interviewee, a candidate on the opposition alliance list in the 2010 municipal elections, declared: "I don't want that now, not now, come next year and make it. But now, the danger is at our door, it is knocking at our door" (Int. 40, civil society actor, November 2015). The danger he refers to are the tensions between local communities in relation to the Syrian civil war and regional divides between Sunni and Shia Muslim groups. In Saida, this materialized in 2013 when the Sunni cleric Al-Assir mobilized against Hezbollah's involvement in the Syrian civil war, leading to roadblocks and deadly clashes inside Saida and neighbourhoods nearby.

Although the clashes of 2013 are extreme events and do not characterize Saida, the local situation did affect practices around the use of municipal infrastructure. For example, the municipality paid careful attention to messages spread by actors using its facilities, as explained by one employee:

'The big building of the municipality, it is used by different actors – political, educational, sometimes religious – if it doesn't affect others. We are always conscious of that point. We never agree with [having] the extremists here in the building.' (Int. 33, municipal employee, November 2015)

All organizations who wanted to use the building had to submit the programme for the meeting, but the municipality also used its local knowledge: "The municipality knows the religious groups and what they are saying. They know which ones to accept and not" (Int. 33, municipal employee, November 2015). Thus, inclusion of local organizations in municipal buildings had its limits. Seen only through the lens of inclusion, the municipality's choice of excluding a few organizations with extreme views may seem disturbing according to the ideal of equality and inclusion of those voices excluded from political arenas. However, considering the, at times, uncertain security situation in Lebanon as a whole and Saida on several occasions, excluding groups that might create animosity and instead working with others that promote unity across diversity presented a locally adapted inclusion that promoted a locally adapted peace through local politics, even if it meant that not all local actors agreed.[1]

In Saida, local and national politics are constantly present and influence the type of needs the municipality attends to. In Saida, the municipal council's close relationship with the Future Movement is seen as one reason for its focus on infrastructural and economic development, as promoted by the late Rafiq Hariri, former head of Future Movement (Miller, 1997, p 246). Reflecting on the lack of municipal involvement in the provision of social needs, one interviewee explained:

'Is it because the municipal council, they don't know that there are social needs? Of course, they know, but it needs a political decision. They cannot come up with any initiative unless they have the stamp of approval from the political leader. For instance, we have this drug problem; the child in the street knows that. We have violence; we have drug addiction. Of course, the municipality is aware. But, is there a green light to work on these social issues? No, in the end, they execute only what they are told to do.' (Int. 44, civil society actor, November 2015)

---

[1] The presence of Al-Assir and allied actors on a third list in the municipal elections of 2016 (*The Monthly*, 2016), suggests that while groups with a religious agenda were excluded from municipal activities in 2015, municipal politics are seen as a relevant space for expressing political ideas and change the direction of local politics and peace.

Instead, civil society organizations in Saida provide for the populations' everyday needs, coordinating their activities through an NGO platform since 1984. During and after the civil war, civil society organizations continued to provide services to the local population and today "the NGOs in Saida are covering almost all its needs; they are covering all the sectors in social life, medical, educational, training, job vacancies" (Int. 43, civil society actor, November 2015).

With the needs of the population covered by civil society actors, the municipality's role is supportive, as one interviewee explained: "they support us in all ways. If we have an event, [if] we need space, [if] we need the crane to work on a high level, they [paid for it] on two consecutive days. If we have any plumbing problem, they solve it very quickly" (Int. 43, civil society actor, November 2015). Although they did not take an active role, the municipality responded to local everyday needs by cooperating with civil society actors, making them legitimate in the eyes of the local population. One interviewee explained: "My view is that the municipality is highly regarded as very perceptive of people's needs; it is because the civil society is giving them this image" (Int. 44, civil society actor, November 2015). As she continued to explain, the cooperation was mutually beneficial, although not an equal cooperation:

> 'Now, the municipality is being applauded not because they are so keen on what is happening on the ground, but it is because the civil society is not doing anything without inviting the municipality to bring sustainability to their projects. Because there are certain projects that if only the civil society implements it the sustainability becomes risky but if the municipality gets involved it becomes rooted and sustainable. So, I would say that the civil society is bringing the municipality along, much more than the municipality is receptive towards.' (Int. 44, civil society actor, November 2015)

For the population, however, who provided for their needs might not be of primary importance. As stated by one interviewee, "I believe that the people if they are in need they are in need. They will go to the one that can serve their need" (Int. 37, civil society actor, November 2015).

Service delivery and peacebuilding in Saida

In Saida, the municipality actively provided for local needs by closing the garbage mountain, initiating less polluting waste management, transforming space into a green area, and rehabilitating places of cultural heritage. As such, the municipality demonstrated capacity, which, according to interviewees, enhanced the perception of the local government and its legitimacy, confirming the notion of service delivery as a peacebuilding function.

However, analysing service delivery through waste management, infrastructural developments and everyday needs in Saida also demonstrates two things. One, that the capacity, or interest, of the municipality is largely focused on infrastructural reform and development. For the municipality, this is a strategic, and political, choice. By focusing on visible changes on the ground, the municipality promotes itself as a local actor capable of fostering change. This strategy was equally used by the former prime minister Rafiq Hariri, infusing the politics of the Future Movement. After the Lebanese civil war, Hariri used infrastructure and property development as a strategy to move Lebanon away from the ideological dividing lines of the civil war. Such developments emphasized a modernization of the Lebanese state towards an ideology of materialism and consumerism (Khalaf, 2012; Miller, 1997, p 246). Simultaneously, it advertised the state as a capable authority (McLoughlin, 2019). Second, the capacity of the municipality of Saida to provide visible services and develop and reform the city came through because national and international connections provided financial and administrative support. This is well known in the local space and service delivery is tainted by the powerful actors involved. The same pattern repeats itself for the provision of everyday needs where civil society actors are the main service providers with the municipality supporting their activities. Although this reflects the lack of decentralization and lack of capacity of Lebanese municipalities in general (Harb and Atallah, 2015), it raises the question of who gets credit for the services delivered. However, as the case of Saida illustrates, who is perceived as providing services and who gets credit for their provision is often blurred. In addition, cooperation between different parties illustrates the different roles involved in service provision, allowing the municipality more or less credit, and more or less legitimacy gains (McLoughlin, 2019).

In terms of answering what role the municipality plays in the peacebuilding function of service delivery, the answer then becomes partial. The municipality, focusing on infrastructural developments that respond to local needs, gain local legitimacy through service provision. At the same time, the municipality is questioned for narrowly addressing infrastructural needs and leaving health care, education or inter-sectarian relationships to other actors. Although the municipality makes some legitimacy gains through cooperating with the civil society, it represents a blurring of boundaries between state and non-state actors as service providers.

Conclusion: three cases of service delivery

This chapter has explored service delivery in the municipalities of Tyre, Bourj Hammoud and Saida and how service provision relates to local peacebuilding through responsiveness, inclusiveness, municipal capacity as well as the idea of economic development. To conclude, this section compares the three municipalities to highlight the diversity present and the complexity inherent in service delivery as a peacebuilding function and the role of local government in local peacebuilding.

In theory, service delivery as a peacebuilding function, builds on the proximity of the local government and its knowledge and awareness of local needs. By knowing local needs, local governments can respond accordingly, and increase their legitimacy gains through responsive service provision (Brinkerhoff, 2011; Roberts, 2011b). Service delivery in Tyre shows that the municipality is responsive to local needs when they autonomously provide services. However, these services were small in scope and might go unnoticed by the population. On the other hand, the more noticeable services provided locally, such as infrastructural developments and waste management solutions, or lack of solutions, were provided through projects that were nationally or internationally initiated and run. In these services, the visibility of projects was high, but the municipality's ability to be responsive was compromised. In Bourj Hammoud, the responsiveness of the municipality was high, as seen by the necessity to respond to acute needs, such as the waste crisis, or responding to everyday needs through their close cooperation with the local civil society. However, the municipality did not respond to other more costly or more progressive needs due to financial and administrative constraints. In Saida, on the other hand, financial and administrative capacity was not a major issue; thus, the municipality was able to respond to local needs that had been troubling the population for many years. As necessary as these services have been, they have also been focused on responding to visible needs, tainted, however, by cooperation with national and international actors that have enabled them. Everyday needs were largely addressed through cooperation with the civil society, where civil society actors took the lead.

The second theme of service delivery as a peacebuilding function is inclusiveness. Inclusiveness implies hearing the voices of those often unheard. Inclusiveness means contextual knowledge of those in need, or locally providing for the needs of those communities that are not addressed nationally (Bland, 2007; Brinkerhoff, 2011). In Tyre, the provision of services on a larger, infrastructural scale has meant that most projects were not inclusive towards a specific group but targeted all inhabitants. Inclusiveness then means the inclusion of all sectarian groups present locally. However, in some instances, the municipality was specifically inclusive towards those it knew to be in need, providing services such as poverty relief or medical support. In Bourj Hammoud, the municipality actively portrayed itself as inclusive to all groups within the local community. However, through its close cooperation with the local civil society in a local space where the local majority is a national minority, the municipality was not always perceived as inclusive towards all. Nevertheless, whether real or perceived, the greater inclusiveness of a national minority has theoretically been argued to be beneficial for national stability and peace. According to the theoretical discussion of this theme, local equality is not an objective, as an unequal local service delivery can level out national inequalities (Brinkerhoff, 2011). However, this study shows that when this is the case, service delivery also furthers already established sectarian dividing lines. Thus, service delivery in Bourj Hammoud does not necessarily offer the potential of overcoming past grievances in the local space but rather re-establishes a power balance achieved during the war. In Saida, just like in Tyre, service provision of infrastructure and the waste management plant targeted the population as a whole. However, sometimes, a particular service targeted an identified population, such as the renovation of the old town, or included some rather than others, such as the ability of groups to use the municipal building. This kind of inclusiveness both ties the municipality to existing local needs and identifies a locally relevant inclusion that fits with the municipality's view of a Saidonian local peace.

The third theme of service provision addresses the municipality's capacity to address local needs through the appropriate financial and administrative resources (Romeo, 2013). While Lebanese municipalities act under financial and decision-making regulations restricting their autonomy, all three cases demonstrate a capacity to provide services through other means. In Tyre, capacity to deliver services was enhanced through cooperation with national and international actors, although the municipality's ability to be responsive was compromised through that cooperation. On the other hand, the municipality demonstrated autonomous capacity to provide services on a smaller scale. As such, the conclusion should not be that the municipality should stay away from larger projects as, sometimes, the larger projects have created the local spaces used by the municipality to provide services in an autonomous way. In Bourj Hammoud, the municipality found its main capacity through its close cooperation with local civil society actors. When the municipality needed to deliver services on its own, it was able to rearrange resources for urgent needs, as in the case of waste management. Nevertheless, municipal councillors generally discussed a situation of having little capacity to autonomously provide services due to a lack of autonomy vis-à-vis the central state. In Saida, on the other hand, the municipality was capable explicitly because of its relationship with national political actors as well as international actors. Here, the external actors enabled capacity, and, unlike both Tyre and Bourj Hammoud, their capacity was not perceived as restricted by external support, even though it also meant that they were not autonomous when providing services.

The fourth theme in the analytical framework claims that a local government that is perceived as prosperous, modern and enhancing the inhabitants' livelihoods, gains increased legitimacy as a local government. As such, showing the image of a local government that pursues the vision or idea of economic development may increase its legitimacy and the acceptance of local developments (Bland, 2007, p 208f; Brinkerhoff, 2011; Hartmann and Crawford, 2008, pp 8, 250). In Tyre, the municipality was perceived as actively pursuing a vision of Tyre as a tourist-friendly city. In their pursuit of this vision, the idea of local economic development was implicitly present in services of infrastructural developments that were believed to enhance commercial spaces. In Bourj Hammoud, the municipality did not discuss a particular vision of economic development. Instead, human, everyday needs were more central to municipal service delivery, which was what they aimed to provide through cooperation with civil society. In Saida, again, the situation was almost the exact opposite to the one in Bourj Hammoud. There, the municipality actively pursued an idea of economic development, mostly through infrastructural developments large and small, but also through taking care of the garbage mountain that had been a nuisance to the image of Saida for many years. Despite its services being highly visible and mostly successful, some interviewees instead questioned the municipality for not attending to the population's everyday needs.

Finally, contrasting the three municipalities' service delivery through responsiveness, inclusiveness, capacity and the idea of economic development, local service delivery has different implications for local government engagement in local peacebuilding. The role of the municipality of Tyre in local service delivery was manifest mostly through external cooperation on infrastructural developments that promoted an idea of economic development and made the municipality visible to the inhabitants. However, as the analysis has shown, external involvement hindered responsiveness and inclusiveness. Nevertheless, the infrastructural developments implemented through external cooperation have given space for smaller, locally created, initiatives, where local service delivery was perceived as a peacebuilding function. As such, external involvement enhanced the municipality's peacebuilding capacity by giving them space to autonomously provide other services for which there was a need. At the same time, external involvement reveals that the municipality is incapable of taking full responsibility for local needs. If legitimacy is key in peacebuilding, as identified by Roberts' (2011a), and service deliveries are the building blocks for increased legitimacy (Mcloughlin, 2015), then peacebuilding through municipal services in Tyre exposes the interconnections between local services and external involvement, proposing that if local service delivery is a peacebuilding function, its practical implementation is not disconnected from national or international levels of governance. Although ingrained in national structures of identity and sect, service delivery as a local peacebuilding function was largely locally created in Bourj Hammoud. Through local cooperation, everyday needs were addressed, enhancing a local peacebuilding that took care of the necessities of life, although the appropriateness and equal access of services delivered was questioned by some interviewees. Nevertheless, service delivery in Bourj Hammoud built on local cooperation. In its local context, service delivery in Bourj Hammoud became a part of enhancing Armenian domination of the local space, in relation to its national subordination. In Saida, external influence was an important component in the role it played in local peacebuilding, as it enhanced the municipality's capacity to deliver services. However, the role of the municipality in service delivery as a peacebuilding function was only partial, as the municipality focused primarily on constructed services such as infrastructural developments, emphasizing the material side of services. Other, more mundane service delivery was delivered by other actors, such as the civil society, who filled constructed spaces with activities and responded to everyday needs, for example health care and education. Thus, the role of the municipality of Saida in service delivery was consequently highly visible, and according to some very successful, but a role that responded only to particular needs.

As evident from this chapter, service delivery does not stand isolated from the surrounding context of the municipality. Service delivery in Tyre, Bourj Hammoud and Saida demonstrates how the three cases engage in local peacebuilding in diverse ways, creating different types of local peace. The local space and its interactions matter, displaying service delivery as a space where power, politics and feelings of belonging interact with local governments' capacity to respond to local needs and, thus become a legitimate actor promoting local peace.

4

Local Interactions: Formal and Informal Everyday Interactions

This chapter investigates local interactions, emphasizing the need to ground peace in the everyday lives of the population to make peacebuilding relevant. Conceptualized as a peacebuilding function, local interactions emphasize participation, influence and fostering trust towards the local government or trust between local communities. The interactions analysed in this chapter are those that occur between local inhabitants, directly or through civil society actors, and the Lebanese municipalities of Tyre, Bourj Hammoud and Saida. In this chapter, municipal councillors, municipal employees or civil society actors offer their views on how interactions are pursued. Through their perceptions, interactions are analysed, furthering our understanding of local interactions and how they relate to the role of local governments in local peacebuilding.

In particular, this chapter investigates how inhabitants interact with the municipality through the constellation of the municipal council and municipal council interaction, as well as how the municipality interacts with the population as a local authority in situations where the municipality issues permits and ensures that they are followed or provides services to the population. Interactions through the constellation of the municipal council offer opportunities to analyse municipal councils as collective decision-making bodies (Sisk and Risley, 2005a). Furthermore, analysing local interactions when the municipality exercises authority or provides services allows for an analysis of continuous practices and negotiations over participation, influence and trust-building. Following the discussion of local interactions in each municipality, the three cases are discussed together, highlighting how interactions are perceived as well as how these interactions relate to local government engagement in local peacebuilding.

Tyre

> 'This is our city. [Interviewee shows me a photo of local religious and municipal leaders posing together]. I like this photo. Sour [Tyre] has the Muslim and the Christian, and the Sunna and Shia … Sour is mixed.' (Int. 2, municipal councillor, May 2015)

Tyre is a city with diversity at its heart. Interviewees described the city as easy-going (Int. 49, civil society actor, December 2015), where people were friends and brothers across religious communities (Int. 48, civil society actor, December 2015), which sometimes resulted in marriages across sects (Int. 6, municipal councillor, June 2015). Although the municipality was not perceived as the main actor in promoting a good relationship between religious communities, the municipality was perceived as inclusive towards the different communities.

In practice, this worked through a division of seats within the municipal council. The majority of the population in Tyre is Shia Muslim, but the 21 seats in the municipal council were divided among thirteen Shia, four Sunni and four Christians. In addition, the division of seats included taking national political parties into consideration. In the municipal council of 2010–2016, five of the municipal councillors were supported by Hezbollah and 16 by Haraket Amal (or Amal), the two main Shiite political parties in Lebanon. Tyre is known for its support of Amal, which came to light in the 2004 municipal elections, an actual contested election according to one interviewee:

> 'In 2004, it was a big competition. Somebody like to call it a big fight. But no, it's a competition. And the surprise was that Amal Movement got 72 [per cent]. That does not say that 72 per cent of the population is Amal Movement. But they support Amal Movement. And sometimes, they support Nabih Berry. We don't have the system of parties in Lebanon. Sometimes people support leaders.' (Int. 1, municipal councillor, December 2014)

Although the interviewee emphasized that it was not a fight, it did bring back memories of the later years of the civil war when Hezbollah and Amal fought with each other because of diverging views on how to resist Israel, as well as diverging prospects for the Lebanese state. In the aftermath of the withdrawal of Israel from the security zone in the south in the year 2000, as well as Hezbollah's self-acclaimed victory and increased influence thereafter, Amal's victory was indeed a bit of a surprise (Chaib, 2009; Hanf, 1993, p 315ff).

In 2010, the leaders of Amal and Hezbollah came together and decided on a common list of 21 names for the municipal council, based on the election results in 2004. The agreed list ensured that both Amal and Hezbollah would get political posts, as he continued to explain:

> 'The present [municipal council] is a mix because in 2010 they had an agreement between Amal and Hezbollah, between President [of parliament Nabih] Berri and Said Hassan [Nasrallah, leader of Hezbollah].' (Int. 1, municipal councillor, December 2014)

As such, in 2010, instead of having an election where the voters could choose between two alliance lists, there was only one list to vote for in the municipal election in Tyre (Int. 1, 2, 5). The representation and participation of different groups in the municipal council was therefore not a result of a democratically contested election, but of consensus among local leaders and top-level leaders. Nevertheless, municipal councillors emphasized that the council brought together representatives of all communities in Tyre, reflecting the proportions of each religious or political group. As such, participation from all groups was ensured, keeping the image of a city for all sects.

The inclusion of councillors from different segments of the society was seen as one important channel for interaction with the local community, ensuring broad participation through representation. In Tyre, councillors openly expressed that they relied on municipal councillors' networks of links to the broader society to learn and keep themselves up to date on what was going on. One municipal employee explained: "the municipality has information about people who live in the city. Every member in the council knows people who need aid" (Int. 6, municipal councillor, June 2015). For the inhabitants of Tyre, participation and influence in the municipality went through personal links.

Similarly, the participation of actors involved in civil society organizations in the municipal council provided a possibility for civil society organizations to influence the work of the municipality. One civil society actor described the relationship as close, because:

> 'there are many members in the municipality that are also members of the administrative committee of a number of associations. That means that the social milieu, the society, or the associations, can penetrate and play a role in the programmes of the municipality.' (Int. 50, civil society actor, December 2015)

In addition, civil society actors described how their participation in events and activities reminded the municipality of their views; as on interviewee described it:

> 'Even if we don't talk, even if there is no venue to convene us, but the simple fact that we exist, it makes them think about our opinion

or our stand in this situation or that. And, sometimes we organize events together. The last one was a bicycle race in Tyre; it was a day of joy. Of course, we didn't discuss any project. But the act itself and the people who were involved and the media, etc. This is positive impact. I cannot have such an activity today, and the next day I forget about you. I should take your views into consideration.' (Int. 51, civil society actor, December 2015)

Because of the many civil society organizations in Lebanon, local politics means navigating between different groups and different interests. As such, the presence of different civil society actors was, in the view of the same interviewee, a way to promote social cohesion between communities, continuously important in post-war Lebanon. In this way, municipal work, allowing for the participation of different actors, could promote trust between groups in the local space. In addition, civil society organizations act as mediators between inhabitants and the municipality by putting inhabitants in direct contact with the municipality or forwarding their views. As one civil society actor maintained, the municipality depends on the civil society, in terms of knowledge exchange in relation to specific issues or projects but also in connecting the work of the municipality to those most in need (Int. 51, civil society actor, December 2015). This demonstrates that there are several avenues via which inhabitants can influence municipal services and projects.

Nevertheless, interactions between civil society organizations and the municipality varied in importance. One municipal councillor described how sectarian divisions and the different interests of local organizations hindered the possibility of developing a fruitful dialogue for cooperation in and influence over municipal programmes. As she explained:

'When I came to the municipality, I was the only woman. There was a suggestion from other members to constitute a group of women from associations in the city. But after four months, I realized that every woman comes for her own goals.' (Int. 6, municipal councillor, June 2015)

According to her, participation did not always promote a positive dialogue between the municipality and societal actors. In this example, the participants were not guided by a common goal, and as such, trust between the actors was not enhanced through cooperation. Neither did this cooperation become a forum for civil society influence over municipal affairs. Interviews with other civil society actors acknowledged the perception of a dispersed local civil society. However, the importance of civil society organizations in providing the municipality with links to the society at large was still emphasized. As one interviewee explained:

'They [civil society organizations] may fight with each other, contradict each other but in general, they have the outreach to detect all those vulnerable and all those people at risk, and to provide them with a minimum of livelihood.' (Int. 51, civil society actor, December 2015)

Thus, interaction between the civil society organizations and the municipality did enhance inhabitants' influence over municipal policies and projects. However, where civil society organizations were guided by their own interests, interaction did not foster trust in the local government, and definitely not between groups in the local space.

However, the political party that allowed municipal councillors their place also influenced them and who gained a voice in local matters. One interviewee claimed that politics silenced municipal councillors into not objecting to the unethical practices of a few local inhabitants. Describing two different situations where property owners with political alliances turned to the municipality to expel tenants with legal contracts or ownership of the apartments, the interviewee claimed that:

'In the municipality, all people, silence ... all [council] members they didn't say anything. Only me and two [others]. From 21 members. They don't want problems with people, because they want to be selected [again].' (Int. 4, municipal councillor, June 2015)

The dependence on political parties for a future political career was emphasized by most municipal councillors. Asked about whether he would run in the upcoming municipal elections in May 2016, one interviewee answered: "It is not up to me [to decide]" (Int. 47, municipal councillor, December 2015).

In addition to formal and informal structures for interactions in the municipality, the municipality interacts with the population through service delivery and as a local authority. One example is the municipality's management of Beit Al-Mamlouk. As part of the infrastructural development plans in the CHUD project, one of the old houses in the town had been renovated to serve as a city hall. Originally, a governmental authority called the General Directorate of Antiquities (DGA) had planned to own and run the house. As the number of buildings for the DGA to manage, in Tyre and elsewhere, grew with the renovations in the CHUD project, the CDR convinced the DGA to give the responsibility for Beit Al-Mamlouk to the municipality. As one CDR employee explained, the DGA "know very well that the central government cannot manage everything in the whole territory ... so why not give some space to the municipality to do some good activities?" (Int. 10, government employee, June 2015).

According to the CDR employee, Beit Al-Mamlouk was a good example of municipal capacity building and local interactions through infrastructural developments. Gaining responsibility over the building, the municipality gained capacity to manage projects on its own, opening up the space to the local population. The municipality used the house for several projects such as awareness campaigns, exhibitions or educational programmes, emphasizing that, "this house is open for any activity for the local community" (Int. 1, municipal councillor, December 2014). With activities run by the municipality, civil society organizations or a collaboration, Beit al-Mamlouk provided a space where interactions could occur. Furthermore, these interactions had positive implications for the CHUD project overall, as one employee of CDR described:

> '[The house] is quite busy throughout the year, women, cultural activities, music, dancing. And one of the projects, that they [the municipality] did alone, they give, during the school year, they give assistance after school, if the students need some assistance after school to do their homework or so. They started with a small number of students and now they have 80 or 90 kids, and all of them are from the surrounding area. And it helped a lot, not only for education but also for awareness. These kids they are from the vicinities, and prior to these activities, this house was not for them. They may throw stones; they don't care about it. But now, they go inside, they play inside, so it is for them. They have access and it is their place. It gives a kind of awareness to the young population, and it helped drop the vandalism in that area.' (Int. 10, government employee, June 2015)

The types of interactive services delivered by the municipality in Beit al-Mamlouk are good examples of how participation in services perceived as responding to local needs provides an opportunity for fostering trust in the local government. Thus, local interaction within the project of Beit al-Mamlouk confirms the argument put forward by, for example, Paffenholz (2015a) and Donais (2012, p 54f) that when interaction provides arenas for meaningful participation, it holds a peacebuilding potential.

Another initiative was the creation of a pedestrian street. For the second summer in a row, one of the seaside streets lined with restaurants closed for traffic every Saturday evening. The open space allowed people to walk, children to bike, local merchants to sell their goods and private people or local associations to create events of different kinds. The event was initiated by the municipality and the organizing team included municipal councillors and a local representative of the international NGO Caritas. However, local associations actively proposed activities for the different evenings, influencing the content as well as using it as a space to engage with the public. As such, the pedestrian street created both a physical space for interaction, as well as a space bringing together the municipality with local associations and businesses.

The importance of this interaction could be seen in the role that the restaurant owners played. When the idea was first proposed by the previous municipal council, their resistance hindered the event. However, as the event came into being, their enthusiasm and active financial involvement enabled an expansion of the event. As one municipal councillor explained:

> 'This year in Ramadan, they [the municipality] decided to do decorations; they did a feasibility study for the decorations, and it will cost them 11,000 dollars. And they cannot only invest that money in this road and leave the other roads. So, what they decided to do, or, the owners of the restaurants said that they will pay 40 per cent and the municipality will pay the rest.' (Int. 2, municipal councillor, May 2015)

With a restricted municipal budget, interaction between the municipality and local merchants enabled the municipality to implement the service proposed. Furthermore, through the inclusion of municipal and civil society actors in the managing team, cooperation with local businesses as well as the use of the space by local associations, the project presents several opportunities for interactions with the local community. Additionally, the pedestrian street became an eye-opener for many people, demonstrating municipal capacity and changing perceptions of Tyre in Lebanon as a whole. One municipal councillor explained:

> 'there are people who do not come to Tyre, because [they] think that Tyre is in the south and there are bombs and so. Even the representative of the minister of tourism, when he came to Tyre he was flattered by what he saw. And even people when they react and they do some comments, it is highly positive. They say that Tyre is like that, and we would never imagine that there is another [city] that is so brilliant and it is not in Jbail [Mount Lebanon]. It is not a comparison because what they have in Jbail is different, but it is more important because of the social attraction and social cohesion between people.' (Int. 3, municipal councillor, May 2015)

As such, the pedestrian street became a meeting place for local inhabitants, and with high media coverage it managed to attract visitors from Beirut and beyond. In addition, the municipality had been approached by several state and non-state investors for further development of other areas of the town, illustrating the increased trust in the municipality as a local government (Int. 3, municipal councillor, May 2015). In sum, the pedestrian street was perceived as creating a space for participation, as well as local influence over the project. Furthermore, it had enhanced trust in the municipality as a local government in the local space and beyond.

While Beit al-Mamlouk as well as the pedestrian street created possibilities for interaction through events and projects, the municipality also plays an important role as the local authority closest to the population. According to one interviewee, both the central and local governments are important for the daily activities in their organization. As he explained:

> 'We cannot construct without permits, and we cannot introduce curriculums and claim the attestation of the government unless we have the certification of the government. ... Well, it is true that the government is weak or absent, but it's there by many means.' (Int. 51, civil society actor, December 2015)

In particular, the issuing of construction permits for renovations and new constructions falls under the municipality's responsibility. As the authority in charge, the municipality was informed about physical developments on the ground. Moreover, exercising this responsibility provided the municipality with an income through the fees paid.

Another responsibility that the municipality has is the employment of the local police force or municipal police. In general, the municipal police force (not to be confused with the national police, the Internal Security Forces, ISF) is responsible for public order, traffic control and parking within the municipality. However, even if it was the municipality's responsibility to enforce laws on public order, it was not always an easy task, as one employee described:

> '[The municipal police] notes, for example, illegal parking, give parking tickets, and the owner of the car must pay to the municipality. If they have not paid within 10 days, then the mayor takes the ticket and sends it to the judge. It is not easy to make people pay; many people don't believe that they have made a mistake.' (Int. 8, municipal employee, June 2015)

According to the interviewee, municipal interaction with the local inhabitants portrayed the municipality as important but, at the same time, its authority was contested or even ignored. Even if the municipality was relevant for the population in authorizing permits and contracts, having daily interactions as a local authority often countered the fostering of trust as permits and decisions were contested.

At the same time, the municipality is the level of government closest to the population's daily lives. Municipal councillors described how inhabitants often approached the municipality with requests, as one interviewee explained:

'They ask the municipality for everything, even things we cannot do. They come to the municipality. It is the closest authority to the people. They cannot go to Beirut to the ministry to ask for their need.' (Int. 1, municipal councillor, December 2014)

However, some requests, for example for electricity and potable water, fall under the authority of central government agencies. Despite the requests being legitimate, in terms of services that the state should provide, the municipality lacked authority as well as resources to address such requests. Interviewees described a mismatch between the population's perception of the role of the municipality and the municipality's capacity to act. One municipal councillor claimed that there is a gap in the understanding between the people and the municipality, that there is a "mental lacuna" (Int. 7, municipal councillor, June 2015), in terms of knowledge on how decisions are made, municipal responsibilities and how projects are created. The same municipal councillor related this mental lacuna to the lack of a municipality during the civil war as well as the limited resources and authority it has had since it was reinstated as a locally elected body in 1998. This illustrates that while local interactions should generate influence over municipal activities and responsiveness to needs, a mismatch in the understanding and capacities of the municipality creates unfulfilled expectations and a lack of trust.

However, sometimes, municipal actors were able to use their position to deliver a positive outcome, possibly one that was not expected by the inhabitants. One municipal employee explained that part of his job was to solve conflicts that arose among the population. As he explained:

'There are many problems between neighbours, and they come to the municipality with their problems. If the municipality is responsible for the problem [if it falls under municipal jurisdiction], we accept it. If we are not responsible for this problem, I send them to the department that is responsible for this case; the council, the mayor, governor or court, all have their different responsibilities.' (Int. 8, municipal employee, June 2015)

As he explained, meeting residents and talking to them bridged the formal and informal domains between the municipality as an authority and part of the Lebanese state structure, and people's private lives. As he continued to explain:

'I examine the case and tell them where they should go. I direct people. Often, I meet both parties of the conflict and if I can I help them to solve the conflict, I help them here [pointing at the couch in his office]. If you write [down] the problem and you sign the paper, it is a case. But if you can solve the problem without writing it down, then both are happy. Many times, it is a success. If it becomes a case, it often takes a long time; if it goes to the court or the governor, it is not solved for a long time.' (Int. 8, municipal employee, June 2015)

The conflict mitigating activity performed by this employee may not solve larger conflicts in the society overall, but it emphasized that the municipality has a role in the daily lives of its inhabitants, separate from collecting fees and keeping the streets clean. The ability of the municipal employee to negotiate with people, a personal trait rather than one included in his job description, increased the relevance of the municipality for the population and made it a part of the local community. Rather than being an entry point into a formalized structure to solve conflicts, personal negotiations solved conflicts in a way that decreased the conflict's impact on their lives. Although part of the formal governance structures of Lebanon, daily interactions such as the ones illustrate how municipal actors negotiate formal and informal structures to accommodate legal requirements and private circumstances of the population. These practices enable participation, as well as space for influence and trust-building between neighbours and towards the municipality.

Local interactions and peacebuilding in Tyre

Local interactions in the municipality of Tyre suggest that there are ways that interactions allow for participation, influence and building trust. Overall, local interactions in Tyre appear to provide ample opportunities for meaningful interactions that can increase participation, influence and foster trust. As such, local interactions provide hope for a grounded approach and a municipal ability to include the local population in municipal affairs.

First, by gathering actors with links to political parties, different families and or civil society organizations, the composition of the municipal council of Tyre provided several avenues for participation in and influence over municipal affairs. As such, the municipal council "lend[s] [itself] to inclusion and consensus-oriented problem solving" (Sisk and Risley, 2005a, p 37), an important trait of local governments' ability to build peace. In Tyre, the municipal council also addressed the competition between Hezbollah and Amal in the local space, a competition that had been violent in the past. Second, local interactions in service delivery such as the pedestrianization of a street or the activities performed in Beit al-Mamlouk portray a picture of a municipality capable of delivering services that are locally relevant, allow for participation as well as influence over services, and foster trust in the local space of Tyre, and in Lebanon as a whole. Third, although the municipality's autonomy is constrained, a consequence of centralizing policies during the civil war, local interactions opened a space for negotiating municipal authority. Such negotiations, between legal requirements and people's individual circumstances, allowed the municipality to become an actor of relevance to local inhabitants, fostering trust in the municipality as a local government.

Bourj Hammoud

In Bourj Hammoud, the constellation of the municipal council is defined by the Lebanese communities present in the local space. The largest community is the Armenian Lebanese, but also Lebanese Christians, mainly Maronite as well as Shia Muslims. The 21 municipal council seats are held by 14 Armenian, six Lebanese Christian and one Shia Muslim councillor (Int. 30, municipal councillor, November 2015). However, just like in Tyre, the constellation of the municipal council was not a result of competitive elections in 2010. As explained by one municipal councillor, "The municipal council was not literally elected, it was elected by unanimity for lack of contestants. Without voting, by consensus" (Int. 12, municipal councillor, May 2015). As one municipal councillor explained, the main political party, the Armenian party Tashnag, invited the other local actors to create a list of consensus, agreeing on one list for the municipal elections rather than holding competitive elections. In this way, the smaller communities were granted access to the municipal council and, according to one interviewee, they were not interested in holding elections that could jeopardize that influence (Int. 15, municipal councillor, June 2015).

The inclusion of Lebanese Christian and Shia Muslim councillors was portrayed as an act of inclusion, to ensure that every community had a fair say. However, control over the municipal council was also a continuation of past animosities and fluctuations of power between groups. During the civil war, the Armenians mobilized to protect the local space. The mobilization was successful as the war front was kept, mostly, outside of Bourj Hammoud's space. At the same time, it increased Armenian influence over that space, a power that the Armenian party, Tashnag, continues to exercise (Nucho, 2016, p 24). Although interviewees described the Armenian domination as rightful, and municipal councillors emphasized discussions in the municipal council as inclusive, it did not hinder questioning of Armenian power. Particularly, Lebanese Christians perceived the Armenian domination through a fragment of nostalgia, longing for a past with more influence (Int. 27, 31). Retelling his family's history in Bourj Hammoud, one interviewee described how Maronite influence had waned. Previously, the vice mayor had been a Maronite councillor, and now both the mayor and vice mayor were Armenians (Int. 31, municipal councillor, November 2015). Another interviewee further emphasized the consequences of Armenian domination when he explained:

'they [the Armenians] are getting weaker because other communities are a bit annoyed about what is going on in the municipality. And they may not know. Maybe, they think that everything is right and that everyone loves them, but it is not true.' (Int. 27, civil society actor, November 2015)

Beyond the inclusion of different sects in the municipal council, one municipal councillor also explained that the council had close connections with the civil society through its councillors:

'The majority of the members of the council come from the civil society. They represent all the major communities in Bourj Hammoud, the confessional groups, the political groups and the associations and NGOs. … So, the municipality has an organic tie with the civil society.' (Int. 12, municipal councillor, May 2015)

In addition, inclusion became a tool for transparency and acceptance of policies, as he continued to explain:

'[because] the 21 members represent various groups, their own community, civil society. You become extremely transparent. The whole municipal council knows exactly what is going on and you have to explain; you have to justify your actions to the whole community. It must be acceptable to the whole community because it is based on consensus, not elections.' (Int. 12, municipal councillor, May 2015)

The inclusion of representatives from different communities also meant a link between the population and the municipal council. One municipal councillor, a shop owner, explained how he was often approached by people around him:

'People come to me and tell me about their problem; I help them up to my limits, or I pass the issue to the municipality. I am the link between the people and the municipality. They all know, the neighbours, the other traders on the street; they all know that I am in the municipality.' (Int. 30, municipal councillor, November 2015)

One civil society actor emphasized how that worked for them. As she explained: "we have the chance that [one member of the organization] is in the municipality and it facilitates a lot of procedures" (Int. 26, civil society actor, November 2015). The interviewee further explained how personal connections worked to promote participation and influence from individuals and civil society organizations towards the municipality, or other Lebanese authorities, as she stated:

> 'Here, it is not by title, it is by person. There are several people who are the ones in the community; through their position in the municipality, you can get information or so.' (Int. 26, civil society actor, November 2015)

As she emphasized the importance of connections, the lack of influence perceived by the Christian interviewees noted previously was also given further meaning, because if you participate but cannot influence according to your perceived need, then the influence you can provide to your constituency also decreases. However, the interviewee continued to explain that having connections was not always beneficial, as your connections, no matter how influential they were, might not always be interested in the issue at stake. As the interviewee explained:

> 'some of the responsible people in this party help us. ... When it is in their interests. Sometimes, it is not the right time, sometimes it is not the right person. Sometimes, they also stop the realization of projects. If it is in their own interests, you get all the help you need, but if it's not.' (Int. 26, civil society actor, November 2015)

In Bourj Hammoud, the structures of inclusion operated through consensus, inviting all groups present locally, making it a case of broad participation. However, it was not necessarily perceived as enabling direct influence. On the other hand, personal connections allowed the population to participate and influence. Such interactions through personal connections were perceived as close, enabling both influence over municipal affairs and the spreading of knowledge about municipal work to the public. Nevertheless, because participation and influence occurred through personal connections, they were also subject to the interests of and possibilities to influence those connections.

In addition to interactions through inclusion in the municipal council or through personal contact with councillors, the municipality interacts with the population as an authority and through different services. In the daily work of the municipality, the authorization of building and restoration permits, providing legal services and paperwork, established the municipality as an authority that mattered to the population and provided a space for interaction with the inhabitants (Int. 13, municipal employee, June 2015). However, as explained by one employee (Int. 25, municipal employee, November 2015), enforcing regulations had a lot to do with being in dialogue with the population. In her job as municipal planner and responsible for construction permits, she described a meandering between legal requirements and people's financial capacity. As municipal regulations aimed at preserving the old character of Bourj Hammoud, her job included informing the public of the regulations as she issued permits for renovations. Nevertheless, the local population often questioned the regulations as they required wooden window frames, which were more expensive than the commonly used aluminium frames. As a compromise, she accepted the aluminium frames if they were painted as wood. The compromise of allowing for another material over the preferred original one might seem like a small detail in the exercise of municipal authority. However, it was through these interactions and compromises that a common understanding between the municipality and the public, and thus trust in municipal authority, could be built. All in all, the interviewee emphasized that buildings were restored for people, even if it meant losing some of the soul of the buildings and neighbourhoods (Int. 25, municipal employee, November 2015).

As she continued to explain her job, she emphasized that it centred around communication and giving information before a project began. Although the municipal police supervised restoration projects, it was difficult to make people change what had already been initiated or finalized. This demonstrates that negotiation between the municipality and the population is part of how the municipality performs as an authority. Here, being an authority is not only about implementing regulations and overseeing projects, but it is also about recognizing inhabitants' capacities to follow regulations. In these circumstances, interactions become crucial, and even more, the possibility of the population to influence decisions, even to a small extent, increases the chances of interaction building trust in the municipality as an authority.

As discussed in the chapter on service delivery, interactions and collaboration between civil society organizations and the municipality were important for service provision in Bourj Hammoud. As one municipal councillor described: "we [the municipality] work with and through the civil society. It's very seldom that we do something as a municipality ourselves" (Int. 12, municipal councillor, May 2015). Civil society actors described a mutually beneficial cooperation on projects, from initiation to completion (Int. 16, 17, 28). Through cooperation, NGOs accessed resources as well as space to perform their activities. At the same time, the collaboration enabled the municipality to promote and take part in meaningful activities for the inhabitants, activities for which it did not have the human resources and expertise (Int. 16, civil society actor, June 2015). Many interviewees described cooperation as equal across all segments of Bourj Hammoud, claiming that: "[The municipality] cooperate with all the NGOs not only the Armenian NGOs" (Int. 16). However, as evident in the previous chapter, not all interviewees agreed, and claims of equal inclusion were perceived as the commonly displayed show of Lebanese unity (Int. 27, civil society actor, November 2015).

However, emphasizing that peoples' perceptions, understandings and expectations are essential to peacebuilding functions, the dissemination of information is crucial. In this regard, it is interesting to note a disinterest in publicly announcing municipal activities, as one interviewee claimed, "we are not eager to get photographed during official ceremonies so that our voters see that we are doing a good job" (Int. 12, municipal councillor, May 2015). Furthermore, in another interview, one municipal councillor claimed that it would be unethical to remind the beneficiaries of who had received aid. As he stated:

> 'if we proclaim it, it would be like making the receiver of aid feel like indebted to you, which is not very good. Even in Christian faith, you say that "let your left hand not know what your right hand has given". If you give aid to a poor person, you don't remind him everyday that you aided him.' (Int. 29, municipal councillor, November 2015)

This chapter makes no claim to judge whose perceptions are right or wrong, but rather emphasizes that how interactions in service delivery are perceived matters for analysing local interactions as a peacebuilding function. However, the tradition of humility as a provider may give a partial explanation as to why different actors perceive the municipality's services differently, as the information is simply not there. Although admirable as an approach to aid provision, the vagueness in their proclamations appears to foster perceptions of doubt rather than trust. In analysing local interactions as a peacebuilding function, the unwillingness to publicly display this information impedes citizens' ability to judge the municipality, countering the peacebuilding potential of interactions, as it is believed to enhance the public's access to information and ability to engage with political elites (Donais, 2012, p 54f). By contextualizing the theoretical arguments, this situation highlights the norms and ideas that are at play in a local context.

Another example demonstrates how knowledge about municipal capacities and limitations is crucial for trust-building. During the waste crisis of 2015, municipal councillors described a clash between inhabitants' expectations of the municipality and their lack of understanding of the circumstances under which the municipality acted. As the situation evolved, local inhabitants requested that the municipality remove the waste on the streets and implement waste management schemes. With the waste crisis rapidly evolving, the municipality put considerable effort into communicating with all the communities in Bourj Hammoud. As a municipal councillor further explained:

'we had meetings with representatives of the local communities and explained to them the details of the problem, and I know that they understood what we explained. We put all the documents, all the facts in front of them, and they realized that the problem lies elsewhere.' (Int. 29, municipal councillor, November 2015)

According to one municipal councillor, this communication with the public, through meetings or conversations with all the leaders of the different communities in Bourj Hammoud, was something they had to do because people turned to the municipality when they had nowhere else to go. However, media coverage and civil society activism also pushed the public opinion into believing that the municipality could be the solution to the problem without considering its actual capacities to act (Int. 29, municipal councillor, November 2015). As civil society mobilized against the waste crisis, they demanded that the municipality take responsibility for waste management, and pushed for recycling and sorting at source as well as the establishing of facilities for composting biodegradable waste (Atallah, 2015; Dakroub and Lakiss, 2015). Although not disagreeing with the need to manage waste in a more environmentally sound way, civil society demands were perceived as ignorant of the conditions under which the municipalities worked. As one municipal councillor explained:

'So, they need to come down from their ivory towers and know what the situation on the ground is and realize what is required. This does not mean that they are not right in the end-result of what they demand. But implementing methodology is not as easy as they think.' (Int. 29, municipal councillor, November 2015)

The lack of understanding of municipal conditions and possibilities for waste management restricted the opportunity for fruitful local interactions between civil society actors and the municipality to promote participation, influence and fostering trust. Whereas collaboration between civil society organizations and the municipality presented opportunities for participation, influence and trust-building when services fell within the prerogatives of the municipality, the cooperative spirit did not traverse into interactions in times of crises.

Local interactions and peacebuilding in Bourj Hammoud

In Bourj Hammoud, interactions between the municipality, local civil society organizations as well as the local population were portrayed as essential to inhabitants' perception of the municipality as a relevant and legitimate local actor. Although these interactions were multiple and plentiful, they also illustrate how, to differing degrees, local interactions act as a peacebuilding function.

First, the composition of the municipal council was seen as giving local majority and minority groups, political parties, religious communities and civil society actors an opportunity to directly participate in and influence municipal affairs. Although these direct connections encouraged participation and influence, the importance of who you know, the interest and influence over power of the one you know, comes to the forefront. Thus, participation can be inclusive but influence is not guaranteed. Second, local interactions are crucial for the municipality to exercise authority as a local government. Interactions and negotiations between the municipality and the public can promote participation that influences municipal interpretations of regulations or have more of an information-spreading character. Such interactions illustrate a dialogue between the municipality and the public, necessary for their ability to build trust and exercise authority over the local space. Third, local interactions are key to municipal and civil society service provision, enabling participation and influence over projects, as well as trust-building between parties. However, because of local divisions some interviewees perceived collaboration as unequal, fuelling distrust.

Analysing local interactions as a peacebuilding function, interviewees described interactions in terms of participation and influence when municipal affairs required an adaptation based on the population's needs. However, in terms of fostering trust in the local government, it appears to be partial, with some civil society actors perceiving the municipality as their most important partner, while others interacted with non-municipal connections to exercise influence and respond to needs. In addition, interactions that fostered trust between communities in the local space appear to be missing, at least as interactions that went through the municipality, which is of interest in this study.

Saida

Compared to Tyre and Bourj Hammoud, the municipal council of Saida differs in how it came about. In Saida, the 2010 election was a competitive election between two different alliance lists. The first list, the 'Loyalty and Development list' included the Future Movement (led by the Hariri family), Islamic Gama'a and the group of Abdul Rahman Bizri, the former head of the municipality. The second list, called 'The Popular Will', gathered the Nasserite movement, colloquially referred to as Saad, with support from Amal and Hezbollah (*The Monthly*, 2016). The contestation for power between the Hariri's and the Saad's that emerged in the aftermath of the civil war is, thus, still part of local politics in Saida.

According to one interviewee and member of 'The Popular Will'-list, they did not expect to win the election. However, its participation was an important message for the Hariri's and the Future Movement that dominate Saida, as he claimed:

> 'I know that I will lose the election, but I want to make a message to the other list, you cannot cancel everybody [from participating in politics]. I am alone with my list, but I have one third of the city.' (Int. 40, civil society actor, November 2015)

As the 2010 election passed, the 'Loyalty and Development list' got 62 per cent of the votes (*The Monthly*, 2016). While the winning list was an alliance between three different political actors, it was not a consensus list such as the ones in Tyre and Bourj Hammoud. Thus, the 2010 elections implied that: "those who are represented in the municipality are the moderate Islamic powers, and Bizri and Hariri" (Int. 34, municipal councillor, November 2015). In Saida, the political parties in power identify with the Sunni Muslim majority of Saida. However, as seen, the inclusion of Sunnis in the municipal council does not mean representation of all political views present locally. Judging representation based on sect is therefore not accurate in the case of Saida. Political representation in Saida illustrates that local-level elections can refocus political contestation for power away from being based only on sectarian belonging, to talking about political goals for the city, enabling an alternative narrative of Lebanese politics (Harb, 2017; Salamey, 2014, p 152).[1]

Despite a contested election, many interviewees (for example, Int. 18, 35, 37, 43, 46) emphasized that politics, or the power game between the two lists, should be kept outside the municipality. As one municipal councillor claimed:

> 'from the start, the mayor took the decision that the political must stay out of the municipality. We have to work for all people of the city, our hands being open to all people of the city.' (Int. 35, municipal councillor, November 2015)

The openness towards the different local actors was emphasized by municipal councillors, municipal employees as well as civil society actors. Asked about the relationship between the competing lists after the election of 2010, one civil society actor explained:

---

[1] The municipal elections of 2016 saw a continuation of this story as a third list entered the elections. The third list gathered Islamist voices, some of them allegedly supporters of the Islamist leader Sheikh al-Assir, who had mobilized protests in Saida in 2013 (*The Monthly*, 2016).

> 'They [the municipality] are on the same distance with all the people. If we are at an event in the municipality, it is remarkable that all people are present. You see the other list that didn't win; they are present in the first row.' (Int. 43, civil society actor, November 2015)

Also, members of the opposition confirmed that political quarrels had been put aside after the elections, as one interviewee claimed: "Hariri and Siniora [Future Movement parliamentarian from Saida] are my friends but we are on different sides in politics" (Int. 40, civil society actor, November 2015). In terms of local interactions, such connections illustrated an interaction characterized by participation, contributing to fostering a continued conversation and trust between local groups. However, while the opposition was invited to municipal events, interactions did not generate influence.

Similar to the municipality of Tyre and Bourj Hammoud, civil society actors in Saida had a close collaboration with the municipal council. One civil society actor emphasized that personal relationships with the municipality were important. Asked whether it was possible to influence the municipality, she explained:

> 'Yes, it is very easy. And more than this, our chairman here of the association is a member of the municipality … we have direct contact with them, we discuss with her on a daily basis. If we have something, she can take it to the mayor; for us it is very easy to accomplish.' (Int. 43, civil society actor, November 2015)

This direct link gave this NGO a particular advantage with the municipality. However, the situation was not exclusive to this NGO. Several of the 21 members of the municipal council were aligned with the civil society. In addition, NGOs in Saida are organized within an NGO platform that works as a mediator. Initiated in the 1980s, the platform connects organizations in and around Saida that work on, for example, social, health and educational matters, as well as developmental issues. As explained by one member of the platform, "The great number of organizations and their diversity in the delivery of services creates a plurality of people that constitutes this coalition" (Int. 19, civil society actor, June 2015). Asked whether the platform's relationship with the municipality changed when there was a new municipal council in 2010, one interviewee explained that because of the diversity of the actors involved in the platform, it has, "granted us impunity to continue our coordination with the municipality regardless of what political power takes over" (Int. 19, civil society actor, June 2015).

Although the municipal elections in 2010 produced a winner whose list occupied the seats in the municipal council, interaction between opposing groups has continued. Nevertheless, these interactions are characterized by participation with little influence over municipal policies, in accordance with the 'winner-takes-it-all' system, which is a feature of Lebanese local elections (Salamey, 2014, p 116). Instead, participation and influence over municipal policies are portrayed as acting through civil society interactions with the municipality, either directly through personal connections or through the NGO platform that coordinates NGOs in Saida.

In its role as the state authority closest to the population, the municipality's role included, for example, issuing building permits, employing municipal police for traffic regulation and keeping order. According to one civil society actor, these services impacted how the population perceived the municipality, as it was, "always papers signed, the things official, the taxes they need to pay" (Int. 37, civil society actor, November 2015). Through these daily services, the municipality was available to the population, and they would express their opinions and needs. As one interviewee recalls, the people will "come and tell the municipality about their problems: a tree they don't want, lights, etc. They give their views in the reception" (Int. 32, municipal employee, November 2015). One municipal councillor proudly described the existence of a mobile app that allowed the population to report directly to the municipality:

> 'We have an application, if someone sees a problem in the street, they can take a photo and directly send it to the municipality. And the whole council of ministers [municipal council] can see the problem and then we take it to the department that is responsible for it to solve. But we are looking to update the app to let the people know if the problem has been solved to give it green, red, orange. But it is not finished yet.' (Int. 35, municipal councillor, November 2015)

Whether opinions were expressed through personal communication to the municipality, smart technology or other fora, several interviewees described situations where local inhabitants commonly approached the municipality about existing problems or suggestions for future developments. Although the municipal councillors interviewed conveyed an interest in such suggestions, the influence of suggestions varies. As one municipal councillor stated about the population:

> 'they come with ideas for the city, and some of them were useful. One of the citizens said, when we are arranging the area, why don't we make a river. Yes, we can do that.' (Int. 18, municipal councillor, June 2015)

However, the same municipal councillor also described situations where public proposals were impossible to implement because of the practical implications of the suggestion. Thus, even if public participation and proposals were welcome, their influence was not as simple.

Municipal interaction with the inhabitants of Saida was, however, often more than just listening to suggestions. Through the municipal staff, the municipality solved issues relating to hazardous buildings, irresponsible use of public spaces, or new or restored constructions on a daily basis. As a local authority, it was the municipality's job to implement local regulations. Such daily activities relied on the ability of the municipality to first ensure the understanding of regulations and then to be seen as legitimate in ensuring compliance with them. The municipal police played a key role in this process:

> 'If they do not follow regulations, they have to pay fees, or the municipality will ask the municipal police to go and take the table and the merchandise and take it here, until he [the shop owner] follows the rules. Sometimes people always try to argue at the first step; they get the documents about the regulations and have to sign to ensure that they received the papers. After that, the police go and see if they have followed the regulations. If not, then they will take away the things and then they will do as we say. First information and discussion. Some people are easy, some more difficult.' (Int. 32, municipal employee, November 2015)

Although the interviewee went on to explain that municipal decisions were accepted in 90 per cent of the cases, the previous quote demonstrates that exercising authority was, to a large extent, about interacting with the local community, mirroring governance practices in Tyre and Bourj Hammoud. In addition, it was through the pursuance of meaningful and repeated interactions that trust in the local authority could grow.

Furthermore, the municipal building was a space for interaction. As one interviewee explained, the level of interactions could be seen in the use of the building itself: "Today, we [the NGO platform] have an office inside the municipality building of Saida, which reflects the strong relationship and partnership between civil society and the municipality" (Int. 19, civil society actor, June 2015). Additionally, local NGOs, schools or other groups frequently used the municipal building for meetings, as one employee explained: "The big building of the municipality, it is used by different actors – political, educational, sometimes religious" (Int. 33, municipal employee, November 2015). As such, the municipal building becomes a concrete example of how the municipality enabled a space for interactions, sometimes between different local actors, or sometimes between the municipality and local organizations. As local actors used this space for interaction, it became a space that fostered trust between communities in Saida.

Especially in times of crisis, the municipal building signified the municipality's role as a local authority. As one municipal councillor explained:

'the municipality is the actor on the ground that the people relate to. If anything happens, the people go to the municipality. We have to be prepared; we have to act.' (Int. 46, municipal councillor, November 2015)

In recent years, the municipal building has become a gathering place when unexpected violence or catastrophes erupt. The municipality became a gathering point for Saida's citizens, or its neighbouring inhabitants, for example, during the Israel–Hezbollah war in 2006, the incidents of violence that surrounded the protests by Sunni Sheikh al-Assir and his followers in 2013, and the fires erupting in the Palestinian camp of Ain al-Hilweh in 2015. One municipal employee described the work of the municipality in 2013:

'When al-Assir was here, some employees and the [municipal] police they stayed in the municipality building; they opened the building as a refuge, they slept there, ate, gave people in need food, cars to transport them, they were ready for everything. And after that the municipality rebuilt the buildings; they helped in rebuilding the ones that were destroyed, picking up the garbage and rubble, and giving money to the people who needed it.' (Int. 32. municipal employee, November 2015)

When the municipality uses its facilities to act as a local authority, being the responsive local government needed at that moment, it demonstrates instances of interaction in which trust in the local authority is built. As the interviewee explained further, the municipality's reaction to the al-Assir situation "changed how the people viewed the municipality" (Int. 32, municipal employee, November 2015). However, the municipality's ability to react depends on an active civil society, and the municipality is a participant in the network of activities initiated and run by the civil society. As one municipal councillor explained:

'Today, the NGOs are very effective, especially in Saida. They are an excellent support for us; we collaborate with them in a lot in different fields. Especially during crisis … those NGOs, they act the same day. If you take the last crisis in Ain al-Hilweh, fires started in the afternoon. In three hours, we had almost 500–600 people downstairs here. The government was not there, so the NGOs were really fast to act and provide food, shelter, everything they needed. Without NGOs, there is something missing. The people came to the municipality and then they [the NGOs] placed them in different shelters, schools that were available in coordination with NGOs.' (Int. 46, municipal councillor, November 2015)

In addition to offering services in times of crisis, several interviewees perceived service delivery in Saida as responsive to local needs, taking the local community into account when delivering everyday services. As one interviewee explained:

> 'The municipality of Saida is working very well. It is a municipality that one can rely on; you can have confidence in the municipality. Always, the politics plays a role, but ... for example, for the feast, now in Saida there are not many Christians [living in the city], very few, but still the municipality, for every religious celebration, Christian or Muslim they do a good job in decorating the city.' (Int. 37, civil society actor, November 2015)

Such services illustrate how small acts of taking different groups into account means that local minorities also influence the making of the public space. In turn, small symbolic considerations for local needs appear to foster trust in the municipality. This is important when considering the sectarian divisions in past and present Lebanon.

In other instances, interactions are more direct. Both civil society actors and municipal councillors emphasized the continuous practice of stakeholder dialogues with the population affected by municipal services and projects. One municipal councillor noted, "You need to tell the people that are affected what will be done, answer some questions and make some changes" (Int. 18, municipal councillor, June 2015). These stakeholder dialogues allow for participation, which spreads information and has an influence over projects. In addition, the municipality constantly cooperates with civil society organizations in implementing local projects, as emphasized by another interviewee: "We work with NGO's in everything" (Int. 34, municipal councillor, November 2015). However, participation does not always imply influence over municipal priorities, as one civil society actor described:

> 'Of course, the municipality have their committees and their municipality board and maybe they make some decision, to hold a marathon, for example, and from this point, [from] the first meeting to have ideas on how to do it [we participate]. We participate in every detail, and later, we coordinate; we are on the ground to prepare and implement the event.' (Int. 43, civil society actor, November 2015)

However, participation also implies challenges, as one municipal councillor described:

'Sometimes, you have a vision for something here and as we come from private sector, we think it's good; this is appropriate. Sometimes, you are faced with different ideas that they don't want them, and that's a big challenge. To understand other people's point of view, to be in their shoes, sometimes to give up on things that you expect to have, or prefer to have, because some other people don't want them. So, public work is completely different; you have to take into account other factors, to be well aware. And it takes time to accommodate. Maybe after 5 years, I am, personally, halfway in accepting that. Really, it's a big challenge.' (Int. 46, municipal councillor, November 2015)

Although challenging and time-consuming, interactions were seen as crucial for local developments, as "neither the municipality alone nor the civil sector alone could accomplish such achievements, but it is rather due to the coordination and partnership efforts between the two" (Int. 19, civil society actor, June 2015). Furthermore, in Saida, the role of participation was often turned around when civil society initiated activities for local development. As one municipal councillor explained:

'the area around the river … we share with an NGO. It was a very dirty area and one of the NGO … they took their own money and cleaned it, and now it is open for people. So, this is the kind of sharing with NGOs.' (Int. 35, municipal councillor, November 2015)

Another municipal councillor described this as the municipality linking up with NGOs: "because the NGOs have resources and funds, we also use this for the development of the city" (Int. 34, municipal councillor, November 2015). As this illustrates, participation and influence in Saida goes beyond civil society actors participating and influencing municipal work, as assumed in the theoretical framework, but the invitation to participate often goes in the other direction. As one civil society actor claimed:

'It happens that the relationship between the municipality and the civil society is so close. My view is that the municipality is highly regarded as very perceptive of the people's needs; it is because the civil society is giving them this image.' (Int. 44, civil society actor, November 2015)

According to this interviewee, the close cooperation was beneficial for the municipality. This seems to contradict theoretical assumptions of service delivery, that if non-state actors provide services, only non-state actors gain legitimacy (Krampe, 2016; Menkhaus, 2006). However, it also confirms what other studies have shown, namely, that it does not necessarily matter who is actually delivering the services, but rather to whom the people attribute (giving either credit or blame) the services provided (Mcloughlin, 2015, p 350). This demonstrates the complexity and link between service delivery and interactions as peacebuilding functions.

Local interactions and peacebuilding in Saida

In Saida, local interactions portray a picture of cooperation between the civil society and the municipality. The municipality was keen on involving the population and civil society actors, and the civil society was devoted to including the municipality. However, although interactions were plentiful, they also display varying sides to participation, influence and trust-building through local interactions, illustrating the different sides of local interactions as a peacebuilding function.

First, in Saida, the local is a politically contested space. Unlike municipal elections in Tyre and Bourj Hammoud, the municipal council was constituted through a competitive election in 2010. As the winning party took position in the municipality, the interactions after the election still provided opportunities for participation by the political opposition. However, it did not provide influence over municipal council priorities. Second, the municipality of Saida acted as a (physical) space for interactions and authority through approachability. As the municipal building became a space used by civil society actors for activities, as well as crisis management, it provided a space for participatory responses to emerging needs, as well as a space for fostering trust between different local communities and the municipality itself. Third, the close cooperation between civil society activities and the municipality implied that the municipality was often the one participating in civil society service provision. While the theoretical argument on interactions assumes that interactions are important for participation in and influence on municipal work, the case of Saida illustrates that interactions could also improve other actors' ability to act. In relation to local interactions, this shows that interactions go both ways. However, this sheds a different light on the peacebuilding function of service delivery, which claims that (local) state legitimacy is attained by provision of services when the public acknowledges that it is delivered by state actors (Krampe, 2016; Mcloughlin, 2015). In Saida, local services delivered by the civil society, with participation from the municipality, seem to suggest that it was not only the main provider that gained legitimacy from such provision.

Conclusion: three cases of local interactions

This chapter has explored local interactions in the municipalities of Tyre, Bourj Hammoud and Saida. The empirical discussions on structures for inclusion, daily interactions and inclusion in service delivery have been analysed through the themes of: participation, influence and fostering trust in the local government and trust between local communities. This provides one piece of the puzzle in furthering our understanding of the role of local governments in local peacebuilding. Here, I turn to comparing the three municipalities to highlight how local interactions are perceived and what diverse views tell us about local interactions as a peacebuilding function. Finally, I discuss what this means for local government engagement in local peacebuilding.

Interactions between people who inhabit the local space and the municipality matters for grounding peacebuilding as it allows local actors to engage with local elites, demand accountability and the adaptation of services to local needs (Donais, 2012, p 54f). Participation is one important aspect. In Tyre, participation is characterized by stakeholder dialogues in relation to specific projects, or the participation of actors in specific projects. Participation does not drive municipal work but is included when needed. In Bourj Hammoud, participation occurs mainly through civil society actors who are involved in co-produced projects and services. Such co-production of municipal work involves close participation between the municipality and civil society actors. In Saida, civil society and other political actors are broadly invited to participate in municipal activities. As in Tyre, this participation is related to specific projects or events. However, in Saida, the municipality is also invited to participate in civil society-initiated activities. In all three municipalities, participation is described as ample. However, the analysis suggests that in all three cases participation is rather specific than broad, either through participation by a particular group or in relation to a particular project.

Influence is the second aspect of local interactions that has been analysed in this chapter. Influence is emphasized because participation risks becoming a rhetorical claim with little meaning (Paffenholz, 2015a). As such, analysing whether participation enables influence over municipal affairs is important. In Tyre, influence over municipal affairs is pursued through the inclusive structures of the municipal council, with councillors representing the families or civil society organizations present in the local community. In addition, the municipality is perceived as conscious of local needs, by being attentive to civil society organizations within the local space. In Bourj Hammoud, influence is also described as performed through a municipal council formed by the inclusion of different actors from different religious sects as well as civil society. In this way, influence goes through personal links, and the municipality is perceived as accessible through such links. However, through the composition of the municipal council, influence is also perceived as more accessible to the ones aligned with the local majority. In Saida, influence over municipal work follows the pattern of participation in that it is available, but mostly in relation to the implementation of projects already decided upon.

This approach towards inclusion of influence also comes to the fore in the municipality welcoming suggestions from the public but acknowledging that not all suggestions are possible to implement.

Thirdly, local interactions are also thought to matter for peacebuilding because they foster trust between the local population and the local communities as well as between different local groups (Jackson, 2013, p 354f; Schou and Haug, 2005). In Tyre, interactions with the local population, which occur within projects or events that are owned and run by the municipality itself, appear to have this feature. The project of the pedestrianized street as well as the number of different activities performed within Beit el-Mamlouk have enhanced the population's view of municipal capacity, as well as enabled spaces for interaction between different groups. However, these possibilities to influence appear to occur within the small projects that the municipality can run by itself. In Bourj Hammoud, interactions with the local community does foster trust in the municipality. However, as the positive image of the municipality is emphasized by some, a feeling of alienation is described by others. As such, when interactions occur, they do foster trust, but as perceptions of unequal interaction are described, the ability of the municipality to be a local actor of relevance for all is questioned. As such, even if interactions are plentiful, if participation and influence are perceived as more attainable for some (even if the municipality contests such claims), it does not foster trust in the municipality within all groups, nor does it foster trust between groups in the local community. In Saida, some interactions foster trust. As seen in the response to acute needs, where the municipality becomes the space where interactions occur, through the use of the municipal building for the coordination of services, trust in the municipality as a capable local actor grows. However, as the NGO platform in Saida plays an important role in coordinating civil society actors and answering to the population's everyday needs, trust between communities is also fostered through their activities, something that 'rubs off' on the municipality through their participation.

Finally, comparing local interactions that allow for participation, influence and the building of trust in the local government as well as between local communities in the three municipalities shows that Tyre, Bourj Hammoud and Saida display slightly different ways of interacting with the local community and, thus, grounding peacebuilding in the local space. In Tyre, interactions that provide participation and influence mostly occur via personal interactions through the inclusion of representatives of different local actors. Such personal connections allow the municipality to gain knowledge of the needs of the population, enabling a personally grounded peacebuilding. In Bourj Hammoud, the municipality is also closely connected with the inhabitants through personal connections. In addition, even if not perceived as equal by all, the municipality closely cooperates with civil society actors, allowing for ample participation and influence. As such, the municipality of Bourj Hammoud engages in a cooperatively grounded peacebuilding, but a peacebuilding that becomes more relevant for some. In Saida, participation of civil society actors implies that the municipality gains knowledge of local needs. However, although participation is ample, influence is only granted to civil society actors in certain projects. In addition, as the municipality cooperates with other local actors, the municipality profits from local knowledge, responsiveness and the trust-building capacity of these other local actors. In the municipality of Saida, local interactions are thus perceived as enabling the municipality to engage in grounding a co-opted process of local peacebuilding.

5

Vertical Relationships: Connecting the Local to the National and Global

This chapter discusses vertical interconnectedness as initiated by Lederach (1997), emphasizing a multi-level approach in peacebuilding that connects actors and actions on the local level with those on the national and international, and vice versa. The idea of vertical relationships argues that relationships matter for local developments, enabling peacebuilding activities that, in turn, mitigate conflict. The notion of vertical relationships as a peacebuilding function highlights complementarity, autonomy and agency. Briefly, complementarity emphasizes local, national and international actors working towards the same goals, aligning interests and adapting activities to local needs (Mitchell and Hancock, 2012, p 175). Autonomy is coupled with vertical relationships, highlighting that the more autonomous a local space is, the less vertical relationships matter for local developments, and vice versa (Brinkerhoff, 2011; Kälin, 2004). Finally, agency emphasizes the need for vertical relationships as a peacebuilding function to allow local actors to define and redefine what local peacebuilding means in the local space. Agency acknowledges power asymmetries between local and national or international actors, while opening our eyes to the ways they are challenged and used by local actors.

This chapter discusses vertical relationships between the municipality of Tyre, Bourj Hammoud and Saida and central state authorities, national political figures and international actors. Throughout the chapter, municipal councillors, employees and civil society actors provide their reflections on how vertical relationships work for local developments and, over time, give local governments a role in local peacebuilding. Vertical relationships in Tyre, Bourj Hammoud and Saida are discussed in the light of vertical relationships within Lebanese multi-level governance, and illustrated by local developments such as infrastructural developments and waste management.

By doing so, the chapter sheds light on how vertical relationships matter for developments on the ground, highlighting the diversity in vertical relationships and what implications it has for understanding local government engagement in building local peace.

Tyre

In Tyre, as in Lebanon as a whole, vertical relationships between the municipality and the central state are influenced by the administrative structures and a high degree of centralized authority. This was explained by municipal councillors as normal and a relationship based on routine. As one municipal councillor described it:

> 'the municipality is a small government, so it is a typical Lebanese government. They [the municipality] can do some actions, but also they have to refer to the higher level of authority.' (Int. 2, municipal councillor, May 2015)

This is regulated by the municipal law of 1977, but in essence power over local policies is in the hands of central authorities. For example, the municipal council can only authorize expenses up to twenty million Lebanese pounds (in 2015, 13,000 USD).[1] Municipal decisions that require more spending need to seek approval from governmental representatives at higher levels, depending on the size of spending or type of decision (Ministry of Interior and Municipalities, 1977/2008). In Tyre, this process was described as part of the municipal routine:

> 'Without doubt, there is a relationship with the state, because the ministry of interior is responsible. ... For example, the ministry of tourism, we propose a project, and if needed we go with the suggestion to the ministry of tourism and hope to get an agreement on this project, typical things.' (Int. 5, municipal councillor, June 2015)

However, approval of decisions was also a time-consuming matter. One municipal councillor described a plan for creating a wastewater plant that had been in the planning stages since the year 2000. Despite Tyre and

---

[1] In 2015, this was equivalent to 13,000 USD with the Lebanese pound pegged to the dollar at the exchange rate of 1,500. With the economic crisis, the Lebanese pound is estimated to have lost 80 per cent of its value. As the municipal budget is still regulated by the 1977 municipal law (Ministry of Interior and Municipalities, 1977/2008), municipal budgets have gone from being small to losing 80 per cent of their purchasing power.

neighbouring municipalities polluting the sea with wastewater, very little had happened in implementing the wastewater plant. However, the interviewee did not portray an image of frustration over the situation but rather something that the municipality was used to and had accepted. The municipal councillor shrugged and further explained, "Everything in Lebanon takes time. Like the turtle, the turtle likes to rest some years" (Int. 1, municipal councillor, December 2014).

The need for central government approval and uncertainty or slowness in reaching results emphasizes the lack of autonomy and capacity of the municipality. This was aggravated by the centralization of power during the civil war, and the continuous delay of initiating the decentralization reform proposed in the Ta'if Peace Agreement (Harb and Atallah, 2015). In 2015, municipal councillors had high hopes for a decentralization reform. Nationally, a draft law on decentralization had been presented in 2014 and there seemed to be an opening in the debate (Baroud, 2021).[2] According to municipal councillors, decentralization would provide municipalities with means and capacities to pursue independent development plans, countering the present lack of autonomy. One municipal councillor claimed that: "We would like to see a real decentralization system in the municipality. Because this will drive development and the right management of the city" (Int. 1, municipal councillor, December 2014). This confirms that complementary vertical relationships can only get you so far in attending to local needs, whereas autonomy for the local government could improve the peacebuilding role of municipalities further.

Ironically, despite the constraints put on the municipality through vertical relations with the central state, the absence of the central government was also an apparent obstacle for the municipality of Tyre. The municipal councillor continued to explain:

> 'The central government is based in Beirut. [The further] you go away from the capital, the [more the] influence and the interest of the central government will decrease gradually. For that reason, you can see that ... they don't take care for the south and same for the north, same for Beqaa. ... So, the best way to substitute the absence of the central government is decentralization.' (Int. 1, municipal councillor, December 2014)

---

[2] However, a parliamentary decision on the law is still pending. As Baroud explains: "The draft had to wait until 2016 before reaching the Lebanese parliament. Five years later, it is still 'under discussion' in an ad hoc parliamentary committee, which says a lot about the pace of reform in Lebanon" (Baroud, 2021).

With current administrative regulations restricting the possibility of the municipality to act freely, the absence of the central state becomes another obstacle leading to ignorance of the local space. With autonomy a prerequisite for local government peacebuilding capacity, the lack of decentralized autonomy, as well as the lack of a central state presence through complementary vertical relationships, restricts the peacebuilding role of the municipality.

In Lebanon, the most common argument against decentralization is found in the carefully engineered division of power on all levels of governments to keep national peace and unity. However, while some fear federalism and a divided state as a consequence of decentralization, sectarian and political elites also gain influence through weak local governments (Harb and Atallah, 2015, p 192; Salamey, 2014, p 152). However, in Tyre, municipal councillors denied the involvement of political parties and portrayed the municipality as non-political. In Tyre, as well as in the other municipalities, the non-political argument was used to distance the municipality from the politicization of the national government and national political debate. However, this does not mean that the political parties were absent from the municipal space. The cooperation with the political parties of Amal and Hezbollah, the two most important political parties in Tyre, was, instead, described in the following way by one interviewee:

'We should work with them on a political level; we are representing the party, not ourselves, regarding high political decisions, of course. Regarding the daily management, they don't ask, they never ask.' (Int. 1, municipal councillor, December 2014)

However, even if political actors are described as not making requests on daily activities, they can have an influence as their approval and encouragement of projects is often needed. As one interviewee described, political but also personal interests are often accommodated within political parties:

'I am talking about this project [with a political party], [asking] why in Tyre you can't do this, people will love you more. I didn't get any answers. Till now. No answer. They tell me, no money for projects. I don't need money from you! Money, we have, we have rich people. For example, we have here a green area, why we don't have a park? Because some people in the political [party] want to grab this area. This area is for [regional organization of Tyre] to get a big project like Maroon el Ras, recreation zone, sports area, big park, why not? For example, I will divide this area into six or seven places; this bank will finance this area, this company this, this … I don't need money from you. I need help from you. In the municipality, if I tell them about this. No we can't. Why not? No answer. In this way political parties give answers.' (Int. 4, municipal councillor, June 2015)

The need for assistance from political parties to make land available for local developments illustrates a continuation of Lebanese clientelism, also in relation to the municipality. By the end of the civil war, many past warlords moved into national politics, maintaining, and expanding, their power base, and becoming political patrons of the post-war era (Hamzeh, 2001, p 174f). While clientelism highlights the provision of services in exchange for political support of the patron, complementary vertical relationships emphasize local and national actors working towards the same goal. When complementarity is absent, requests from the municipality are met with no response, constraining local developments and showing whose interests are taken into account. Thus, analysing vertical relationships as a peacebuilding function emphasizes the need to examine whose interests are pursued through an existing relationship.

At the same time, municipal councillors describe vertical relationships to national and international actors as a precondition for local development projects. In Tyre, the main project for local development is the Cultural Heritage and Urban Development (CHUD) project, run by the government agency Council for Development and Reconstruction (CDR) and financed by the World Bank and other international actors. CHUD is put forward as one of the bigger accomplishments in the city. As expressed by one municipal councillor:

'the main project in our city is the CHUD project. It is concerned with the old city, but we look forward to expanding it to other parts of the city. At least, they are doing something really special.' (Int. 1, municipal councillor, December 2014)

Directed and implemented by the CDR, CHUD implements visible changes in the local space. Several infrastructural developments, such as a new vegetable market, pavements and parking, have taken place since 2004. According to one CDR employee, it is a cooperative project relying on a stable relationship between the central state and the municipality. Since the start of the project in 2004, municipal elections have been held in 2004 and 2010,[3] but, as he claimed, the decisions and political direction of the municipality (in relation to CHUD) are the same (Int. 10, government

---

[3] While the first local elections after the civil war were held in 1998 in most of Lebanon, Tyre held its first local elections in 2004 due to its proximity to the security zone in south Lebanon, occupied by Israel until the year 2000 (Chaib, 2009).

employee, June 2015). This is not surprising since the composition of the municipality has not really changed. The interviewee further emphasized that the municipality is involved in all stages, from preparation to implementation and in handling the unexpected consequences as well as gaining capacity to ensure the sustainability of the project. Furthermore, he praised the growing capacity of the municipality, explaining that:

> 'we are confident that by being exposed to this project, Tyre municipality and the other three [municipalities that are involved in CHUD] acquired good knowledge of how to deal with such situations to be used in other projects. Managing a project, managing a city, preparing a business plan, avoiding impact, communication. Some of the skills they had, some a little, some they didn't have.' (Int. 10, government employee, June 2015)

Thus, the project not only delivers infrastructure but also develops local capacity and allows it to grow over time. The growth in capacity, and the possible advances for local autonomy that the project implies, relates to the idea of peacebuilding as a continuous process. Acknowledging the reinstatement of the municipality as a local government in 1998, increased autonomy was not achieved overnight, but is a process over time.

However, although there was a growth in capacity through the partnership with the CDR, municipal councillors interviewed did not share this perception. Perhaps because they did not relate to the project with the same patience and long-term perspective, municipal councillors emphasized the lack of municipal autonomy instead. When asked whether projects were initiated by external actors, one municipal councillor responded: "Yes. We have our ideas after" (Int. 4, municipal councillor, June 2015). Another municipal councillor further elaborated on the division of tasks:

> 'We are in this project as the final beneficiary, but we have to approve the project. There is a special unit in the CDR called Project Manager Unit. This unit is controlling the projects [and] based in Beirut. And they contracted a specialized company to supervise and design the project.' (Int. 1, municipal councillor, December 2014)

Thus, in this project, and others like this, local decision-making power was only considered once the project had been initiated. The inability to initiate local developments of infrastructural changes emphasizes the lack of local autonomy but also the importance of complementary vertical relationships with the central state to enable developments on the ground. In addition, CHUD works under the influence of international actors. Organized under the auspices of UNESCO and financed mainly by international donors such as the World Bank, France and Italy, the project comes with guidelines to be followed and audits from international donors. As one CDR employee noted:

> 'Tyre, it is a world heritage site, so UNESCO is involved in this case. They are directly involved. They have the upper hand. We cannot do anything if we don't have the approval of UNESCO on any intervention we do there.' (Int. 10, government employee, June 2015)

As seen, the involvement of international actors influences the autonomy of the municipality. Nonetheless, UNESCO is seen as an essential actor for the municipality and its emphasis on the historical particularity of Tyre was an object of pride. One municipal councillor described the relationship between the municipality and UNESCO as a good one, encouraging the municipality "to accomplish the project without making any faults [mistakes]" (Int. 5, municipal councillor, June 2015). Again, this emphasizes that the relationship with international actors is a complementary one when the municipality accepts the project proposed.

Thus, municipal councillors in Tyre perceived vertical relationships to international actors as advantageous, claiming that when international actors work "we see the results" (Int. 6, municipal councillor, June 2015). The common acceptance, and often enthusiasm, of the work done by national and international actors illustrates a situation where local and national or international actors work towards common goals in a complementary manner. Nevertheless, it is a complementarity that aligns with internationally set agendas, and, coupled with the municipality's lack of means and decision-making power, hindered the creation of a municipal strategy for local development (Int. 1, 4). Also, the lack of autonomy hindered the municipality from addressing local needs through projects run in collaboration, as one interviewee claimed:

> 'When the World Bank came here, I told them we need your help, but through our strategies, our vision, not yours. [But] they have everything, and we have to get money and do what they need.' (Int. 4, municipal councillor, June 2015)

Thus, the rigidity of internationally initiated projects hindered the municipality from adopting projects to local needs. Rather, as receivers of projects or initiatives the municipality had one particular role, as one municipal councillor explained:

> 'And you may ask me "what is your role [in this process]?" We are shouting, and pushing. We are following these projects to ask questions,

and to provide them with local help if they need it.' (Int. 1, municipal councillor, December 2014)

Hence, while local to international relationships are described as complementary, it is a complementarity that encourages local developments only when local and international goals align. This does bring important projects to the local space, but it limits the municipality's ability to adopt projects to local needs, thus limiting the possibility of municipal engagement in local peacebuilding.

At the same time, the insufficient waste management capacity of the municipality of Tyre demonstrates that with a lack of local autonomy, complementary vertical relationship are crucial for solving local issues. In 2015, the waste management plant in Ain el-Baal had the capacity to handle about half of the daily production of waste in the district of Tyre. To solve the issue, the municipality was collaborating with UN-Habitat to build a new plant. While plans moved ahead, the problem was access to land. According to one municipal councillor, the government controlled access to land. To ask for land, the municipal councillor described how he made use of vertical relationships with national political actors, visiting the ministry of finance to push for a resolution. In 2015, the finance minister was Ali Hassan Khalil, member of the Amal movement, the most important political party in Tyre. This description suggests that although the municipality must abide by the institutional structures available for vertical relationships with the central state and international actors, there are still other avenues through which these relationships work and through which individual agency is used to push for local needs. However, the municipal councillor was uncertain whether it would provide the preferred results, stating, "The connection to state authorities and the ministry of finance is good, but it does not mean that he will obey my request" (Int. 47, municipal councillor, December 2015).[4] Nonetheless, it does hint at vertical relationships working more in a reciprocal manner than noted earlier.

However, the reciprocity is described in personal terms, rather than institutional. The individual that is of most importance to the municipality is Nabih Berri, the speaker of parliament and leader of the Amal Party, the party that holds most the municipal council posts in Tyre. Thus, even if the municipality is described as non-political, one interviewee also claimed that, "We cannot do anything without Berri. People are very loyal to him

---

[4] In November 2021, the plan for a new waste management plant and landfill was yet to be implemented. Once again, a municipal councillor described using personal connections to get the necessary permits. This illustrates a continuation of local developments depending on vertical relationships, but in a process that is extraordinarily slow.

in Tyre, and he is very proud of his influence in Tyre" (Int. 47, municipal councillor, December 2015). The vertical relationships with national elites are a common feature for all three municipalities, but the level of involvement differs. In Tyre, the large developments come from international involvement channelled through national government agencies. In interviews with municipal councillors, personal vertical relationships with national elites are not presented as necessary for bringing developments to the local space. However, in Tyre, interviewees described personal vertical relationships as an avenue for solving problems that occur along the way. As the example of asking for land from the ministry of finance, headed by a minister from Nabih Berri's Amal movement, suggests, personal national–local connections are used to support the municipality's case. The agency of the municipality of Tyre is therefore to be understood in relation to ongoing projects, rather than a driver of new developments. In addition, agency is used within vertical relationships with a particular national political actor, having a position within the central state. Thus, vertical relationships exercised in Tyre emphasize the clientelism present in Lebanese political affairs, a clientelism that is sectarian and political in character, and a factor behind the civil war as well as its resolution through the Ta'if Agreement (Hamzeh, 2001; Khalaf, 2002, p 290).

Vertical relationships and peacebuilding in Tyre

In the municipality of Tyre, vertical relationships with national and international actors are perceived as important to developments within the city. Vertical relationships have enabled infrastructural developments through CHUD as well as other projects. As such, vertical relations are a blessing in the attention they give the local space. Arguing that vertical relationships matter for peace through the developments they enable on the ground (Brinkerhoff, 2011; Kälin, 2004; Mitchell and Hancock, 2012), the municipality of Tyre offers an illustration of how this works. However, vertical relationships appear to be complementary and allow for local influence when local, national and international interests align within a vision proposed from above. Thus, they do not allow for municipal autonomy or ownership over local developments. Nevertheless, even if the municipal councillors described the power asymmetry inherent in vertical relationships, as well as the administrative structure of Lebanon, as constraining, they did not challenge the asymmetry in their narratives. In the vertical relationships as they appear today, the agency of the municipality is expressed as acceptance, support and encouragement of externally developed goals and projects, and when obstacles arise, personal relations with national political elites are used to move projects forward. Thus, the municipality of Tyre engages in vertical relationships on the terms set by the most powerful (McCandless et al, 2015;

Ramsbotham, 2005, p 295). However, by using the power hierarchies, the municipality also acknowledges that it is a hierarchy that they can, sometimes, actively use to their benefit.

Bourj Hammoud

In Bourj Hammoud, municipal councillors and civil society actors describe vertical relationships with the central state as complicated and a matter of formalities and paperwork (Int. 30, 31). In Bourj Hammoud, the vertical relationship with the Lebanese central state occurs mainly within the Lebanese administrative structure. Like the other two municipalities, Bourj Hammoud is required to interact with the central state and seek permission for proposed local developments. However, even though the procedure is the same for all three municipalities studied, the interaction with the central state is continuously described as complicated by municipal councillors in Bourj Hammoud (Int. 15, 30), as opposed to the feeling of municipal–central state interactions being normal and a matter of routine as put forward in Tyre. One municipal councillor in Bourj Hammoud (Int. 31), even went so far as to claim that there was no relationship with the central state – a statement that reflects the perception of an absence of central state attention, policies and procedures that matter for the local space.

This feeling of an absent central state also refers to the periods of no government or no president, as faced by Lebanon in recent years (discussed in Chapter 4). Even if this too is not particular to the municipality of Bourj Hammoud, it is described in Bourj Hammoud as influencing the daily work of the municipality, a notion that does not come to the forefront in the other two cases. Particularly in Bourj Hammoud, the complicated relationship between the central state and the municipality was described as pertaining to the politicization and stagnation of national politics. When asked about the relationship with the government, one interviewee observed:

> 'It is a bit complicated. Because Lebanon is divided between 8 March, with Armenians, Mr Aoun, with the Shiite, the other 14 March are the Sunnites, Druze and all that, they are divided into two. Now, we don't have a president. For one and a half years; it is too long. Now, there are seven Armenians in the parliament. Only two from the Tashnag party. ... No we have relations, but it doesn't help us.' (Int. 30, municipal councillor, November 2015)

This illustrates a general feeling of limited possibilities to influence national politics to the advantage of the municipality through vertical relationships with national political actors. The political party that dominates the political scene in the municipality of Bourj Hammoud is the Armenian Revolutionary

Federation (ARF or Tashnag in colloquial Lebanese), which is also the party that fills the parliamentarian posts pertaining to the electoral district to which the municipality belongs. In the national parliament, six out of 128 posts are allocated to Armenians, but not all of them are from Bourj Hammoud. In addition, the Armenian political parties filling the six posts are divided between supporting March 14 or March 8, thus split by the core dividing line in Lebanese politics (Salamey, 2014, pp 115, 211). Consequently, the feeling of having a lack of influence in the national arena, described in the previous quote, is also based in the fact that Armenian parliamentarians are a minority in national politics. Compared to the municipality of Tyre, where the speaker of parliament, Nabih Berri, is put forward as their main national connection, the situation in Bourj Hammoud is a different one. In addition, because in Lebanon, projects, services or other benefits are often pursued through, or helped by, personal connections to national elites (Hamzeh, 2001), the limited influence of the Bourj Hammoudi representatives on the national level has an impact on local life. The description of the complicated vertical relationship with the central state can therefore also be explained by the limited possibility of influencing political decisions nationally for the benefit of Bourj Hammoud. The case of Bourj Hammoud illustrates the importance of vertical relationships with national political actors for the acceptance of local policies in dealing with municipal issues. The case of Saida, discussed in the following, will further demonstrate the importance of relations with national political actors within the construction of the Lebanese state.

While vertical relationships to national actors were complicated, relationships with international actors enabled developments locally. As part of the UNDPs increasing support to Lebanese communities that host a large number of Syrian refugees, the UNDP proposed a project to restore Manash Street in Bourj Hammoud. With UNDP engineers making plans for the street, the municipality enhanced the opportunity to beautify the city. The hope of developing a market place as a touristic attraction, similar to local developments in other parts of Lebanon, was of particular interest to one interviewee:

'We need to have the tourists. That is why we are going to do this project. Have you been to Byblos? It is the UNDP that made that market. All the shops have wooden doors, all that is the UNDP. We hope that also here we will make it a good market place, to bring in tourists.' (Int. 30, municipal councillor, November 2015)

Although not through a municipal initiative initially, the vertical relationship with the UNDP enabled the local development of a neglected, but locally cherished, space, which was not possible for the municipality to restore by itself. In this sense, vertical relationships not only deliver projects of infrastructural change but also provide a vision of subsequent tourism and hopes for a brighter future through attractive spaces, echoing the perceptions of municipal councillors in Tyre towards the CHUD project. In light of the complicated vertical relationships with the central state, Bourj Hammoud's vertical relationships with the UNDP encompass a feeling of the possibility to counter nationally initiated projects that are perceived as locally harmful but also the ability to alleviate existing local hardships.

On the other hand, when the municipality proposed projects on infrastructural developments or improvements the relationship to the central state was described as slow, bureaucratic and filled with double standards. A complementary local–national relationship was far from reality in Bourj Hammoud. The infrastructural project of social housing, an apartment block with affordable apartments for Bourj Hammoud's residents, parking areas and shops illustrates the lack of complementarity and a relationship that does not pursue a common goal. As described by one municipal councillor, the national authority took its time to give approval for the project, which strengthened the municipality's view of it being opposed by the central state:

> 'This project, if you look at the municipal law, it is within the authority of the municipality; it is also one of its obligations. Now this project has now been doing the bureaucratic circle of the Lebanese government and various ministries and departments for 8 years, to get the final approval.' (Int. 12, municipal councillor, May 2015)

Although the approval for this project eventually came, and the first phases of the construction began in November 2015, the complicated vertical relationship with the central state was a continuous struggle. In all interviews, municipal councillors described the lack of governmental approval for suggested projects, indicating a lack of complementarity in local–central state relationships. In Bourj Hammoud, the lack of complementarity continued to obstruct local developments, thus hindering the advancement of needed local developments that might have enhanced the living situation of the local population. As such, it appears that when vertical relationships lack complementarity, vertical relationships do not act as a peacebuilding function, illustrating how vertical relationships are a double-edged sword (Ramsbotham, 2005, p 21).

Another example of obstructed local development was the creation of a fund for solar panel water heating that would lend money to organizations such as small clinics, local associations, etc. As borrowers returned the money, the fund would slowly become a self-sustaining fund for solar panel investments. The response to that project was described in the following way:

'It wasn't ratified because of a legal principle that came into play, out of nowhere because in other places, it [the legal principle] was ignored; you have no right to spend public funds on improvement of private property. This was the pretext. But in other places, public funds were spent to improve private properties.' (Int. 12, municipal councillor, May 2015)

This demonstrates a feeling of double standards held by the government and the perception that Bourj Hammoud was often disadvantaged compared to other areas in Lebanon.

The lack of complementarity in the relationship between the municipality and the central state hampers local developments when proposed by the local level. However, as will be seen, the lack of complementarity and inability to pursue a common goal also characterize the municipality's response to governmentally proposed projects. As the lack of proper facilities to treat wastewater threatens the environment in all of Lebanon, the government had put forward a plan to build a wastewater plant in Bourj Hammoud. The proposed plant would collect wastewater from a large surrounding area and take it to Bourj Hammoud. According to Nucho (2016), the wastewater plant was based on an outdated design from 1982, which needed considerable revision to reach current standards. Although the project was only at the planning stage in 2015, the interviewees described an environmentally harmful project. Municipal councillors referred to experiences from other wastewater plants in Lebanon, where water was filtered rather than properly treated to remove harmful substances, thus continuing to pollute the already polluted coastline of the municipality. In addition, interviewees feared that the accumulation of wastewater could cause flooding in areas around Bourj Hammoud.

With the perceived negative effects of the wastewater plant, municipal councillors also described how the municipality mobilized international connections to oppose the governmental plan. Through its cooperation with Nice on the Côte d'Azur, the municipality strategically used its vertical relationship to bring in expertise to study the supposed effects of the plant. This relationship was evasively described as having been started through a mutual friend by finding gaps in the regulations of the municipality's international relationships to evade governmental approval of the cooperation (Int. 12, municipal councillor, May 2015). Once established, the relationship enabled the municipality to study the environmental impact of the wastewater plant on the coastline of Bourj Hammoud. One interviewee described it as follows:

'We are cooperating with Nice Côte d'Azur; they are bringing the technical knowhow to study the whole project [of the wastewater plant] and what would make it less harmful for Bourj Hammoud and the surrounding areas.' (Int. 12, municipal councillor, May 2015)

This illustrates how the municipality actively uses its agency outside of their non-complementary vertical relationships with the central state to resist or oppose governmental interventions. In this case, the municipality's vertical relationships with international actors enabled them to confront a national development plan that they perceived as locally harmful. Another example of a governmentally run infrastructural project that concerned Bourj Hammoud was the building of eight kilometres of solar panels over the Beirut River. Again, it was the environmental impact on the ground that sparked the resistance to the project. One interviewee noted that:

> 'when the project was proposed to us as a municipality, it was within our district. We hired experts and since we were not authorized to spend money on expertise, we found donors for these experts. So they gave the grants; they made the studies and they warned us that there is sewage water being thrown into the Beirut River. Experiences in Europe, from France and Italy, urban engineering [has] warned that whenever you have water running that has sewage, you should not cover it because the ultraviolet rays contribute to the reduction of the [rate of] increase in bacteria.' (Int. 12, municipal councillor, May 2015)

The objection was overruled because "even if the river is within our municipal district, the coastline and the river bed is under the authority of the ministries of water and transports. They have the last word on the issue" (Int. 12, municipal councillor, May 2015). However, the project did not evolve further. After constructing the initial 800 metres that are in the vicinity of Bourj Hammoud, the project stopped due to lack of funds. Nevertheless, this does not imply that the municipality expressed feelings of relief or of having been able to convince the government of rethinking the project, because "whenever they [the government] can get funds, [they will] continue another segment, and there is still wastewater in the river. This is a huge concern to us" (Int. 12, municipal councillor, May 2015).

As these examples demonstrate, when needed, international vertical relationships are strategically used to promote the interests of Bourj Hammoud in relation to governmental plans. In the case of Bourj Hammoud, the agency of the municipality and municipal actors is then rather used outside vertical relationships with the central state and, in practice, to oppose the central state. This illustrates the notion of agency and that local actors can use their agency to act also within asymmetric power relations.

Nevertheless, this was not always the case. In 2015, the waste crisis obliged the municipality to take on the waste collecting duties previously performed by the private company Sukleen. In addition, Bourj Hammoud became the centre of governmental attention for solving the crisis as a whole. As space to accumulate waste was sparse, the Bourj Hammoud landfill site, which had accumulated waste from Beirut and neighbouring regions from the time of the civil war until its closure in 1997, was to be reopened according to a government proposal. To accommodate the waste from all of Beirut, the Bourj Hammoud landfill site was proposed to be one of two temporary landfills until a better solution was found (Abu-Rish, 2015; Färnbo, 2018). In November 2015, the municipality's position was that it should remain closed:

> 'we had the [garbage] mountain of Bourj Hammoud, which closed 17 years ago. All the garbage of Lebanon used to come here for 20 years. Now it is closed. The political party of Tashnag and the municipality say that it was the end.' (Int. 30, municipal councillor, November 2015)

Another municipal councillor explained that the governmental proposal to reopen the landfill site lacked sufficient details and strategies to deal with the environmental concerns. Nevertheless, pressure on the municipality to comply with the governmental plan was strong. Asked whether the municipality was under pressure from the government, one municipal councillor answered, "a lot. And still are" (Int. 29, municipal councillor, November 2015). In relation to the vertical relationships with the central state, the interviewee denied that the proposed reopening of the Bourj Hammoud landfill site would encourage relationships to take on a more positive note. Instead, he claimed that the relationship to the government "was never easy" (Int. 29, municipal councillor, November 2015). The uneasy story continued after my interviews in 2015 and the Bourj Hammoud landfill site reopened in 2016, promising an income of 25 million USD to the municipality for hosting the temporary landfill site for another four years (Massena, 2017; Reuters, 2016).

The issue of waste is a pressing problem in Lebanon. Throughout my interviews in Bourj Hammoud, several municipal councillors acknowledged that for a long-term solution the municipality could play a role if adequate funding and authority was granted to it. Referring to the delayed and irregular distribution of revenues to all municipalities through the national Independent Municipal Fund (IMF), as discussed in Chapter 2 (Atallah, 2011), one interviewee claimed that municipalities should be part of the solution:

> 'Municipalities should get the money from the government to solve the garbage problem for the government. Now they are talking about the money and distributing it to the municipalities, but we still don't have the money.' (Int. 31, municipal councillor, November 2015)

Another municipal councillor pointed to the lack of authority rather than funding, when he claimed that:

> 'The municipality is until now not free. We do not have decentralization; it is still centralized. From the Ta'if Agreement, where it says that there should be decentralization, but until now we don't have it. If we have decentralization, all the municipalities can collect the garbage and recycle and have a lot of money, but until now we don't have decentralization. Until now, the municipality can't solve this problem, only small problems.' (Int. 30, municipal councillor, November 2015)

In the narratives of the municipal councillors, the issue of waste becomes yet another illustration of a non-complementary vertical relationship between the central state and the municipality of Bourj Hammoud. The relationship, as it was described in 2015, mirrored a similar lack of cooperation and conflicting interests, which hindered the possibility of achieving the, assumed,[5] mutual goal of solving the waste crisis.

Vertical relationships and peacebuilding in Bourj Hammoud

In Bourj Hammoud, vertical relationships to the central state are perceived by the municipality as obstructing local development, hindering the municipality from providing for local needs, and thus hindering local peacebuilding. Municipal councillors blame the bureaucracy surrounding municipal–state interactions and also the lack of influence through personal relationships as the main reasons. The frequent obstruction of local developments through complicated and vertical relations with the central state offers an illustration of the importance of complementary local–national relations, and its effects if they do not exist. Although the municipality of Bourj Hammoud does challenge the central state, the narratives on the lack of complementarity reveal a source of conflict, which latently spills over to issues that need to be addressed within the local–central state relationship. In addition, the municipality's opposition to governmental projects suggests the state's cost to uphold the asymmetric relationship is high. However, the cost does not appear to be too high. Thus, decentralization reforms to increase local government autonomy are still not in sight, hindering the municipality's prospect of engaging in local peacebuilding.

---

[5] In Lebanon, a commonly expressed view is that the inability of the national elite to solve the waste crisis is due to sectarian preferences as to who should get the waste management contracts, and thus who gains financially from managing the waste (Färnbo, 2018).

The counter argument of vertical relationships suggests that even though the power asymmetry inherent in national–local relations matters, it does not determine every possibility for local leaders. While local–national relations are restrained in Bourj Hammoud, the municipality makes use of international connections to further its interests towards the central state, as noted by Nucho (2016, p 116ff). Thus, while the central state–municipality interplay does not allow the municipality to pursue peacebuilding practices, the municipality uses other types of vertical relationships to alleviate local needs and, possibly, put off future environmental catastrophes. This echoes Nucho's claim that '[s]ometimes good development is what does not get done rather than what does' (2016, p 116). Thus, in the municipality of Bourj Hammoud, complementary vertical relationships with non-Lebanese actors enable the obstruction of national plans to promote locally preferred developments. As such, the peacebuilding function of vertical relationships appears to work against the central state by preventing developments rather than enabling them. However, it also reinforces Bourj Hammoud as a particular space, similar to what was described as an 'Armenian fortress' during the civil war (Nucho, 2016, p 24).

Saida

In Saida, vertical relationships have contributed to some of the major changes since 2010. For example, there have been renovations in downtown Saida, a new wastewater plant, the closing of the 'garbage mountain', and the building of a plant to separate organic and non-organic wastes. When asked what made these changes possible during their term (2010–2016), one municipal councillor pointed to the importance of personal relationships and support from external actors. As he claims, changes have come about:

> 'because I have a good relation with the gentlemen [laughter]. ... I have to say I have very good support from the politicians. With Hariri, Siniora, the other, Mikati one of the ministers, also the minister of environment, minister of interior, I have good support. Very good support. Also financial support. ... We cannot do anything from within the budget of the municipality. Government support or borrowing or we had some donations, from Saudi Arabia, United Arab Emirates, and from UNDP recently.' (Int. 18, municipal councillor, June 2015)

Several interviewees highlight the connections to national political elites as an avenue to move development forward. One municipal councillor described the relationship with the Lebanese central state as "[v]ery good, because of Mrs Bahia [Hariri] and [Fouad] Siniora. It makes it easier, it facilitates problems that may occur. We contact them if there is something we need" (Int. 45, municipal councillor, November 2015). Another municipal councillor further explained:

> 'They [national actors] are very important, I would say they are behind all these projects that we have now. Getting the funding from international donors or central government; they have Saida in their hearts. They are in the centre of political life in Lebanon. And Lebanon is different. You need here more push, we have to have connections. We have to have a say in the government to enforce in some places a budget for your city. You have to defend your city you have to have it always in mind. We don't expect the central government to have plans for the local places. So, you have to bring your projects, you have to go to the prime minister, you have to talk to the ministers, seek budgets, maybe some political factors are involved. I would say that we wouldn't have succeeded without their support.' (Int. 46, municipal councillor, November 2015)

This demonstrates that the local government is an important agent and initiator of plans for the local space but good vertical relations are crucial in implementing such plans. In comparison with Tyre and Bourj Hammoud, Saida illustrates how different the nature of vertical relationships with the central state can be in Lebanon and how they matter. In Saida, when the municipality has ideas for projects, it uses its relationship with the central state and important political actors to market its ideas and to convince the government of investing in and supporting Saida (Int. 18, municipal councillor, June 2015). Although there is always an element of negotiation involved, municipal councillors do not perceive it as difficult. As such, the municipality described a situation of local and national authorities working in a complementary manner, enabling developments on the ground. This is key for vertical relationships to have a peacebuilding function.

In Saida, national actors and the close ties that national actors have to the municipality and the city is explicitly pointed out in many of the interviews. One municipal councillor assessed the importance of these relationships as one of its main resources, "This is one of the assets of this municipality. The municipality is really coordinating and cooperating with parliamentary representatives in an excellent and very successful way" (Int. 46, municipal councillor, November 2015). The municipality, interpreting the relations as of great importance, clearly engages in vertical relationships and channels its agency through these relationships. The complementarity of the vertical relationships with the central state, and national political representatives, builds on shared goals and a shared interest in the local space, which also allows the municipality to actively engage in the vertical relationships to put forward ideas for new developments.

However, this is not a one-way street and national political elites are closely involved in the municipality. Referring to the divide between March 8 and March 14 in national politics, one civil society actor claimed: "March 14, the Future Movement [is] leading Saida now" (Int. 44, civil society actor, November 2015). The Future Movement, the political party of Hariri (or 'the Hariris'), is both the largest party in the coalition that won the municipal elections in 2010, and a major player in March 14. As such, the national level is perceived as being directly involved in municipal politics, assigning municipal councillors, the mayor and keeping a close relationship with them. One civil society actor expalined, "[t]he current municipality head is known to be assigned from this party [Future Movement]" (Int. 44, civil society actor, November 2015). However, the involvement of the Hariris goes beyond the municipal council. In Saida, one of the largest civil society organizations is the Hariri Foundation, a non-governmental organization founded by Rafiq Hariri in the late 1970s with close ties to the political party. The Hariri Foundation is put forward by the municipality as an actor of great support to the municipality: "we often cooperate with Hariri Foundation, we are working a lot together" (Int. 33, municipal employee, November 2015). Although it brings positive developments, it is also contested. In the eyes of one civil society actor, it is yet another example of party influence on the local space. As she described it, the Hariri political party "put[s] all the people in [their] pocket" (Int. 38, civil society actor, November 2015), referring to an Arabic proverb where everyone is aligned to the same actor. This practice has also been illustrated by Ghaddar (2016), who describes politics in Saida as a Hariri-run family operation, infiltrating individual clientelism on the local level all the way through national and international alliances.

The vertical relationships at work in the municipality of Saida are described by municipal councillors as well as civil society actors as two-way encounters, which enable local initiatives through national acceptance but also imply national involvement locally. As these relationships are perceived as highly beneficial, the municipal council of 2010–2016 made it an explicit strategy to extend vertical relations towards the international arena and pursue international networking to enhance development on the ground:

> 'We try to cooperate with the Italians, City Alliance, Marseille Office of Development, and attended several international conferences for the UN, one in Geneva, one in Tokyo, etc. Previous municipalities, maybe for several reasons, they didn't open on such platforms, but we did.' (Int. 46, municipal councillor, November 2015)

In Saida, vertical relationships, with national as well as international actors, are portrayed as complementary, enabling local developments. As the municipal councillor continued, he described the developments that were enabled through international networking and the synergy effects it has had on the municipality's work:

> 'Our city was working, lots of projects going on, but we didn't have a strategy. Now we have a strategy, a vision. If it wasn't for the collaboration with these international agencies, we wouldn't have learned about this step. Collaboration with Barcelona is really beneficial for the city. We are learning from them about sewage treatment and their urban infrastructure. We learn and cooperate with them. Now we have a plan for the fishermen's port, and [we have] cooperated with the best urbanist in the world. Now we are seeking a budget for it, hopefully in a year or two. Hopefully, it will be there.' (Int. 46, municipal councillor, November 2015)

However, despite positive vertical relations between the municipality and national and international actors, Saida is not exempt from the administrative procedures of the Lebanese central state with regard to financing and the need for approval for projects that cost more than twenty million Lebanese pounds (in 2015, 13,000 USD). Although aided by good relations with the political elite, the relationship with the central state was also related to bureaucratic procedures. Similar to the situation described in Tyre and Bourj Hammoud, the bureaucracy was perceived as slow, as one municipal councillor explained: "Here in Lebanon, all decisions take a lot of time to get approvals" (Int. 46. municipal councillor, November 2015). Also for Saida, municipal regulations and administrative procedures limited the municipality's work, as he continued to explain:

> 'I always say in Saida, thanks to our representatives, Mrs Bahia Hariri and Mr Fouad Siniora, we can have projects for 10 million USD, 20, 30. But we don't have projects for 200,000 USD. This is really a challenge. For example, people want to light the promenade, really, we don't have 300,000 USD to invest there. This represents a challenge; you want to do something. You know the solution, but you cannot do it.' (Int. 46, municipal councillor, November 2015)

Thus, despite good connections, the municipality was still suffering from a lack of capacity in terms of resources and autonomy over decisions. The lack of autonomy and capacity on the local level have long been connected to the lack of decentralization in Lebanon (Harb and Atallah, 2015, p 192). However, none of the municipal councillors in Saida mentioned the lack of decentralization as an obstacle, while it was a common topic in Tyre and Bourj Hammoud. Instead, the municipal councillors of Saida appeared satisfied with the current political structure and not bothered by restrictions due to administrative structures. According to one municipal employee, the work of the municipality was not really affected by the political paralysis and presidential vacuum in Lebanon, present at the time of the fieldwork. This is because, as she explained:

> 'It is possible to keep working, according to the municipal law that already exists. So still they are continuing to work in the same manner. For bigger decisions, for sure, there needs to be a president. But, for Saida city, the bigger decisions are already taken.' (Int. 33, municipal employee, November 2015)

As we have seen, this was possible largely because of complementary vertical relationships with the central state, national political elites and international actors, creating a space for autonomy, allowing the municipality to suggest local developments and push for their implementation. As such, the complementarity of relationships and autonomy granted to the municipality through the vertical relationships enables vertical relationships to work as a peacebuilding function.

By enabling restorations in the old town, creation of green areas, building of a new stadium and the opening of the new waste management plant, to name a few examples, vertical relationships have managed to solve development challenges and enhanced the living standards of many Saidonians. According to Roberts (2011b), this matters for a locally legitimate peacebuilding. However, the aura of positive developments in Saida leaves a taste of sectarianism and political elitism in its trail. According to civil society actors in Saida, the importance of political relations is confirmed. However, the interviewees also reveal that, as much as political connections enable present success, they have previously hindered development. Asked about the implementation of the garbage factory, one civil society actor emphasized the politicization of development and clearly linked the start-up of the factory to the change in the municipal council in 2010:

> 'the factory should have been established a long time ago, during the presence of Dr Abdul Rahman el Bezri [former Mayor of Saida, 2004–2010]. Prince Walid granted 5 million USD to the municipality to establish it but no decree. The law that says that you can start was not passed during the presence of the last municipality. They want to do this law during the presence of the municipality who is affiliated to the Hariri political party.' (Int. 38, civil society actor, November 2015)

With close interactions between the national and local level within the Future Movement, the image of the political party of the Hariris is enhanced by its involvement in local municipal developments. Although that is to be expected by the election victory of 2010, these reflections also highlight that the municipality is part of the political structure of Lebanon with sectarianism at its core. One civil society actor reflected on the duality of such a relationship in the following way:

> 'For the sake of Saida, being under the rule of the sectarian Sunni entity, it is not helping. … On the ground, he [the mayor] is doing good work together with the civil society, a well selected municipal council. But in the end, they are representing a certain political party.' (Int. 44, civil society actor, November 2015)

The representation of a certain political party in the local space implies that the municipality has difficulties to move beyond the political positions that the national political party takes. This close alignment to one party was a major concern to one member of the opposition in the municipal elections in 2010. As Lebanon was suffering from national political paralysis, the close ties to one of the national parties also restrained the local government and its actions in the local space:

> 'The most important for the municipality in this bad time for Lebanon is the conflict between Sunni and Shia. The municipality must play an important role; they must pay more attention to this problem, [but] we are suffering from the government, from Hariri's way in politics. … This is a very big problem. As a representative, I must work to make them come together. I do not want street [infrastructural development]; this [situation] is very dangerous.' (Int. 40, civil society actor, November 2015)

The very good relations with influential national elites, which are particular to Saida among the three cases, appear to be beneficial in some ways but restricting in others. The room to manoeuvre in the local space, emphasized in theories on local peacebuilding, is here shown to play out through national influence, affecting the ways in which interactions take place on the ground. The emphasis on the local government as non-political in local interactions, discussed in the previous chapter, is here shown to be influenced by political national standpoints. Similar to Mitchell and Hancock's discussion on national relationships between opposing groups affecting relationships between the national and the local (Mitchell and Hancock, 2012), the case of Saida demonstrates how national political divides in Lebanon manifest themselves in municipal politics. As such, vertical relationships in Saida locally reproduce the dividing lines that run through Lebanese politics, but also exist in the regional, and sometimes, global arena. This emphasizes the connection between local and national and international events and discourses, in the past part of fuelling the civil war, but, in recent times, part of the polarization between Sunni and Shia influencing the whole Middle East (Dakroub, 2014b; Geukjian, 2017).

Vertical relationships and peacebuilding in Saida

In Saida, vertical relationships are at the centre of all developments. Since the vertical relationships of the municipality are influential, both nationally but also internationally, they enable important advancements on the ground such as infrastructural developments and the implementation of the waste management plant. In particular, Fouad Siniora and Bahia Hariri are mentioned as crucial for local developments, echoing Ghaddar's (2016) claims on the patronage networks in Saidonian politics, consolidated under Bahia Hariri and the Future Movement. The vertical relationships between Saida and national and international actors are described as complementary and working towards the same goal. In addition, because of complementary vertical relationships, Saida perceives itself as capable of promoting local developments, and the constraints put on municipal autonomy through Lebanese regulations of multi-level governance is less of a concern. For Saida, autonomy, or room to manoeuvre, is negotiable through vertical relationships. Nonetheless, complementary vertical relationships do not imply autonomy from national approval.

Illustrated by the delayed building of the waste management plant, the case of Saida suggests that peacebuilding, understood as needs-based local development, is effectively hindered if complementary vertical relationships with the central state are lacking and promoted when complementary relationships are in place. However, Saida also illuminates that vertical relationships to national political elites provides advancements in some areas but restraints in others. In Saida, the close relationship with national elites influences the municipality's freedom to act on local needs that fall within the interests of these elites.

Conclusion: three cases of vertical relationships

This chapter has explored vertical relationships between the municipalities of Tyre, Bourj Hammoud and Saida and their respective national and international connections. The introduction to this chapter discussed the notion of vertical relationships as imperative for peacebuilding because they enable local developments that are adapted to and influenced by the local space (Brinkerhoff, 2011; Kälin, 2004; Mitchell and Hancock, 2012). The three municipalities have been analysed in relation to complementarity, autonomy and agency, to highlight how vertical relationships are perceived and how they relate to peacebuilding. Having analysed the vertical relationships in Tyre, Bourj Hammoud and Saida, the most important take away is that vertical relationships with the central state and/or international actors matter for local developments, but they also differ. Thus, vertical relationships matter as a peacebuilding function in some local spaces while less so in others. This resonates with Mitchell and Hancock's view that complementarity in vertical relationships varies in impact on the local space and the locals' peacebuilding potential (Mitchell and Hancock, 2012). In addition, the fact that vertical relationships with national and international actors are important in the municipalities emphasizes a continuation of international interference in Lebanese politics (Khalaf, 2012). This chapter illustrates how such interference goes local, manifested through top-down collaboration, but also bottom-up use of agency.

Scrutinizing vertical relationships as a peacebuilding function, the first theme is complementarity, emphasizing that goals and interests on different levels need to align to coordinate activities in the local space (Mitchell and Hancock, 2012). In the municipality of Tyre, vertical relationships with the central state and international actors are at times both complementary and non-complementary. As has been shown, when interests align, local developments are encouraged. However, if local interests clash with national and/or international interests, there is considerable difficulty in accommodating opposing views. In Bourj Hammoud, the vertical relationships with the central state are far from complementary, and municipal councillors tend to describe them as oppositional. The vertical relationships with the central state, therefore, have little positive impact on local developments. There, the municipality uses its vertical relationships with international actors to oppose central governmental projects and pursue its local interests. As such, the transnational interlinkages described in Bourj Hammoud are actively used to further local interests against the central state. This contests the idea that vertical relationships always work towards integrating local zones of peace into a national context (McCandless et al, 2015; Öjendal et al, 2017, p 36). In Saida, vertical relationships are described as the bread and butter of municipal work. Relationships are their main asset; it is how the municipality influences and how it achieves local developments. As such, vertical relationships with national political elites matter a lot, confirming the theoretical assumptions that complementary vertical relationships enable developments on the ground (Brinkerhoff, 2011; Kälin, 2004; Mitchell and Hancock, 2012).

The second theme is autonomy, building on the claim that if the local government is autonomous, complementary vertical relationships matter less, but if autonomy is non-existent, complementarity is essential (Brinkerhoff, 2011; Kälin, 2004). In Tyre, although the vertical relationships with national and international actors do make changes on the ground, the municipality perceives itself as having little autonomy and little capacity to act on its own.

In Bourj Hammoud, the vertical relationships with the central state are not complementary, and, since the municipality is constrained by regulations in Lebanese multi-level governance, the municipality also perceive that they have very little autonomy. In Saida, complementary vertical relationships are perceived as equipping the municipality with a feeling of autonomy, or at least the resources needed for capacity. As all three cases have described a lack of autonomy in relation to the Lebanese system of multi-level governance, the perceived autonomy in Saida illustrates that complementarity and autonomy are interdependent, more so than a municipality having either/or, as assumed by the theoretical framework (Brinkerhoff, 2011; Kälin, 2004; Mitchell and Hancock, 2012). However, further studies are required to assess whether this holds in other Lebanese municipalities.

The notion of vertical relationships as a peacebuilding function also emphasizes the agency of the municipality or municipal actors. As such, the local government chooses to accept, oppose, promote, cooperate or resist national or internationally proposed policies and projects (Donais, 2012; Mac Ginty, 2010a; Richmond and Mitchell, 2012, pp 5, 8, 11, 16). In Tyre, much of the municipality's agency is directed towards accepting nationally and internationally initiated developments. Sometimes, its role is to promote those developments or to try to accelerate their implementation. However, if interests do not align, the municiplty does use its agency within vertical relationships with the central state to push for changes of importance in the local context. In Bourj Hammoud, because the municipality has an oppositional relationship with the central state, it uses its agency to connect with actors outside, connecting to international actors to oppose governmental proposals. In Saida, the municipality uses its agency within the vertical relationships with the central state, national political elites and international actors to enable local developments. Because vertical relationships work in a complementary manner, the municipality does not use its agency to oppose or resist, but rather promotes local initiatives, cooperates and accepts national or international proposals for local developments.

Recalling the conceptualization of peacebuilding as a wide range of activities, defined through the everyday, that prevent the relapse of violence, local developments enabled through vertical relationships can provide a clue as to what local peacebuilding looks like in local spaces. In this chapter, the analysis of vertical relationships through the themes of complementarity, autonomy and agency illustrates that vertical relationships matter for how and what local developments are implemented and, over time, what role local governments have in local peacebuilding. In Tyre, vertical relationships do create something, as they are present in every infrastructural change and developmental aspect discussed by the municipality. However, through exploring the vertical relationships in Tyre, what emerges is a peacebuilding role that relies heavily on international actors. The present vertical relationships, therefore, enable a peacebuilding that is internationally run. In Bourj Hammoud, the vertical relationships with international actors enable the municipality to keep struggling for a locally defined development, against negative implications of vertical relationships with the central state and nationally proposed projects. Since the municipality is necessarily part of the Lebanese multi-level governance, vertical relationships with the central state must be sustained, even if oppositional in character. The peacebuilding role of the municipality therefore becomes one of a struggle for local influence in national plans, in part aided by vertical relationships with international actors. In Saida, the vertical relationships enable the material development of services and the local infrastructure that are crucial to everyday life, such as waste and sewage management. For the municipality's peacebuilding role, vertical relationships are crucial in enabling the creation of a materially good everyday life, manifesting a peacebuilding that is materially sustained. In the analysis of these three Lebanese municipalities, Saida is the case that shows the clearest impact of vertical relationships on the municipality's peacebuilding ability.

This chapter has analysed the vertical relationships pursued in Tyre, Bourj Hammoud and Saida and discussed what developments are made possible due to these relationships, thus, vertically connecting the local government to national and international actors and goals. Starting out from a theoretical understanding of the need for verticality for peacebuilding to prosper, the chapter concludes that vertical relationships do matter for peacebuilding, as they become avenues for the municipality to attract capacity and gain a negotiated autonomy to pursue local developments within a centralized Lebanese state. At the same time, non-complementary vertical relationships do not necessarily restrict the municipality's use of agency as a locally preferred development can be pursued through hindering externally initiated plans.

Conclusion

The local turn in peacebuilding is at a crossroads. Despite a rich field of empirical research and brave theorizations of peacebuilding flaws, there has been little connection between the two. This book addresses this gap. Through an empirical study of service delivery, local interactions and vertical relationships as local peacebuilding functions, this book contributes to our understanding of the role of local governments within a world that is globally connected but increasingly pays attention to the particular. To achieve this aim, the book has emphasized perceptions and local interpretations of municipal officials, municipal and state employees as well as civil society actors within the local spaces of Tyre, Bourj Hammoud and Saida. In previous chapters, the peacebuilding functions of service delivery, local interactions and vertical relationships have been analysed separately. In this chapter I conclude the book by drawing together the findings and theoretical implications, discussing local peacebuilding by combining the separate pieces of the puzzle. Picking up on the particularities of service delivery, local interactions and vertical relationships as peacebuilding functions in the three municipalities, the chapter illustrates how Tyre, Bourj Hammoud and Saida play different roles and promote different types of peace(s).

Tyre: a municipality to 'relate to' in local peacebuilding

By combining our insights from the peacebuilding functions of service delivery, local interactions and vertical relationships, the role of the municipality of Tyre emerges as a local actor to 'relate to' in local peacebuilding. In Tyre, service delivery is closely interlinked with vertical relationships with national and international actors and services that require resources or capacities, such as infrastructural developments and waste management operations, are delivered through external actors. The municipal councillors claimed that external actors shared their vision of Tyre as a touristic city, emphasizing the cultural heritage and Roman ruins as well as Tyre's attraction as a coastal town. As such, vertical relationships are perceived as complementary, as working towards the same goal, and infrastructural changes have been implemented, such as a new vegetable market, the restoration of old buildings, cultural heritage promenades, parking lots, etc., making the municipality visible to the local population. This resonates with the argument that the building of infrastructure allows for greater state visibility, an important aspect of state consolidation through service delivery and vertical relationships as peacebuilding functions (Bachmann and Schouten, 2018; Brinkerhoff et al, 2012; Mcloughlin, 2015; Mitchell and Hancock, 2012).

Nevertheless, in Tyre, visible developments are not always perceived as legitimizing the local government in the eyes of civil society actors. On the contrary, such advancements have spurred criticism, and civil society actors perceive the municipality as swept away, or seduced, by global perceptions of what is a beautiful and attractive city for tourists, ignoring or, according to civil society actors, not fighting enough, for the adaptation of international projects to the local way of life. Thus, the complementarity of the vertical relationship appears to be top-down rather than bottom-up. In addition, the empirical exploration of infrastructural developments in Tyre has shown what Bachman and Schouten (2018) argue, that infrastructural developments are not necessarily beneficial for peace in themselves, but the inclusion of the local in the creation of services is key to how service delivery works as a peacebuilding function.

At the same time, nothing is ever this black or white. Some activities that interviewees described as strengthening the legitimacy of the municipality, such as after-school activities or public lectures in Beit al-Mamlouk, would not have been possible without national and international assistance in developing the infrastructure within which the activities take place. Thus, through its involvement in externally funded projects, run by national agencies, the interviewees described how the municipality has gained the capacity to autonomously implement activities. Consequently, despite the risk of external interference in Tyre, making the municipality look incapable, some of its activities, which from a peacebuilding point of view enable local inclusion, address local needs and ground policies, could not have come about without external involvement. This illustrates the interconnections between the local and the national and international. Also, peacebuilding cannot be seen as a static tool, but peacebuilding is non-linear and evolving within the local context. This emphasizes the continuous change and evolvement of peacebuilding or the interlink between place-making and space-making for defining peace(s), as argued by Björkdahl and Kappler (2017). In addition, the claim that the municipality of Tyre finds its capacity in local developments implemented through national and international relations, or more bluntly put, top-down interventions, complicates Bargués-Pedreny and Randazzo's (2018) critique against the interventionism inherent in critical peacebuilding approaches. Because even if it confirms the presence of international intervention, contextualizing local peacebuilding within the specificities of the municipality of Tyre tells us that, currently, no intervention would give the municipality fewer opportunities to play a role in local peacebuilding.

In addition, the analysis of service delivery, local interactions and vertical relationships in Tyre has shown that activities which appear to have peacebuilding potential for the local context may seem small and insignificant. Examples include the pedestrian street, which creates a space for different communities to interact, as well as Beit al-Mamlouk, with its after-school activities for local children. Although small in scope, their smallness allows the municipality room to manoeuvre to gain and make use of local knowledge, cooperate with local actors to create locally responsive policies, and thus, ideally, legitimating local governance. These practices highlight how, in the restricted autonomy of local governance in Lebanon's centralized state, local governments can be an actor for change. Or, as claimed by Romeo (2013, p 78f), 'democratically elected councils [can] fight back against marginalization and start taking responsibilities and obtain powers to participate in the core regulatory and service delivery business of the state.' Such small acts of local governance can bring people together across sectarian divides in the local space as well as across different Lebanese spaces, making a difference in relation to the violence of the past. As south Lebanon, including Tyre, has been the scene for Israeli intervention, occupation and violence, most recently during the 2006 war, for some Lebanese the area has gained a reputation for insecurity. These perceptions are not only related to external intervention, as the increasing fear of sectarianism on a national level has given the south an image of a Shia-space, mainly controlled by Hezbollah (although the local space is mixed), and a locality to stay away from for others (Bou Akar, 2018, p 4; Zeidan, 2017). In this context, activities that bring together communities as well as visitors from farther away matters for what a contextually defined local peacebuilding becomes. As such, the everyday needs, expressed by the interviewees in Tyre, included issues of managing waste as well as festive events, echoing Mitchell's emphasis on the diversity of the everyday (Mitchell, 2011).

Through the functions of service delivery, citizen–local state interactions and vertical relationships, the role of the municipality of Tyre is understood as part of national and international collaborations as well as local connections. However, although the municipality has connections, personal connections to international and national actors and to local communities, or within the Lebanese central state governance, the municipality is not perceived as making these connections but being part of them. As such, the role of the municipality is not to initiate and drive relationships or projects, but pushing, proposing and connecting top-driven connections to the local space or between the local space and the national and international. As such, it is an actor of relevance which has relationships, and it is an actor to 'relate to' in the local space. However, the municipality is not necessarily an actor that would get things done, as it lacks the capacity and autonomy to act independently in most cases.

In Tyre, unlike in Bourj Hammoud and Saida, the roles of sectarian groups are not highlighted to the same extent. In a few instances, connections to a particular person or political party in the national arena is mentioned, but more frequently interviewees described how every group has its own agenda and how it is important to keep the municipality away from politics, understood as divisions in national Lebanese politics. Possibly, this is because of the majority of Shia Muslims in the Lebanese south, and the domination of the Shia political party Amal in the local elections in 2004 and its majority in the 2010 municipal council through political bargaining between Amal and Hezbollah. However, also outside of politics, relations between sectarian groups are emphasized as good. One example was the municipal councillor who showed me a picture of municipal leaders together with leaders from different sectarian communities, demonstratively saying that 'this is our city'. This can be compared to the contestations of Bourj Hammoud as an Armenian or Lebanese space, as well as the municipal emphasis on connections to politicians in the Future Movement for enabling local developments in Saida, thus two cases that particularly emphasize a sectarian or political connection as defining the local space. Connecting this back to the relational role of the municipality, the municipality of Tyre is an actor to relate to, but not necessarily an actor that defines the local space.

Bourj Hammoud: a municipality to 'go to' or 'pass by' in local peacebuilding

In the municipality of Bourj Hammoud, local peacebuilding in relation to service delivery, local interactions and vertical relationships is not decided by external influence, but the role of the municipality is still shaped by it. In fact, the lack of external support, or, as perceived, a lack of support from the central state, shapes the way the municipality delivers services, interacts with the local space and pursues its vertical relationships. Without complementarity between the local and the central state the municipality is left outside, or strategically positions itself outside of governmental projects for local developments. As the local and the national visions for these projects do not align, difficulties arise in their implementation. Instead, the municipality has chosen to cooperate with local and non-Lebanese actors to gain knowledge of local needs and provide, or oppose, services. The proximity of the municipality and the active choice of the municipality to acquire knowledge of local needs confirms the theoretical argument that localized service deliveries hold greater potential for the local state to deliver locally relevant services, thus, highlighting service delivery as a peacebuilding function (Mcloughlin, 2015). The inclusiveness emphasized by the municipality in their cooperatively delivered services promotes an image of a municipality that actively listens to the voices on the ground.

However, in Bourj Hammoud, inclusiveness promotes the responsiveness of the municipality to the needs of the Armenian community. From a peacebuilding perspective, the inclusion of a local group that is a national minority is one of the benefits of local government. Through greater decentralized governance, national minorities may be listened to locally, preventing grievances from arising against an ignorant central state (Brinkerhoff, 2011). In Lebanon, the Armenians form such a group. As such, the municipality of Bourj Hammoud performs that which, according to the peacebuilding literature, is one of the benefits of building peace locally. However, what the actions performed in Bourj Hammoud also illustrate is that even if locally responsive, inclusion is defined within a local context of sectarian belongings, where the Armenians may be the majority but not the only local community present in the municipality. Nevertheless, since a national minority with little national influence dominates the municipal council, the council also perceives itself as possessing few avenues for central state support. Instead, the municipality approaches the local space and cooperates with actors on the ground, as well as international actors who can advocate for the municipality's locally defined needs. As this local and global cooperation shapes what is achieved in everyday life, cooperating with their connections, often with the same sectarian belonging, builds on past power struggles justifying Armenian domination, but it also constructs the possibilities and the direction municipal work takes. As discussed by Nucho (2016) in her analysis of Bourj Hammoud, it is through these interactions that the local is continuously made. As such, while the local (and the particular) is presently enjoying a phase of popularity (Hughes et al, 2015; Rosanvallon, 2011a), contextually analysing the fluid creation of the local cannot be ignored, as Nucho claims:

> while 'local' decision making and decentralization may appear to be a solution to the oversights of broad-based 'national' planning initiatives, the municipality cannot really be called a 'local' institution. Defining the 'local' can potentially produce forms of exclusion through identifying, evicting, or preventing the circulation of many kinds of *others* who do not belong. (Nucho, 2016, pp 118, emphasis in original)

This is a clear reminder of the pitfall of romanticizing the local as legitimate because of its proximity. In addition, as this study has shown, the local, in my case Bourj Hammoud as well as Tyre and Saida, are not territories of small scale (Lambek, 2011), but local spaces created through actions and agency. In Bourj Hammoud, local actions, namely municipal governance, actively aim at preserving the Armenianess of the local space, alluding to their role as the guardians of Bourj Hammoud during the civil war but also to a more distant past as Armenian refugees fleeing genocide to become yet another sectarian community in Lebanon (Geukjian, 2014; Joseph, 1975; Nucho, 2016).

However, the reproduction of sectarian affiliations through actions of service delivery, local interactions and vertical relationships also occurs within the Lebanese state system. With no civil legislation to rule matters of family law, and the division of state power according to sectarian quotas (in parliament, state agencies and the military), as well as the delivery of services through patronage networks, means that governing through sectarianism is 'business as usual' in Lebanon (see Cammett and Issar, 2010; Egan and Tabar, 2016). In Bourj Hammoud, where municipal resources are not necessarily abundant and where local cooperation makes up the bulk of municipal activities, the sectarian networks are perceived as a necessity and not necessarily a choice. In addition, we must not forget that within Bourj Hammoud, other communities maintain their own external sectarian connections. As such, the municipality may be cheered or disliked for including or excluding certain actors and developments, but for most local communities the municipality is not the only actor of relevance.

Through the analysis of service delivery, local interactions and vertical relationships in Bourj Hammoud, the municipality's role in local peacebuilding is understood as performed through close interactions within the local space, which allows for influence by local actors and responsiveness to local needs. Responding to what the municipality perceives as needs in the local space is also what is emphasized in their vertical relationships. In relation to the central state, such responsiveness implies opposing governmental projects with local consequences that are perceived as harmful or cooperating with actors that can promote their views in relation to the government. The role of the municipality is therefore perceived as struggling, mainly because of a lack of autonomy and resources, but it is also that struggle that facilitates its cooperative strategy within the local space. However, the local cooperative strategy of the municipality has also emphasized its cooperation with some local actors more than others. Thus, the role of the municipality appears to be that of an actor that some local communities would 'go to', whereas for others, the municipality is an actor they mostly 'pass by'. Again, this emphasizes that the municipality of Bourj Hammoud is one of several actors involved in creating the local space. This highlights that in order to understand local peacebuilding, we need to analyse the local within its particular political order (Debiel and Rinck, 2016, p 247ff).

Saida: a partial actor in local peacebuilding

In the municipality of Saida, the peacebuilding functions of service delivery, local interactions and vertical relations are shaped by the close connections the municipality has with national and international actors. This is manifested in the implementation of larger projects such as the waste management plant, restoration of the old part of town as well as the building of the new stadium, to name a few. In Saida, the services delivered are mostly visible infrastructural developments. In theory, such projects aim to increase the visibility of the state and foster state legitimacy, advancing peacebuilding (Bachmann and Schouten, 2018; Brinkerhoff et al, 2012; Mcloughlin, 2015).

As the analysis has shown, the visible infrastructural developments in Saida have attended to local needs through complementary vertical relationships with the central state and international actors. Vertical relations in Saida are perceived as complementary, in that they allow the local government to make local needs known as well as channel resources in response to those needs. This can be compared to Tyre, where vertical relationships are perceived as complementary only when pursuing the vision portrayed from above, and Bourj Hammoud, where complementary relationships to the central state are lacking. In Saida, the close interaction between vertical relationships and service deliveries demonstrates that complementary vertical relationships enable other developments on the ground (Mitchell and Hancock, 2012). Through the eyes of the municipal councillors, these vertical relationships are the key to local success.

However, Saida also demonstrates that even if services answer local needs, those needs are not necessarily pursued by including the local population or civil society, and the needs addressed only answer to a particular type of existing need. Although interviewees perceive civil society participation as important in municipal activities, participation that allows for influence is often ignored. Rather, local actors are not invited to decide *what* policies to pursue, but only *how* to pursue those already decided upon. In keeping its close connections to the central government, the municipality may be able to attend to existing local needs, but what comes forward is that the municipality is attentive to certain kinds of needs, mainly infrastructural developments. Other, 'softer', local needs, are instead addressed by civil society actors and the division of tasks between the local government and the civil society is prominent in Saida. However, in Saida, this is amplified by the municipality's perception of local development as achieved through infrastructural improvements (similar to Rafic Hariri's post-war reconstruction of Lebanon), whereas the civil society focuses on empowerment and provision for social needs. The complementarity of the vertical relationship thus also appears to have a price, the price of partial attendance to local needs.

In addition, vertical relationships in Saida are not just to any central state actors, but to particular actors within the Lebanese state. Through the division of power on the national level, the vertical relationships that matter for the municipality are with those who are in the top positions within the same political party as the municipal councillors, the Future Movement. In Lebanon, political actors and parties are framed within sectarian logics, divided within the two alliances of March 8 and March 14, who in turn pertain to the pro-Syria (March 8) or the pro-Saudi (March 14) side of the polarization of politics in the Middle East. Thus the implementation of local developments occurs through a reproduction of sectarian networks and political divides, drawing on regional and, sometimes, also global alliances.

As in Bourj Hammoud, the sectarianism infused in municipal activities does not go unnoticed by civil society actors. Once in place, local developments with a high visibility are appreciated for the services they deliver, but, as the sectarianism and political alliances involved in their implementation are well known, there is no direct connection between the services delivered and legitimation of the state. This is because there is no one state that delivers the service, but rather a divided state where the municipality receives assistance through cooperating with a particular side. However, scholars on Lebanese governance have argued that instead of perceiving the sectarian divide of the state as a state weakness, the fact that the state performs through sectarian networks makes the state, or a part of it, relevant in the everyday life of the population (Egan and Tabar, 2016). As such, the Lebanese state is not absent or weak, but in fact made up of formal and informal organizations and their practices (Nucho, 2016, p 110).

Nevertheless, as interviews with civil society actors have shown, the obvious politicization of those organizations is critiqued, hampering their peacebuilding function. The civil society actors interviewed are divided between those who perceive municipal services as responsive, passively agreeing on the use of sectarian connections to further local needs, and those who appreciate municipal services but actively oppose their sectarian implementation. Thus, if we acknowledge the theoretical link between service delivery and state legitimacy (Mcloughlin, 2015), the interviews in Saida suggest that services delivered either legitimize the Sunni Future Movement way of politics (aligned to the Saudi Arabia divide in the Middle East) or de-legitimize the municipality, precisely because of its national and international links. The peacebuilding function of service deliveries is thus confirmed as a complex web of existing needs, individualized expectations and perceived value of the services delivered, relating both to how services are implemented and what is achieved (Bachmann and Schouten, 2018; Mcloughlin, 2015, 2019; Roberts, 2011b).

Through the empirical analysis of the three peacebuilding functions of service delivery, local interactions and vertical relationships in the municipality of Saida, the role of the municipality is understood as performed through national and international connections. It is these connections that enable municipal councillors to promote an image of a well-functioning local government, able to attend to badly needed local needs. At the same time, through its vertical connections to particular actors, the services delivered locally, as well as the interactions performed locally, are characterized by the municipality's vertical relationships, meaning that they engage in some activities, and allow, or rely on, other local actors to take care of activities of a more social character. This makes the municipality of Saida a partial actor in local peacebuilding. However, if the partiality of the municipality is about different actors considering the municipality relevant or not in Bourj Hammoud, in Saida the distinction is rather related to what kind of services are provided through the municipality and in what matters the population is better served by others.

Furthermore, Saida illustrates that even if the municipality is perceived as a competent actor that works for local development, the avenues through which the municipality gains capacity to deliver local development impacts on how those developments are perceived. As such, we can understand the role of the municipality as competent in achieving local (infrastructural) development but questioned as a legitimate actor for local peacebuilding, as its actions make use of sectarian as well as political dividing lines. Thus, Saidan governance reproduces divisions in Lebanese politics and the sectarian system, a system of governance that has continuously been used as a bargaining tool for ending violence but which has, in itself, hindered reconciliation and reproduced violence in Lebanon (Bou Akar, 2018; Khalaf, 2002, p 290).

Navigating local peacebuilding in Lebanon and beyond

In this book, local peacebuilding is conceptualized as a continuous struggle, performed by multiple actors and their agency in relation to but also going beyond structural forms. The role of the municipalities of Tyre, Bourj Hammoud and Saida is to navigate the local space, consisting of legal and customary structures, external influences and local specificities by connecting the local government to local actors and communities, national and international actors and structures through personal, political, sectarian or professional networks. Through these activities, the municipalities use their agency to strategically push for inclusion of the local or actively withdraw from national and international plans, although with varying success. As such, the municipality is part of creating localized versions of peacebuilding but simultaneously re-emphasizing a system of governance based on a divided consensus, which, in Lebanon, has been partly responsible for repeated periods of violence as well as for ending violence. This means that the municipality is a political agent (or compilation of actors), and one that is connected to the larger context of Lebanon, countering the romanticized picture of the legitimate local and the local as isolated from national and international actors and structures (Björkdahl et al, 2016; Debiel and Rinck, 2016; Kappler, 2013b; Paffenholz, 2015b).

As a study on Lebanon, this book emphasizes the need to see local governments as relevant actors in a post-conflict setting that has failed to deliver the decentralization reform promised by the Ta'if Peace Agreement (Harb and Atallah, 2015, p 191f). Although clearly constrained in their autonomy, the municipalities offer a potential to ground peacebuilding functions within the local space. Such knowledge opens up the possibility of engaging with local governments as also actors in Lebanon's ongoing economic crisis, provided that they have capacities to act and autonomy to attend to local needs. At the same time, the comparison of three municipalities illustrates the politicization of the local space and how sectarianism as well as politics is reproduced through local policies. This is not unique to individual municipalities, but ingrained in the Lebanese model of multi-level governance. The many writings on the sectarian division of the Lebanese state (for example Fawaz, 2009, 2014; Ghaddar, 2016; Khalaf, 2002; Mackey, 2006; Nucho, 2016; Salamey, 2014; Stel and van der Molen, 2015) is here shown to have ramifications all the way down to the local level. As claimed in this study, this is also the case in local spaces beyond the capital Beirut (for studies on Beirut see Bou Akar, 2018; Egan and Tabar, 2016; Fawaz, 2014; Fawaz et al, 2012; Larkin, 2010). This adds further nuance to the field of urban peacebuilding (Björkdahl, 2013; Gusic, 2013), showing also that in urban spaces not divided during the civil war, the post-war period continues to be influenced by national as well as regional, political and sectarian dividing lines. In Lebanon's current state of economic crisis, and lack of political legitimacy and accountability, the local is, thus, not isolated from national events.

Contributing to the need to bridge the gap between theory and everyday practices of local peacebuilding, this study empirically explores the theoretically conceptualized local peacebuilding functions of service delivery, local interactions and vertical relationships. By contextualizing service delivery, this book has shown that how services are delivered matters for how they are perceived and for the consequential gains that can be made for legitimacy, and thus for the building of peace. By contextualizing citizen–local state interactions, this book has shown that although local interactions ground local policies, analysing how interactions occur, for whom and for what matters for understanding in what way local interactions relate to local peacebuilding. Finally, by contextualizing vertical relationships, this study has shown that vertical relationships matter, but that the complementarity of vertical relationships is a double-edged sword which both empowers the local government as well as constrains the local government from using its agency in a particular way. Thus, studying vertical relationships should not be about characterizing them as beneficial or not, but as seeing what opportunities open up and what opportunities close because of them. The findings of this book emphasize that if we are to understand local peacebuilding, we need to underline how local peacebuilding processes evolve rather than what measures to implement. As such, this study re-emphasizes the need for contextualization of peacebuilding as crucial for understanding local peacebuilding (see for example de Coning, 2013; Mac Ginty, 2010a; Roberts, 2011b). As the three municipalities provide somewhat different scenarios of how the peacebuilding functions are perceived and relate to local peacebuilding, the book shows that the localization of peace is not local in a particular way, but locally contextualized peacebuilding builds locally contextualized types of peace(s).

Furthermore, by re-emphasizing the importance of contextually defined local peacebuilding, this book contributes to the critical local peacebuilding debate by challenging one of its common narratives. In particular, the study questions the often-assumed absence of the state in local peacebuilding. By positioning the local state as one actor within a local space of local peacebuilding, this study illustrates how the local government is also part of a frictional peacebuilding, creating the local place as well as local space (as conceptualized by Björkdahl and Kappler, 2017). This blurs the often-assumed dichotomy between an 'absent', but presumably legitimate and ordering state, and the everyday friction(s) and local agency(ies) that represent the realities on the ground. By placing processes of local peacebuilding within the political order of the Lebanese state, this study has taken a first step in responding to the critique of a 'methodological reductionism' inherent in the local turn literature (Debiel and Rinck, 2016), emphasizing that the local is also a political space. Moreover, by studying local governments, the book highlights what role the local state has, or can have, in post-conflict spaces. By analysing the local government as an actor that is not ignored but also not able to be the sole actor of relevance locally, the study confirms that in the overlap between peacebuilding and state-building, claims to authority and legitimacy are continuously negotiated by the actors involved (Lemay-Hébert, 2009; Lottholz and Lemay-Hebert, 2016). In Lebanon, this becomes apparent on the sub-national level through the peacebuilding functions of service delivery, local interactions and vertical relationships.

In addition, the book accentuates the definition of the local as continuously changing by highlighting the differing interpretations within the three municipalities of what the local is and should be. This further adds to research that defines the local as dynamic rather than static (Kappler, 2015). The study of the dynamic local government has also shown local peace as contextual and created through the interaction between the local, national and international, highlighting global interconnectedness but emphasizing the need to account for the particularities of each local space (Rosanvallon, 2011a, 2011b). Furthermore, this mirrors some of the processes emphasized in the conceptualizations of peacebuilding as friction (Björkdahl et al, 2016), but also within the spatial turn of peacebuilding (Björkdahl and Buckley-Zistel, 2016; Björkdahl and Kappler, 2017; Macaspac and Moore, 2022).

To sum up, I return to my conceptualization of peacebuilding as a broad concept, including:

> Efforts aimed at political, institutional, social, and economic transformations in post-war societies engaging a variety of actors ... to reduce the risk of overt violent conflict and to pave the way for durable peace and development. (Björkdahl and Höglund, 2013, p 291)

In this book, this includes practices as diverse as state legitimization, fostering good relationships and providing for local needs. Such a broad definition of peacebuilding has been argued to make the concept useless as it captures just about anything that peacebuilding actors may choose to perform (Roberts, 2011a, p 8). However, I argue that the necessary interaction between service delivery, local interactions and vertical relationships demonstrates that a broad concept does not mean that the peacebuilding term is a list of activities from which we can pick and choose, but the broad definition must be considered as a whole. Although it may appear as a long stretch to analyse waste management, infrastructural developments and the issuing of construction permits as peacebuilding activities, combining these in an analysis of three interdependent peacebuilding functions shows that only by analysing the whole can we further understand local peacebuilding that moves a post-conflict context away from violence towards locally defined peace(s). As such, this book argues that peacebuilding is all encompassing, but any one piece is not peacebuilding in itself.

References

Abu-Rish, Z. (2015). Garbage politics. *Middle East Report, Winter* (MER277). Available from: http://www.merip.org/mer/mer277/garbage-politics

Abu-Rish, Z. (2016). Municipal politics in Lebanon. *Middle East Research*, 46(280).

Arandel, C., Brinkerhoff, D. W., and Bell, M. M. (2015). Reducing fragility through strengthening local governance in Guinea. *Third World Quarterly*, 36(5): 985–1006.

Atallah, S. (2011). *The Independent Municipal Fund: Reforming the Distributional Criteria*. Policy Brief, Issue 1. Beirut: Lebanese Center for Policy Studies. Available from: https://www.lcps-lebanon.org/publications/1331312295-imf-policybrief-eng.pdf

Atallah, S. (2015). *Liberate the municipal fund from the grip of politicians*. Beirut: The Lebanese Center for Policy Studies. Available from: https://www.lcps-lebanon.org/featuredArticle.php?id=52

Aziz, J. (2015). Standstill persists in Lebanon. *Al-Monitor*. 21 September. Available from: http://www.al-monitor.com/pulse/originals/2015/09/lebanon-president-vacuum-parliament-elections-christian-bloc.html

Azzi, E. (2017). *Waste Management Systems in Lebanon: The Benefits of a Waste Crisis for Improvement of Practices*. Stockholm: KTH Royal Institute of Technology.

Bachmann, J., and Schouten, P. (2018). Concrete approaches to peace: infrastructure as peacebuilding. *International Affairs*, 94(2): 381–98.

Bargués-Pedreny, P., and Randazzo, E. (2018). Hybrid peace revisited: an opportunity for considering self-governance? *Third World Quarterly*, 39(8): 1543–60.

Barnard, A. (2013). Civilians flee and soldiers die in clashes in Lebanon. *The New York Times*. 23 June. Available from: https://www.nytimes.com/2013/06/25/world/middleeast/clashes-continue-on-second-day-in-south-lebanon-city.html

Baroud, Z. (2004). *Gouvernance Locale et Réforme Institutionnelle au Liban: Les Municipalités, un outil d'innovation? Analyse et étude de cas (1998–2004)*. Governance Knowledge Sharing Program (GKSP) Policy Initiatives and Reforms in the MENA Region. Beirut: The World Bank/Lebanese Center for Policy Studies.

Baroud, Z. (2021). Decentralization in Lebanon is not neutral. Washington, DC: Middle East Institute. 5 April. Available from: https://www.mei.edu/publications/decentralization-lebanon-not-neutral

Beirut Report (2015a). Invisible garbage, visible activism. *Beirut Report*. 15 August. Available from: http://www.beirutreport.com/2015/08/invisible-garbage-visible-activism.html

Beirut Report (2015b). Lebanon's garbage crisis: a blessing in disguise? *Beirut Report*. 5 August. Available from: http://www.beirutreport.com/2015/08/lebanons-garbage-crisis-a-blessing-in-disguise.html

Bevir, M. (2009). *Key Concepts in Governance*. Thousand Oaks, CA: SAGE Publications.

Bhabha, H. K. (1994). *The Location of Culture*. New York: Routledge.

Björkdahl, A. (2013). Urban peacebuilding. *Peacebuilding*, *1*(2): 207–21.

Björkdahl, A., and Buckley-Zistel, S. (2016). Spatializing peace and conflict: an introduction, in A. Björkdahl and S. Buckley-Zistel (eds), *Spatializing Peace and Conflict: Mapping the Production of Places, Sites and Scales of Violence* (pp 1–22). Basingstoke: Palgrave Macmillan.

Björkdahl, A., and Gusic, I. (2015). 'Global' norms and 'local' agency: frictional peacebuilding in Kosovo. *Journal of International Relations and Development*, *18*(3): 265–87.

Björkdahl, A., and Höglund, K. (2013). Precarious peacebuilding: friction in global–local encounters. *Peacebuilding*, *1*(3): 289–99.

Björkdahl, A., Höglund, K., Millar, G., Lijn, J. v. D., and Verkoren, W. (2016). *Peacebuilding and Friction: Global and Local Encounters in Post Conflict-Societies*. Abingdon: Taylor & Francis.

Björkdahl, A., and Kappler, S. (2017). *Peacebuilding and Spatial Transformation: Peace, Space and Place*. Abingdon: Routledge.

Bland, G. (2007). Decentralization, local governance and conflict mitigation in Latin America, in D. W. Brinkerhoff (ed.), *Governance in Post-conflict Societies: Rebuilding Fragile States* (pp 207–25). Abingdon: Routledge.

Booth, D., and Cammack, D. (2013). *Governance for Development in Africa: Solving Collective Action Problems*. London: Zed Books.

Bou Akar, H. (2018). *For the War Yet to Come: Planning Beirut's Frontiers*. Stanford, CA: Stanford University Press.

Brancati, D. (2006). Decentralization: fuelling the fire or dampening the flames of ethnic conflict and seccesionism? *International Organization*, *60*(3): 651–85.

Brenner, N. (1999). Globalisation as reterritorialisation: the re-scaling of urban governance in the European Union. *Urban Studies*, *36*(3): 431–51.

Brinkerhoff, D. W. (2011). State fragility and governance: conflict mitigation and subnational perspectives. *Development Policy Review*, *29*(2): 131–53.

Brinkerhoff, D. W., Wetterberg, A., and Dunn, S. (2012). Service delivery and legitimacy in fragile and conflict-affected states: evidence from water services in Iraq. *Public Management Review*, *14*(2): 273.

Burgis-Kasthala, M., and Saouli, A. (2022). The politics of normative intervention and the special tribunal for Lebanon. *Journal of Intervention and Statebuilding*, *16*(1): 79–97.

C.A.I.MED. (2004). *Administrative Reform in the Mediterranean Region: Summary of Lebanon*. Center for Administrative Innovation in the Euro-Mediterranean Region. Available from: http://unpan1.un.org/intradoc/groups/public/documents/caimed/unpan019338.pdf

Cammett, M., and Issar, S. (2010). Bricks and mortar clientelism: sectarianism and the logics of welfare allocation in Lebanon. *World Politics*, *62*(3): 381–421.

Carrascal, I. H. (2020). Decentralising Lebanon: utopia or a feasible next step? *The Lebanon Papers*, (2(10): 1–20.

Castree, N., Kitchin, R., and Rogers, A. (2013). Scale, in A. Rogers, N. Castree and R. Kitchin (eds), *A Dictionary of Human Geography*. Oxford: Oxford University Press.

Causevic, S., and Lynch, P. (2011). Phoenix tourism: post-conflict tourism role. *Annals of Tourism Research*, *38*(3): 780–800.

Chaib, K. (2009). Les identités chiites au Liban-Sud: Entre mobilisation communautaire, contrôle partisan et ancrage local. *Vingtième Siècle*, *103*: 149–62.

Chandler, D. (2017). *Peacebuilding: The Twenty Years' Crisis, 1997–2017*. Cham: Springer International Publishing.

Chambers, R. (1983). *Rural Development: Putting the Last First*. London: Longman.

Cheema, G. S., and Rondinelli, D. A. (eds) (2007a). *Decentralizing Governance: Emerging Concepts and Practices*. Washington, DC: Brookings Institution Press.

Cheema, G. S., and Rondinelli, D. A. (2007b). From government decentralization to decentralized governance, in G. S. Cheema and D. A. Rondinelli (eds), *Decentralizing Governance: Emerging Concepts and Practices*. Washington, DC: Brookings Institution Press.

Clark, J. A., and Zahar, M.-J. (2015). Critical junctures and missed opportunities: the case of Lebanon's Cedar Revolution. *Ethnopolitics*, *14*(1): 1–18.

Collier, P. (2003). *Breaking the Conflict Trap: Civil War and Development Policy*. Washington, DC: World Bank and Oxford University Press.

Curle, A. (1971). *Making Peace*. London: Tavistock Publications.

Curle, A. (1994). New challenges for citizen peacemaking. *Medicine and War*, *10*(2), 96–105.

Dakroub, H. (2014a). Bleak future for Lebanon as Syria war enters fourth year. *The Daily Star*. 7 March. Available from: http://www.dailystar.com.lb/News/Analysis/2014/Mar-07/249519-bleak-future-for-lebanon-as-syria-war-enters-fourth-year.ashx#axzz34VH8IotC

Dakroub, H. (2014b). Saudi-Iranian thaw to help defuse tensions, elect president. *The Daily Star*. 16 May. Available from: http://www.dailystar.com.lb/News/Analysis/2014/May-16/256618-saudi-iranian-thaw-to-help-defuse-tensions-elect-president.ashx#axzz36Icmhp2P

Dakroub, H. (2018). Lebanon vote peaceful; turnout weak. *The Daily Star*. 7 May. Available from: http://www.dailystar.com.lb/News/Lebanon-News/2018/May-07/448320-lebanon-vote-peaceful-turnout-weak.ashx

Dakroub, H., and Lakiss, H. (2015). Cabinet OKs plan to lift country out of garbage. *The Daily Star*. 10 September. Available from: http://www.dailystar.com.lb/News/Lebanon-News/2015/Sep-10/314665-cabinet-oks-plan-to-lift-country-out-of-garbage.ashx#

de Certeau, M. (1988). *The Practice of Everyday Life*. Berkeley, CA: University of California Press.

de Coning, C. (2013). Understanding peacebuilding as essentially local. *Stability*, 2(1): 1–6.

Debiel, T., and Rinck, P. (2016). Rethinking the local in peacebuilding, in T. Debiel, T. Held and U. Schneckener (eds), *Peacebuilding in Crisis: Rethinking Paradigms and Practices of Transnational Cooperation*. Abingdon: Routledge.

Debiel, T., Held, T., and Schneckeneret, U. (2016). *Peacebuilding in Crisis: Rethinking Paradigms and Practices of Transnational Cooperation*. Abingdon and New York: Routledge.

della Porta, D. (2008). Comparative analysis: case-oriented versus variable-oriented research, in D. della Porta and M. Keating (eds), *Approaches and Methodologies in the Social Sciences* (pp 198–222). Cambridge: Cambridge University Press.

Donais, T. (2012). *Peacebuilding and Local Ownership: Post-Conflict and Consensus-Building*. New York: Routledge.

Donais, T. (2015). Bringing the local back in: Haiti, local governance and the dynamics of vertically integrated peacebuilding. *Journal of Peacebuilding and Development*, 10(1): 40–55.

Duffield, M. (2007). *Development, Security and Unending War: Governing the World of Peoples*. Cambridge: Polity Press.

Egan, M., and Tabar, P. (2016). Bourdieu in Beirut: *wasta*, the state and social reproduction in Lebanon. *Middle East Critique*, 25(3): 249–70.

El-Mikawy, N., and Melim-McLeod, C. (2010). *Lebanon: Local Governance in Complex Environments Project Assessment*. Beirut: UNDP Lebanon.

ESCWA (United Nations Economic and Social Commission for West Asia) (2021). Multidimensional Poverty in Lebanon (2019–2021): Painful reality and uncertain prospects. Policy Brief, Issue 2. Available from: https://www.unescwa.org/sites/default/files/news/docs/21-00634-_multidimentional_poverty_in_lebanon_-policy_brief_-_en.pdf

Fakhoury, T. (2009). *Democracy and Power-Sharing in Stormy Weather: The Case of Lebanon*. Wiesbaden: VS Research.

Fakhoury, T. (2018). Multi-level governance and migration politics in the Arab world: the case of Syria's displacement. *Journal of Ethnic and Migration Studies*, 45(8): 1310–26.

Färnbo, M. (2018). Skräpet som kväver Libanon. *Omvärlden*. Available from: https://omvarldenberattar.se/libanon-sopkrisen/

Fawaz, M. (2009). Hezbollah as urban planner? Questions to and from planning theory. *Planning Theory*, 8(4): 323–34.

Fawaz, M. (2014). The politics of property in planning: Hezbollah's reconstruction of Haret Hreik (Beirut, Lebanon) as case study. *International Journal of Urban and Regional Research*, 38(3): 922–34.

Fawaz, M. (2017). *Urban Policy: A Missing Government Framework*. Lebanese Center for Policy Studies featured analysis. May. Available from: http://lcps-lebanon.org/featuredArticle.php?id=116

Fawaz, M., Harb, M., and Gharbieh, A. (2012). Living Beirut's security zones: an investigation of the modalities and practice of urban security. *City and Society*, 24(2): 173–95.

Financial Times (2006). Fearful residents flee city of Tyre. 3 August. Available from: http://tinyurl.galegroup.com/tinyurl/8YfKf5

Geukjian, O. (2014). An ignored relationship: the role of the Lebanese Armenian diaspora in conflict resolution (1975–90). *Middle Eastern Studies*, 50(4): 554–67.

Geukjian, O. (2017). *Lebanon after the Syrian Withdrawal: External Intervention, Power-Sharing and Political Instability*. London and New York: Routledge.

Ghaddar, S. (2016). Machine politics in Lebanon's alleyways. New York: The Century Foundation. Available from: https://tcf.org/content/report/machine-politics-lebanons-alleyways/

Ghosn, F., and Khoury, A. (2011). Lebanon after the civil war: peace or the illusion of peace? *The Middle East Journal*, 65(3): 381–97.

Gizelis, T. I. (2011). A country of their own: women and peacebuilding. *Conflict Management and Peace Science*, 28(5): 522–42.

Grindle, M. S. (2007). *Going Local: Decentralization, Democratization, and the Promise of Good Governance*. Princeton, NJ: Princeton University Press.

Gusic, I. (2013). *Bringing Cities In: The Urbanisation of Critical Peacebuilding*. Contested Administrations Working Paper Series. Department of Political Science, Lund University.

Haddad, T. (2017). Analysing state-civil society associations relationship: the case of Lebanon. *Voluntas*, *28*(4): 1742–61.

Hameiri, S., and Jones, L. (2017). Beyond hybridity to the politics of scale: international intervention and 'local' politics. *Development and Change*, *48*(1): 54–77.

Hameiri, S., Hughes, C., and Scarpello, F. (2017). *International Intervention and Local Politics*. Cambridge: Cambridge University Press.

Hamzeh, A. N. (2001). Clientalism, Lebanon: roots and trends. *Middle Eastern Studies*, *37*(3): 167–78.

Hamzeh, A. N. (2004). *In the Path of Hizbullah*. Syracuse: Syracuse University Press.

Hancock, L. E., and Mitchell, C. R. (2018). *Local Peacebuilding and Legitimacy: Interactions between National and Local Levels*. Abingdon: Routledge.

Hanf, T. (1993). *Coexistence in Wartime Lebanon: Decline of a State and Rise of a Nation*. London: Centre for Lebanese Studies in association with I.B. Tauris.

Harb, M. (2017). Diversifying urban studies' perspectives on the city at war. *International Journal of Urban and Regional Research*, 2. Available from: https://www.ijurr.org/spotlight-on/the-city-at-war-reflections-on-beirut-brussels-and-beyond/diversifying-urban-studies-perspectives-on-the-city-at-war/

Harb, M., and Atallah, S. (2015). Lebanon: a fragmented and incomplete decentralization, in M. Harb and S. Atallah (eds), *Local Governments and Public Goods: Assessing Decentralization in the Arab World*. Beirut: The Lebanese Center for Policy Studies.

Harb, M., and Fawaz, M. (2020). *Leave No One Behind: For an Inclusive and Just Recovery Process in Post-Blast Beirut*. Beirut: UNDP Lebanon.

Hartmann, C., and Crawford, G. (eds) (2008). *Decentralisation in Africa: A Pathway Out of Poverty and Conflict?* Amsterdam: Amsterdam University Press.

Haugbolle, S. (2010). *War and Memory in Lebanon*. Cambridge: Cambridge University Press.

Hooghe, L., and Marks, G. (2002). *Multi-Level Governance and European Integration*. Lanham, MD: Rowman & Littlefield Publishers.

Horst, C. (2017). Implementing the women, peace and security agenda? Somali debates on women's public roles and political participation. *Journal of Eastern African Studies*, *11*(3): 389–407.

Hudson, H. (2012). A double-edged sword of peace? Reflections on the tension between representation and protection in gendering liberal peacebuilding. *International Peacekeeping*, *19*(4): 443–60.

Hughes, C. (2013). Friction, good governance and the poor: cases from Cambodia. *International Peacekeeping*, *20*(2): 144–58.

Hughes, C., Öjendal, J., and Schierenbeck, I. (2015). The struggle versus the song – the local turn in peace building: an introduction. *Third World Quarterly*, *36*(5): 817–24.

International Center for Transitional Justice (2013). *Lebanon's Legacy of Political Violence: A Mapping of Serious Violations of International Human Rights and Humanitarian Law in Lebanon, 1975–2008.* New York: International Center for Transitional Justice. Available from: https://www.ictj.org/publication/lebanon-legacy-political-violence

Jackson, D. (2013). Who won and who lost? The role of local governments in post-conflict recovery, in J. Öjendal and A. Dellnäs (eds), *The Imperative of Good Local Governance.* Tokyo: United Nations University Press.

John, A. W.-S., and Kew, D. (2008). Civil society and peace negotiations: confronting exclusion. *International Negotiation,* 13(1): 11–36.

Joseph, S. (1975). *The Politicization of Religious Sects in Borj Hammoud, Lebanon* (Publication Number 7527428), Columbia University: ProQuest Dissertations and Theses Global.

Kaldor, M. (1999). *New and Old Wars: Organized Violence in a Global Era.* Cambridge: Polity Press.

Kappler, S. (2012). Divergent transformation and centrifugal peacebuilding: the EU in Bosnia and Herzegovina. *International Peacekeeping,* 19(5): 612–27.

Kappler, S. (2013a). Everyday legitimacy in post-conflict spaces: the creation of social legitimacy in Bosnia-Herzegovina's Cultural Arenas. *Journal of Intervention and Statebuilding,* 7(1): 11–28.

Kappler, S. (2013b). Peacebuilding and lines of friction between imagined communities in Bosnia-Herzegovina and South Africa. *Peacebuilding,* 1(3): 349–64.

Kappler, S. (2015). The dynamic local: delocalisation and (re-)localisation in the search for peacebuilding identity. *Third World Quarterly,* 36(5): 875–89.

Kappler, S., and Richmond, O. (2011). Peacebuilding and culture in Bosnia and Herzegovina: resistance or emancipation? *Security Dialogue,* 42(3): 261–78.

Kent, S., and Barnett, J. (2012). Localising peace: the young men of Bougainville's 'crisis generation'. *Political Geography,* 31(1): 34–43.

Khalaf, S. (2002). *Civil and Uncivil Violence in Lebanon: A History of Internationalization of Communal Conflict.* New York: Columbia University Press.

Khalaf, S. (2012). *Lebanon Adrift: From Battleground to Playground.* Beirut: Saqi Books.

Khazen, F. (n.d.). *Lebanon's First Postwar Parliamentary Election, 1992: An Imposed Choice.* Created by the Digital Documentation Center at AUB in collaboration with Al Mashriq of Høgskolen i Østfold, Norway. Available from: http://almashriq.hiof.no/ddc/projects/pspa/elections92.html

Klick, M. T. (2016). The effect of state-local complementarity and local governance on development: a comparative analysis from post-war Guatemala. *World Development,* 82(1). Available from: https://search.proquest.com/docview/1777966278?accountid=11162

Kraidy, M. M. (2016). Trashing the sectarian system? Lebanon's 'You Stink' movement and the making of affective publics. *Communication and the Public*, 1(1):19–26.

Krampe, F. (2016). Empowering peace: service provision and state legitimacy in Nepal's peace-building process. *Conflict, Security and Development*, 16(1): 53–73.

Kälin, W. (2004). Decentralized governance in fragmented societies: solution or cause of new evils?, in A. Wimmer, R. J. Goldstone, D. L. Horowitz, U. Joras and C. Schetter (eds), *Facing Ethnic Conflicts: Toward a New Realism*. Lanham, MD: Rowman & Littlefield Publishers.

Lambek, M. (2011). Catching the local. *Anthropological Theory*, 11(2): 197–221.

Larkin, C. (2010). Remaking Beirut: contesting memory, space, and the urban imaginary of Lebanese youth. *City and Community*, 9(4): 414–42.

LCPS (2012). *The Role of Regional Administrations in the Context of Decentralization*. Roundtable Report Series. Beirut: Lebanese Center for Policy Studies. Available from: https://www.lcps-lebanon.org/publications/1347614622-the_role_of_regional_administrations.pdf

LCPS (2020). *Has the October 17 Revolution Accomlished Anything at All? Setting the Agenda*. Beirut: Lebanese Center for Policy Studies. Available from: https://lcps-lebanon.org/agendaArticle.php?id=197

Lederach, J. P. (1997). *Building Peace: Sustainable Reconciliation in Divided Societies*. Washington, DC: United States Institute of Peace Press.

Lee, S. Y. (2015). Motivations for local resistance in international peacebuilding. *Third World Quarterly*, 36(8): 1437–52.

Leenders, R. (2012). *Spoils of Truce: Corruption and State-Building in Postwar Lebanon*. Ithaca, NY: Cornell University Press.

Leeuwen, M. v., Verkoren, W., and Boedeltje, F. (2012). Thinking beyond the liberal peace: from Utopia to heterotopias. *Acta Politica*, 47(3): 292–316.

Leino, H., and Puumala, E. (2020). What can co-creation do for the citizens? Applying co-creation for the promotion of participation in cities. *Environment and Planning C: Politics and Space*, 39(4): 781–99.

Lemay-Hébert, N. (2009). Statebuilding without nation-building? Legitimacy, state failure and the limits of the institutionalist approach. *Journal of Intervention and Statebuilding*, 3(1): 21–45.

Lemay-Hébert, N. (ed.) (2019). *Handbook on Intervention and Statebuilding*. Cheltenham: Edward Elgar Publishing.

Leonardsson, H. (2011). Between diversity and unity: young Lebanese's visions of a legitimate social and political system 20 years after civil war. *Peace, Conflict and Development: An Interdisciplinary Journal*, 17: 102–17.

Leonardsson, H., and Rudd, G. (2015). The 'local turn' in peacebuilding: a literature review of effective and emancipatory local peacebuilding. *Third World Quarterly*, 5(36): 825–56.

Liden, K., Mac Ginty, R., and Richmond, O. P. (2009). Introduction: beyond northern epistemologies of peace – peacebuilding reconstructed? *International Peacekeeping*, 16(5): 587–98.

Lottholz, P., and Lemay-Hebert, N. (2016). Re-reading Weber, re-conceptualizing state-building: from neo-Weberian to post-Weberian approaches to state, legitimacy, and state-building. *Cambridge Review of International Affairs*, 29(4): 1467–85.

Lundqvist, M. O., and Öjendal, J. (2018). Atomised and subordinated? Unpacking the role of international involvement in 'the local turn' of peacebuilding in Nepal and Cambodia. *Journal of Peacebuilding and Development*, 13(2): 16–30.

Mac Ginty, R. (2007a). Hizbullah: a short history. *International Affairs*, 83(5): 997.

Mac Ginty, R. (2007b). Reconstructing post-war Lebanon: a challenge to the liberal peace? *Conflict, Security and Development*, 7(3): 457–82.

Mac Ginty, R. (2010a). Hybrid peace: the interaction between top-down and bottom-up peace. *Security Dialogue*, 41(4): 391–412.

Mac Ginty, R. (2010b). No war, no peace: why so many peace processes fail to deliver peace. *International Politics*, 47(2): 145–62.

Mac Ginty, R. (2013). Indicators+: a proposal for everyday peace indicators. *Evaluation and Program Planning*, 36(1): 56–63.

Mac Ginty, R. (2015). Where is the local? Critical localism and peacebuilding. *Third World Quarterly*, 36(5): 840–56.

Mac Ginty, R., and Richmond, O. P. (2013). The local turn in peace building: a critical agenda for peace. *Third World Quarterly*, 34(5): 763–83.

Macaspac, N. V., and Moore, A. (2022). Peace geographies and the spatial turn in peace and conflict studies: integrating parallel conversations through spatial practices. *Geography Compass*, 16(4), e12614.

Mackey, S. (2006). *Lebanon: A House Divided*. New York: W. W. Norton.

Mahdawi, D. (2008). Analysts link Ain al-Hilweh violence to regional issues. *The Daily Star*. 22 July. Available from: http://www.dailystar.com.lb/News/Lebanon-News/2008/Jul-22/50010-analysts-link-ain-al-hilweh-violence-to-regional-issues.ashx

Mahmood, S. (2001). Feminist theory, embodiment, and the docile agent: some reflections on the Egyptian Islamic revival. *Cultural Anthropology*, 16(2): 202–36.

Mahmood, S. (2011). *Politics of Piety the Islamic Revival and the Feminist Subject*. Princeton, NJ: Princeton University Press.

Majed, R. (2020). In defense of intra-sectarian divide: street mobilization, coalition formation, and rapid realignments of sectarian boundaries in Lebanon. *Social Forces*, 99(4): 1772–98.

Majoor, S. J. H., and Salet, W. G. M. (2008). The enlargement of local power in trans-scalar strategies of planning: recent tendencies in two European cases. *GeoJournal*, *72*(1): 91–103.

Manor, J. (ed.) (2007). *Aid That Works: Successfull Development in Fragile States*. Washington, DC: The World Bank.

Maroun, C. E. (2017). *Saida Garbage Mountain, Lebanon*. Environmental Justice Atlas. Available from: https://ejatlas.org/conflict/garbage-mountain-saida

Massena, F. (2017). Trash situation still stinks as Lebanon leans on 'temporary' landfills. *Al Monitor*. 14 November. Available from: https://www.al-monitor.com/originals/2017/11/lebanon-cabinet-asks-cdr-study-expanding-landfills.html

McCandless, E., Abitbol, E., and Donais, T. (2015). Vertical integration: a dynamic practice promoting transformative peacebuilding. *Journal of Peacebuilding and Development*, *10*(1): 1–9.

McLoughlin, C. (2015). When does service delivery improve the legitimacy of a fragile or conflict-affected state? *Governance – An International Journal of Policy and Administration*, *28*(3): 341–56.

McLoughlin, C. (2019). Non-state actors, service delivery and statebuilding, in N. Lemay-Hébert (ed.), *Handbook on Intervention and Statebuilding*. Cheltenham: Edward Elgar.

Menkhaus, K. (2006). Governance without government in Somalia: spoilers, state building, and the politics of coping. *International Security*, *31*(3): 74–106.

Mercy Corps (2014). *Policy Brief: Engaging Municipalities in the Response to the Syria Refugee Crisis in Lebanon*. Portland, OR: Mercy Corps. Available from: https://d2zyf8ayvg1369.cloudfront.net/sites/default/files/Mercy%20Corps%20Lebanon%20Policy%20Brief%20Engaging%20Municipalities%20%28English%29.pdf

Migdal, J. S. (1988). *Strong Societies and Weak States: State-Society Relations and State Capabilities in the Third World*. Princeton, NJ: Princeton University Press.

Millar, G. (2018). Decentring the intervention experts: ethnographic peace research and policy engagement. *Cooperation and Conflict*, *53*(2): 259–75.

Millar, G. (2020). Toward a trans-scalar peace system: challenging complex global conflict systems. *Peacebuilding*, *8*(3): 261–78.

Millar, G. (2021). Trans-scalar ethnographic peace research: understanding the invisible drivers of complex conflict and complex peace. *Journal of Intervention and Statebuilding*, *15*(3): 289–308.

Miller, J. (1997). *God Has 99 Names: Reporting from a Militant Middle East*. New York: Touchstone.

Milton-Edwards, B., and Hinchcliffe, P. (2008). *Conflicts in the Middle East since 1945*. Abingdon: Routledge.

Ministry of Finance (2006). *Update on the Stockholm Conference for Lebanon's Early Recovery*. Beirut: Ministry of Finance. Available from: http://www.finance.gov.lb/en-US/finance/DonorCoordination/Documents/Donor%20Coordination/Aid%20Coordination/International%20Conferences/Stockholm%20Conference%20(31%20August%202006)/Stockholm%20Conference%20for%20Lebanon's%20Early%20Recovery/Update%20on%20Stockholm%20Conf.pdf

Ministry of Interior and Municipalities (1977/2008). Municipal Act. Decree – law no. 118, Government of Lebanon and Ministry of Interior and Municipalities.

Mitchell, A. (2010). Peace beyond process? *Millennium-Journal of International Studies*, 38(3): 641–64.

Mitchell, A. (2011). Quality/control: international peace interventions and 'the everyday'. *Review of International Studies*, 37(4): 1623–45.

Mitchell, C. R., and Hancock, L. E. (2012). *Local Peacebuilding and National Peace: Interactions between Grassroots and Elite Processes*. London: Continuum.

The Monthly (2016). Saida's Municipal Elections 2016. Available from: http://monthlymagazine.com/article-desc_3928_

Moosa, Z., Rahmani, M., and Webster, L. (2013). From the private to the public sphere: new research on women's participation in peace-building. *Gender and Development*, 21(3): 453–72.

Mouly, C. (2013). The Nicaraguan Peace Commissions: a sustainable bottom-up peace infrastructure. *International Peacekeeping*, 20(1): 48–66.

Mourad, L. (2017). 'Standoffish' policy-making: inaction and change in the Lebanese response to the Syrian displacement crisis. *Middle East Law and Governance*, 9(3): 249–66.

Nagel, C., and Staeheli, L. (2015). International donors, NGOs, and the geopolitics of youth citizenship in contemporary Lebanon. *Geopolitics*, 20(2): 223–47.

Nilsson, D. (2012). Anchoring the peace: civil society actors in peace accords and durable peace. *International Interactions*, 38(2): 243–66.

Nordstrom, C. (1997). *A Different Kind of War Story*. Philadelphia: University of Pennsylvania Press.

Nucho, J. R. (2016). *Everyday Sectarianism in Urban Lebanon: Infrastructures, Public Services, and Power*. Princeton, NJ: Princeton University Press.

Öjendal, J., and Dellnäs, A. (2013). *The Imperative of Good Local Governance: Challenges for the Next Decade of Decentralization*. Tokyo: United Nations University.

Öjendal, J., and Kim, S. (2013). Reconciliation in Cambodia? Decentralization as a post-conflict strategy, in J. Öjendal and A. Dellnäs (eds), *The Imperative of Good Local Governance*. Tokyo: United Nations University Press.

Öjendal, J., Leonardsson, H., and Lundqvist, M. (2017). *Local peacebuilding: challenges and opportunities*. Stockholm: Expert Group for Aid Studies (EBA). Available from: https://eba.se/wp-content/uploads/2017/04/Local-turn-of-peacebuilding-webbversion.pdf

Osoegawa, T. (2013). *Syria and Lebanon: International Relations and Diplomacy in the Middle East*. London: I.B.Tauris.

Paffenholz, T. (2010). *Civil Society and Peacebuilding: A Critical Assessment*. London: Rienner.

Paffenholz, T. (2013). International peacebuilding goes local: analysing Lederach's conflict transformation theory and its ambivalent encounter with 20 years of practice. *Peacebuilding*, 2(1): 11–27.

Paffenholz, T. (2015a). Inclusive politics: lessons from and for the new deal. *Journal of Peacebuilding and Development*, 10(1): 84–9.

Paffenholz, T. (2015b). Unpacking the local turn in peacebuilding: a critical assessment towards an agenda for future research. *Third World Quarterly*, 36(5): 857–74.

Paffenholz, T. (2016). Peacebuilding goes local and the local goes peacebuilding, in T. Debiel, T. Held and U. Schneckener (eds), *Peacebuilding in Crisis: Rethinking Paradigms and Practices of Transnational Cooperation* (pp 210–26). Abingdon: Routledge.

Paris, R. (2010). Saving liberal peacebuilding. *Review of International Studies*, 36(2): 337–65.

Paris, R., and Sisk, T. D. (2007). Managing contradictions: the inherent dilemmas of postwar statebuilding. New York: International Peace Academy. Available from: http://www.ipinst.org/2007/11/managing-contradictions-the-inherent-dilemmas-of-postwar-statebuilding

Paris, R., and Sisk, T. D. (2009). Introduction: understanding the contradictions of postwar statebuilding, in R. Paris and T. D. Sisk (eds), *The Dilemmas of Statebuilding* (pp 1–20). London: Routledge.

Pogodda, S., Richmond, O., Tocci, N., Mac Ginty, R., and Vogel, B. (2014). Assessing the impact of EU governmentality in post-conflict countries: pacification or reconciliation? *European Security*, 23(3): 227–49.

Porter, L. (2017). Is Tyre the Mediterranean's best-kept secret? *CNN*. 25 August. Available from: https://edition.cnn.com/travel/article/mediterranean-tyre-lebanon/index.html

Ramsbotham, O. (2005). *Contemporary Conflict Resolution: The Prevention, Management and Transformation of Deadly Conflicts*. Cambridge: Polity.

Randazzo, E. (2016). The paradoxes of the 'everyday': scrutinising the local turn in peace building. *Third World Quarterly*, 37(8): 1351–70.

Randazzo, E. (2017). *Beyond Liberal Peacebuilding: A Critical Exploration of the Local Turn*. Abingdon: Routledge.

Reuters (2012). Bomb in south Lebanon restaurant injures five. *Reuters.* 23 April. Available from: https://www.reuters.com/article/us-lebanon-bomb-idUSBRE83M0CL20120423

Reuters (2016). Lebanon's trash crisis threatenes return in summer heat. *Reuters.* 29 August. Available from: https://www.reuters.com/article/us-lebanon-rubbish/lebanons-trash-crisis-threatens-return-in-summer-heat-idUSKCN1141SO

Richards, P. (2005). *No Peace, No War: An Anthropology of Contemporary Armed Conflicts.* Athens, OH: Ohio University Press.

Richmond, O. P. (ed.). (2010). *Palgrave Advances in Peacebuilding: Critical Developments and Approaches.* Basingstoke: Palgrave Macmillan.

Richmond, O. P. (2011a). Peacebuilding and critical forms of agency: from resistance to subsistence. *Alternatives: Global, Local, Political, 36*(4): 326–44.

Richmond, O. P. (2011b). *A Post-Liberal Peace.* Abingdon: Routledge.

Richmond, O. P. (2012). Beyond local ownership in the architecture of international peacebuilding. *Ethnopolitics, 11*(4): 354–75.

Richmond, O. P., and Mitchell, A. (2012). *Hybrid Forms of Peace: From Everyday Agency to Post-Liberalism.* Basingstoke: Plagrave Macmillan.

Rigual, C. (2018). Rethinking the ontology of peacebuilding: gender, spaces and the limits of the local turn. *Peacebuilding, 6*(2): 1–26.

Roberts, D. (2011a). *Liberal Peacebuilding and Global Governance: Beyond the Metropolis.* New York: Routledge.

Roberts, D. (2011b). Post-conflict peacebuilding, liberal irrelevance and the locus of legitimacy. *International Peacekeeping, 18*(4): 410–24.

Rogan, E. L. (2013). The emergence of the Middle East into the modern state system, in L. Fawcett (ed.), *International Relations of the Middle East.* Oxford: Oxford University Press.

Romeo, L. (2013). Decentralizing for development: the developmental potential of local autonomy and the limits of politics-driven decentralization reforms, in J. Öjendal and A. Dellnäs (eds), *The Imperative of Good Local Governance: Challenges for the Next Decade of Decentralization* (pp 60–89). Tokyo: United Nations University Press.

Rosanvallon, P. (2011a). *Democratic Legitimacy: Impartiality, Reflexivity, Proximity.* Princeton, NJ: Princeton University Press.

Rosanvallon, P. (2011b). The metamorphoses of democratic legitimacy: impartiality, reflexivity, proximity. *Constellations, 18*(2): 114–23.

Rose, S. (2018). Musa Sadr and the 40-year disappearance that landed Gaddafi's son in prison. *The National.* 2 September. Available from: https://www.thenational.ae/world/mena/musa-sadr-and-the-40-year-disappearance-that-landed-gaddafi-s-son-in-prison-1.766249

Safa, O. (2006). Lebanon springs forward. *Journal of Democracy, 17*(1): 22–37.

Salamey, I. (2014). *The Government and Politics of Lebanon.* Abingdon: Routledge.

Schakel, A. H., Hooghe, L., and Marks, G. (2014). Multilevel governance and the state, in S. Leibfried, E. Huber, M. Lange, J. D. Levy and J. D. Stephens (eds), *The Oxford Handbook of Transformations of the State*. Oxford: Oxford University Press.

Schneckener, U. (2016). Peacebuilding in crisis? Debating peacebuilding paradigms and practices, in T. Debiel, T. Held and U. Schneckener (eds), *Peacebuilding in Crisis: Rethinking Paradigms and Practices of Transnational Cooperation*. Abingdon: Routledge.

Scholte, J. (2014). Reinventing global democracy. *European Journal of International Relations*, 20(1): 3–28.

Schou, A. (2014). Conflict resolution attempts in self-determination disputes: the significance of local minority groups concerns in the Philippines and Sri Lanka. *Ethnic and Racial Studies*, 37(2): 302–21.

Schou, A., and Haug, M. (2005). *Desentralisation in Conflict and Post-Conflict Situations*, 139. Oslo: Norwegian Institute for Urban and Regional Research.

Scott, J. C. (1991). *Domination and the Arts of Resistance: Hidden Transcripts*. London: Yale University Press.

Siegel, A. (2021). *How Lebanese Elites Coopt Protest Discourse: A Social Media Analysis*. Policy Report. Beirut: Lebanese Center for Policy Studies.

Simangan, D. (2017). The pitfalls of local involvement: justice and reconciliation in Cambodia, Kosovo and Timor-Leste. *Peacebuilding*, 5(3): 305–19.

Sisk, T. D. (2009). Pathways of the political, in R. Paris and T. D. Sisk (eds), *The Dilemmas of Statebuilding* (pp 196–223). London: Routledge.

Sisk, T. D., and Risley, P. (2005a). *Democracy and Peacebuilding at the Local Level: Lessons Learned*. Stockholm: International IDEA (Institute for Democracy and Election Assistance).

Sisk, T. D., and Risley, P. (2005b). *Democracy and United Nations Peace-building at the Local Level: Lessons Learned*. Stockholm: International IDEA (Institute for Democracy and Election Assistance).

Spivak, G. C. (1988). Can the subaltern speak?, in C. Nelson and L. Grossberg (eds), *Marxism and the Interpretation of Culture* (pp 271–315). Chicago: University of Illinois Press.

Stel, N. (2014). Is there anything local about local governance? Decision-making in an institutional vacuum. *Maastricht School of Management blog*. 17 October. Available from: https://www.msm.nl/is-there-anything-local-about-local-governance-decision-making-in-an-institutional-vacuum/

Stel, N., and van der Molen, I. (2015). Environmental vulnerability as a legacy of violent conflict: a case study of the 2012 waste crisis in the Palestinian gathering of Shabriha, South Lebanon. *Conflict, Security and Development*, 15(4): 387–414.

Stern, M., and Öjendal, J. (2010). Mapping the security – development nexus: conflict, complexity, cacophony, convergence? *Security Dialogue*, *41*(1): 5–29.

Synaps (2020). *Grand Theft Lebanon*. Available from: https://www.synaps.network/post/lebanon-finance-economy-ponzi-bankrupt

Taslakian, P. (2016, June 2016). Curfews and human rights within the Syrian context in Lebanon. *The Peace Building in Lebanon*, 12: 1–11.

Themnér, A., and Ohlson, T. (2014). Legitimate peace in post-civil war states: towards attaining the unattainable. *Conflict, Security and Development*, *14*(1): 61–87.

Tueni, G. (1985). *Une guerre pour les autres*. Beirut: Lattes.

UNESCO (2006). UNESCO Director-General launches 'heritage alert' for the Middle East. *UNESCO News*, 11 August. Available from: https://whc.unesco.org/en/news/276/

UNESCO (2017). *World Heritage List*. Paris: United Nations. Available from: http://whc.unesco.org/en/list/

United Nations (2012). *Peace Dividends and Beyond: Contributions of Administrative and Social Services to Peacebuilding*. Paris: United Nations. Available from: http://www.un.org/en/peacebuilding/pbso/pdf/peace_dividends.pdf

World Bank (2011). *The State and Peace-Building Fund: Addressing the Unique Challenges of Fragility and Conflict*. Washington, DC: World Bank. Available from: http://siteresources.worldbank.org/EXTLICUS/Resources/511777-1240930480694/OPCFC_fragility-brochure-final-150.pdf.

World Bank (2021). Lebanon Sinking (to the Top 3). *Economic Monitor*. Spring. Washington, DC: World Bank.

Zaatari, M. (2012). Two killed, three wounded in Sidon clashes. *The Daily Star*. 11 November. Available from: https://www.dailystar.com.lb/ArticlePrint.aspx?id=194667&mode=print

Zaatari, M. (2013). Lebanese Army deploys after one killed in Sidon clashes. *The Daily Star*. 22 June. Available from: http://www.dailystar.com.lb/News/Local-News/2013/Jun-18/220785-explosions-heard-east-of-lebanons-sidon.ashx

Zaatari, M. (2018). Ain al-Hilweh to go on strike after Army ramps up security measures. *The Daily Star*. 15 November. Available from: http://www.dailystar.com.lb/News/Lebanon-News/2018/Nov-15/469212-ain-al-hilweh-to-go-on-strike-after-army-ramps-up-security-measures.ashx

Zahar, M.-J. (2005). Power sharing in Lebanon: foreign protectors, domestic peace, and democratic failure, in P. G. Roeder and D. S. Rothchild (eds), *Sustainable Peace: Power and Democracy after Covol Wars*. Ithaca, NY: Cornell University Press.

Zahar, M.-J. (2009). Liberal interventions, illiberal outcomes: the United Nations, Western powers and Lebanon, in E. Newman, R. Paris and O. Richmond (eds), *New Perspectives on Liberal Peacebuilding*. New York: United Nations University Press.

Zahar, M.-J. (2012). Norm transmission in peace - and statebuilding: lessons from democracy promotion in Sudan and Lebanon. *Global Governance*, *18*: 73–88.

Zanker, F. (2014). Legitimate representation: civil society actors in peace negotiations revisited. *International Negotiation*, *19*(1): 62–88.

Zeidan, D. (2017). Municipal management and service delivery as resilience strategies: Hezbollah's local development politics in South-Lebanon, in L. Baker, K. Kao, E. Lust and M. Lynch (eds), *Local Politics and Islamist Movements* (Vol. 27, pp 37–40). The Project on Middle East Political Science. Available from: https://www.researchgate.net/profile/Melissa_Marschall/publication/320592315_Municipal_Service_Delivery_Identity_Politics_and_Islamist_Parties_in_Turkey/links/59ef4946a6fdccd492871a9f/Municipal-Service-Delivery-Identity-Politics-and-Islamist-Parties-in-Turkey.pdf#page=38

Index

References to tables appear in **bold** type.
References to footnotes show both the
page number and the note number (97n1).

1958 crisis, Lebanon 38

A
activism/protests 44, 45, 95
actors, individual 25
actors, international 21, 118–19
actors, local 20–1, 100, 105, 139, 140, 142
 and agency 30, 108, 121
 and local governments 11, 75, 95, 106, 134
agencies, national government 116
agency, local 2, 3, 9–11
 and actors 30, 108, 121
 and local governments 9, 11, 12, 30, 143
 and vertical relationships 30, 108, 132
agency-oriented approach 8, 11
aid 13, 66, 94
Ain al-Hilweh refugee camp 51, 101
Ain el-Baal waste treatment plant 55, 115
alienation of population **16**, 17
Amal movement 45–6, 47, 111, 115
 and local interactions 81–2, 89, 96
approvals processes 68, 109–10, 119, 127
apps 99
Arab Fund 71–2
Armenian people, Bourj Hammoud 13, 48–50, 90–1, 118, 137–8
 and service delivery 64, 66, 67, 79
Armenian Revolutionary Federation (ARF) *see* Tashnag, political party
Assad, Bashar al- 43, 52
Assir, Ahmed al- 51, 97n1, 101
authoritarianism 21
authority, centralized 109
authority, exercising 29, 96, 100
autonomy
 and local governments 20, 33, 60, 110, 135, 136, 137
 and vertical relationships 29, 113, 114, 115, 116, 128

 and service delivery 20, 77
 Tyre 60, 77, 110, 116, 131–2, 135, 136, 137
 and vertical relationships 26, 108, 131–2, 133
 and local governments 29, 113, 114, 115, 116, 128

B
Barcelona 127
Bargués-Pedreny, P. and Randazzo, E. 4, 135
Beirut 35, 41
 see also Bourj Hammoud, Lebanon
Beirut River solar panel project 121
Beit al-Mamlouk, Tyre 55, 84, 85, 136
Beqaa, Bourj Hammoud 49
Berri, Nabih 46, 47, 82, 115–16
Bizri, Abdul Rahman El- 70, 96
Björkdahl, A. and Kappler, S. 11, 135, 145
Bland, G. 21
bottom-up approach 21, 23
Bourj Hammoud, Lebanon 5, 6, 12, 48–50, 137–9
 central government 61, 117–19, 137, 140
 and decentralization 124, 138
 and regulations 92–3, 96, 120, 132
 civil society 64–5
 and local interactions 91–2, 93–4, 96, 105
 and service delivery 64–5, 68, 77
 civil war, Lebanon 49, 90
 cooperation 77, 78–9, 93, 138, 139
 demographic change 49, 64
 displaced people 49, 50
 housing, social/affordable 63–4, 119
 inclusiveness 90–2, 138–9
 and minority groups 66, 137–8
 and sectarianism 77, 138–9
 and service delivery 64, 65–6, 67, 76–7, 137

162

INDEX

infrastructural developments 63, 119–20
international relationships 120–1, 124, 133
legitimacy 65, 68, 138
local interactions 90–6, 139
  and civil society 91–2, 93–4, 96, 105
  and communication 93, 94–5
  and connections, personal 91–2, 106–7
  and inclusiveness 93–4, 96
  and information, dissemination of 93, 94, 96
  and participation 89, 96, 105
  and power/influence 91, 92, 96, 105
  trust in local government 93, 94–5, 96, 106
minority groups 13, 79, 137–8
  Christians 49, 64, 66–7, 90, 91
  see also Armenian people, Bourj Hammoud
needs, local/everyday 78, 124, 137
NGOs 65, 93
personal connections 91–2, 106–7, 118
responsiveness 137, 139
sectarianism 48, 68, 77, 138–9
service delivery 61–8, 78–9, 137–8
  and civil society 64–5, 68, 77
  and inclusiveness 64, 65–6, 67, 76–7, 137
  and legitimacy, local 65, 68
  and resource availability 68, 77
  and sectarianism 65–6, 67, 68
Tashnag, political party 48–9, 50, 90, 118
tourism 118, 119
trust 67, 93, 94–5, 96, 106
vertical relationships 13, 117–24, 139
  and complementarity 119–20, 123, 124, 131, 132, 137, 140
  and development, local 118–20, 124
  and international relationships 120–1, 133
  and politics, national 117, 118
  and tourism 118, 119
waste disposal 50, 59, 61–2, 121–3
  Naameh landfill site 44, 61, 122
Brancati, D. 21
Brinkerhoff, D. W. 21
Britain 37
buildings, public
  Beit al-Mamlouk, Tyre 55, 84, 85, 136
  municipal building, Saida 100–1, 104, 106

C

Cammett, M. and Issar, S. 67
capacity, local 59, 60, 113
  and local interactions 85, 86
  and service delivery 28
    Saida 75, 76
    Tyre 55, 58–9, 60, 77, 135
  and vertical relationships 113, 115, 127, 131, 132

capitalism, global 41
Cedar Revolution 41
central government 33, 34–5, 144
  decentralization of central government
    and local governments 12, 36, 110–11, 124, 127–8, 138, 143
    and service delivery 20, 59–60, 75
    and Ta'if Agreement 34, 40
    and vertical relationships 122–3, 124
  and infrastructural developments 112–13, 119–20
  and local governments 12, 55–6
    and decentralization 12, 34, 36, 110–11, 124, 127–8, 138, 143
    and expenses, authorization of 35, 109–10
    and regulations 92–3, 96, 100, 111, 120, 127, 132
    and relationships, asymmetric 26, 27, 29–30
    and resource availability 36, 122–3, 127
    and vertical relationships 109–11, 116, 117–26, 130, 133
    and waste disposal 55, 61
  and local interactions 21, 84, 87, 88
  and permits 55, 87, 92–3
  and service delivery 17–18, 20, 35–6, 59–60, 75
  and taxation 35, 61
  and vertical relationships
    and complementarity 123, 131, 132, 137, 140
    and local governments 109–11, 116, 117–26, 130, 133
  see also Bourj Hammoud, Lebanon; Saida, Lebanon; Tyre, Lebanon; vertical relationships
centralized peacebuilding **16**, 17, 32–53
centralized system of governance 35–6, 109
Chamoun, Camille 38
Chebab, Fuad 38
Christians/Christian Maronite community 51
  Lebanon 37, 38, 39, 40, 48
  and local governments 49, 64, 66–7, 81, 90, 91
  and service delivery 64, 66–7
citizenship 63
civil society
  Lebanon 34, 35–6, 39–40, 45
  and legitimacy 103–4, 135
  and local governments
    and cooperation 74, 103, 104
    and legitimacy, local 135
    and local interactions 82–4, 86, 91–105
    and service delivery 57–8, 65, 68, 76–7, 79
  and local interactions 20–3
    and cooperation 83, 93

163

and inclusiveness 20, 93–4
and local governments 82–4, 86, 91–105
and NGOs 93–4, 106
and needs, local/everyday 57–8, 74, 76, 140, 141
and NGOs 65, 93–4, 106
and service delivery 35–6
 and local governments 57–8, 64–5, 68, 69, 75, 76–7, 79
 and needs, local/everyday 74, 75
 and waste disposal 53, 95
 see also Bourj Hammoud, Lebanon; Saida, Lebanon; Tyre, Lebanon
civil war, Lebanon 32–4, 39–40, 50–1
 Bourj Hammoud 49, 90
 and local interactions 88, 90
 Tyre 46, 81, 88, 110, 116
civil war, Syria 43, 72
clientelism 39, 41, 53, 112, 116, 126
communication 93, 94–5
community involvement 85–6
complementarity in vertical relationships 27, 29, 108, 133, 143
 Bourj Hammoud 119–20, 123, 124, 131, 132, 137, 140
 and central government 123, 131, 132, 137, 140
 Saida 125, 128, 130, 131, 132, 140
 Tyre 112, 113, 114, 115, 116, 131, 134–5, 140
conflict resolution 23, 26, 27
connections, personal 91–2, 106–7, 115, 118, 124–5, 136–7
constructivist approach 12
consumerism 41, 71, 75
cooperation 26
 and civil society 74, 103, 104
 and inclusiveness 138, 139
 and local governments 74, 103, 104
 and local interactions 83, 93
 and service delivery 77, 78–9
corruption 36
Council for Development and Reconstruction (CDR) 35, 84, 112, 113
councils, municipal *see* local governments
councils, regional 34
Cultural Heritage and Urban Development (CHUD) 55, 60, 84, 85, 112–14
Curle, A, 26

D

Debiel, T. and Rinck, P. 4
decentralization of central government
 and local governments 12, 36, 110–11, 124, 127–8, 138, 143
 and service delivery 20, 59–60, 75
 and Ta'if Agreement 34, 40
 and vertical relationships 122–3, 124

democracy 22, 37, 49, 82
 decentring of democracy 6–8
demographic change 49, 64
development, economic 40–1
 and local governments 28, 78
 and service delivery 19–20, 28, 71, 72
development, local 13
 and local governments 103, 112–13, 143
 and vertical relationships 112–13, 118–20, 124, 130, 131, 132
development assistance 53
dialogues, stakeholder 102, 105
displaced people 34, 43, 49, 50
diversity 36–45, 50, 81
Doha Agreement 43
Donais, T. 27, 85
donors, international 33, 36, 41, 42, 114–15
double standards 119, 120
drug abuse 65, 73

E

economic crisis, Lebanon 44–5, 52, 109n1, 143
education 64
elections, Lebanon 34, 38, 42, 43, 47, 53, 104, 112
 and local interactions 82, 90, 96–7
elites 9–10, 40
 elitism **16**, 17
 local 21, 22, 105
 and local governments 36, 105
 and local interactions 21, 22
 national 36, 118
 and vertical relationships 116, 118, 123n5, 124–5, 126, 128–9, 130, 131
 and sectarianism 32–3, 43, 45, 128
elites, Syrian 41
emergency/crisis situations 101–2
environmental issues 55, 62, 69, 120–1
 see also waste disposal
ethnic cleansing 49
European Union 43, 70
European Union Election Observation Mission 42
exclusion, social 21, 66, 67, 138

F

financial matters
 economic crisis 44–5, 52, 109n1, 143
 economic reform 38–9, 41
 expenses, authorization of 35, 109–10
 financial resources 35, 36, 122–3, 124–5, 127
France 37, 38
Future Movement 50
 and local interactions 96, 97
 and service delivery 73, 75
 and vertical relationships 126, 130, 141

INDEX

G
garbage factory, Saida 128
gardens, public 55, 69
gender 4, 21, 34
General Directorate of Antiquities (DGA) 84
Ghaddar, S. 130
golden age, Lebanon 38
governance, centralized 35–6, 109
governance, local 11, 13, 32–53, 136, 143
  and local governments 12, 29
  and service delivery 20, 63
  and vertical relationships 13, 108–33
governance, multi-level 5–6, 12, 24, 25, 108–33, 143
governance, trans-scalar 24–5
Guatemala 27

H
Haiti 27
Hameiri, S. and Jones, L. 24
Hamzeh, A, N, 36
Hariri, Bahia 50, 51, 124, 127, 130
Hariri, Rafiq 41, 50, 51, 73, 75, 126
Hariri, Saad 50
Hariri family 50, 51, 96, 97, 126, 128–9
Hariri Foundation 126
health/medical care 64, 76
heritage, cultural 47–8, 55–6, 70–1, 84, 85
Hezbollah 43, 47, 51–2, 111, 136
  and local interactions 81–2, 89, 96
Hezbollah-Israel war 42, 47
'home-grown' peacebuilding 1–2, 24
Horst, C. 22
housing, social/affordable 63–4, 119
humility 94
Hussein-MacMahon agreement 37
hybridity 4, 10

I
identity politics 6
impunity 40, 98
inclusiveness
  and cooperation 138, 139
  and local governments 30, 57, 60, 89, 90–2, 138–9
    and minority groups 66, 73, 76–7
    and service delivery 19, 28, 57, 66, 76–7
  and local interactions 20, 22, 81, 82, 93–4, 96
  and minority groups 73, 76–7, 137–8
    religious groups 66, 67
  and sectarianism 77, 138–9
  and service delivery
    and local governments 19, 57, 64, 65–6, 67, 76–7, 137
    and responsiveness 67, 68
  see also Bourj Hammoud, Lebanon; Saida, Lebanon; Tyre, Lebanon
independence, Lebanon 37–8

Independent Municipal Fund (IMF) 35, 122
individualism 2, 71
inflation, Lebanon 44
influence *see* power/influence
information, dissemination of 93, 94, 96, 102
infrastructural developments
  and central government 112–13, 119–20
  and local governments 63, 71–3, 75, 119–21, 130, 140
  and service delivery 36, 54, 63
    and local governments 55–8, 60, 71–3, 75, 76, 78, 140
  and vertical relationships 118–19, 120–1, 130
    and central government 112–13, 119–20
    and local governments 112–14, 116, 119–21, 132, 134–5
  see also Bourj Hammoud, Lebanon; Saida, Lebanon; Tyre, Lebanon
interactions, local 16–17, 20–3, 31, 80–108, 143
  and capacity 85, 86
  and central government 21, 84, 87, 88
  and permits 55, 87, 92–3
  and civil society 20–3
    and cooperation 83, 93
    and inclusiveness 20, 93–4
    and local governments 82–4, 86, 91–105
    and NGOs 93–4, 106
  and civil war, Lebanon 88, 90
  and democracy 22, 82
  and elections, Lebanon 82, 90, 96–7
  and elites 21, 22
  and everyday life 15–16, 21, 87–9
  and inclusiveness 20, 22, 81, 82, 93–4, 96
  and legitimacy 20, 100
  and local governments 5, 9, 21–3, 80
    and civil society 82–4, 86, 91–105
    and information, dissemination of 93, 94, 96, 102
    and life, everyday 21, 87–9
    and participation 28–9, 85, 89, 96, 98, 99, 105
    and power/influence 90–1, 92, 96, 97, 98, 99, 105
  and minority groups 20, 21, 22
  and needs, local/everyday 20, 21, 22, 105, 107
  and NGOs 85, 93, 98, 106
  and police 87, 93
  and politics, local 81–2, 84, 89, 96–9
  and power/influence 22, 29
    and local governments 90–1, 92, 96, 97, 98, 99, 105
  and religious groups 81–2, 90, 102
  and resource availability 86, 88, 93

165

and trust 83, 98
and women 20, 21, 83
see also Bourj Hammoud, Lebanon; Saida,
   Lebanon; trust in local government;
   Tyre, Lebanon
interconnectivity 15, 24–5, 135, 144
and service delivery 59, 60, 65, 78
international relationships 4, 5, 108–33
international donors 33, 36, 41, 42,
   114–15
and local governments 36, 42–3
   Bourj Hammoud 120–1, 133
   Saida 124–5, 126–7, 140
   Tyre 114–15, 132–3, 135–6
involvement, external 78, 135
Iran 39, 46
Islamic Gama'a 96
Israel 39, 46–7
Israel-Hezbollah war 42
Israel-Palestinian conflict 39, 46

J
'Jabal al-Zbeleh' waste mountain 68–9

K
Khalil, Ali Hassan 115
Klick, M. T. 27
knowledge, lack of **16**
Krampe, F. 8

L
land availability 55, 111–12, 115
law, family 38, 66, 139
law, municipal 33–4, 109, 119, 128
leaders, middle-range 23–4
League of Nations 37
Lebanese municipalities 32–53
see also Bourj Hammoud, Lebanon; Saida,
   Lebanon; Tyre, Lebanon
Lederach, John Paul 23–4, 108
legitimacy 6–8, **16**, 20
legitimacy, local 3, 13
and legitimacy, state 7, 9
and local governments 11, 100, 136, 138
   and civil society 103–4, 135
   and service delivery 28, 57, 60–3, 65,
      68, 70, 72, 75, 77–8
and local interactions 20, 100
and service delivery 54, 70, 143
   and local governments 28, 57, 60–3, 65,
      68, 70, 72, 75, 77–8
legitimacy, state 9, 17–19, 140, 141
Libya 39
life, everyday 10, 15–16, 18, 21, 87–9,
   141
life, quality of 44, 69, 128
'local' 8–12
local, indigenous 10
local, spatial 8–9
local government officials 11

local governments 5, 10–12, 28–31, 144
and actors 11, 75, 95, 106, 134
and agency 9, 11, 12, 30, 143
and authority, exercising 29, 96, 100
and autonomy 20, 33, 60, 135, 136, 137
   and vertical relationships 29, 110, 113,
      114, 115, 116, 128
and central government 55–6
and decentralization 12, 34, 36, 110–11,
   124, 127–8, 138, 143
and expenses, authorization of 35,
   109–10
and regulations 92–3, 96, 100, 111, 120,
   127, 132
and relationships, asymmetric 26, 27,
   29–30
and resource availability 36, 122–3, 127
and vertical relationships 109–11, 116,
   117–23, 133
and waste disposal 55, 61
and civil society 64–5
   and cooperation 74, 103, 104
   and legitimacy, local 103–4, 135
   and local interactions 82–4, 93, 95, 96,
      97–8, 99–101, 102–3, 104
   and service delivery 57–8, 65, 68, 76–
      7, 79
and development, economic 28, 78
and development, local 103, 112–13, 143
and elites 36, 105
and governance, local 12, 29
and inclusiveness 30, 89, 90–2, 138–9
   and minority groups 66, 73, 76–7
   and service delivery 19, 28, 57, 60,
      66, 76–7
and infrastructural developments
   and service delivery 72, 75
   and vertical relationships 112–14,
      119–21
   and international relationships 36,
      42–3, 124
and legitimacy 11, 100, 136, 138
   and civil society 103–4, 135
   and service delivery 28, 57, 60–3, 65,
      68, 70, 72, 75, 77–8
and local interactions 5, 9, 21–3, 80, 81–
   90, 96–104
   and civil society 83–4, 92–3, 95, 96, 97–
      8, 99–101, 102–3
   and everyday life 21, 87–9
   and information, dissemination of 93,
      94, 96, 102
   and NGOs 93, 98, 99, 100, 101–2, 103
   and participation 28–9, 85, 89, 96, 98,
      99, 105
and minority groups 28, 66, 73, 76–7
   and inclusiveness 66, 73, 76–7
   and religious groups 72–3, 81, 90, 91
and politics, local 73, 117–18

INDEX

and local interactions 81–2, 84, 89, 96–9, 111
and power/influence 29, 105
and reciprocity 57, 115
and responsiveness 60, 76, 88, 139
and service delivery 57–8, 59, 76
and sectarianism 34, 68, 77, 143
and service delivery 13, 54–79
  and civil society 57–8, 65, 68, 76–7, 79
  and inclusiveness 19, 28, 57, 66, 76–7
  and infrastructural developments 72, 75
  and legitimacy, local 28, 61–3, 68, 72, 75
  and needs, local/everyday 28, 73, 78
  and resource availability 35, 36, 77, 93, 122–3
  and waste disposal 69–70, 74–5
and vertical relationships 27, 29–30, 109–26, 140, 141–2, 144–5
  and autonomy 29, 113, 114, 115, 116, 128
  and central government 109–11, 116, 117, 119–26, 130
  and decentralization 122–3, 124
  and infrastructural developments 112–14, 119–21
see also Bourj Hammoud, Lebanon; Saida, Lebanon; Tyre, Lebanon; vertical relationships
'Loyalty and Development list' 96, 97

M

Mahmood, S. 22
Manash Street, Bourj Hammoud 118
March 14 movement 41, 52, 126, 141
March 8 movement 42, 52, 141
McCandless, E. 24, 26
McLoughlin, C. 65
men, young 20
Middle East, partition of 37
Migdal, J. S. 7
Millar, G. 24
Ministry of Interior and Municipalities, Lebanon 35
minority groups
  Armenian people 13, 48–50, 90–1, 118, 137–8
  and service delivery 64, 66, 67, 79
  and inclusiveness 66, 67, 73, 76–7, 137–8
  and local governments 28, 66, 73, 76–7, 90
  and local interactions 20, 21, 22
  and service delivery 19, 28, 79
  see also religious groups
Mitchell, A. 136
Mitchell, C. R. and Hancock, L. E. 26, 27, 129, 131
Mouly, C. 27

Mount Lebanon 37
Movement of the Deprived 45
municipalities, Lebanese 13, 33–5
  see also local governments
Muslims 49
  Shia Muslims 37, 38, 39, 40, 42, 52, 90
    Tyre 45–6, 47, 81, 136, 137
  Sunni Muslims 37, 38, 39, 40
    Saida 51, 52, 97, 128–9
    Tyre 48, 81

N

Naameh landfill site, Bourj Hammoud 44, 61, 122
Nabaa, Bourj Hammoud 48, 49
Nasrallah, Said Hassan 82
Nasserite movement 38, 39, 51, 96
nationalism, Lebanese 37, 38, 39
National Pact 38
needs, local/everyday
  and civil society 57–8, 74, 76, 140, 141
  and local governments 28, 73, 76, 78, 140
  and local interactions 20, 21, 22, 105, 107
  and service delivery 17, 18, 19, 20, 54–79
  and local governments 28, 73
  and vertical relationships 114, 124, 133
neglect 15, **16**
negotiators of peace 20, 21
NGOs 34
  and civil society 65, 93–4, 106
  and local interactions 85, 93
    and civil society 93–4, 106
  and local governments 93, 98, 99, 100, 101–2, 106
  and service delivery 65, 70–1, 74
Nicaragua 27
Nice, Côte d'Azur 120–1
non-state organizations 25
Nucho, J. R. 120, 124, 137

O

October revolution, Lebanon 44
Ottoman Empire 33, 37
overcrowding, Bourj Hammoud 63

P

Paffenholz, T. 85
Palestine Liberation Organization (PLO) 46, 51
pan-Arabism 37, 38, 39
participation in local interactions 20–1, 22
  and local governments 28–9, 85, 89, 96, 98, 99, 105
particularity 6–8, 9
patronage 130, 139
peacebuilding 1, 30–1, 142–5
  definitions 5–6, 15
  liberal peacebuilding 2, 3, 4, 9, 15, 41

167

failures of 10, 16–17, 30
  see also autonomy; central government; centralized peacebuilding; complementarity in vertical relationships; inclusiveness; interactions, local; legitimacy, local; liberal peacebuilding; local governments; responsiveness; service delivery, local; vertical relationships
pedestrian street, Tyre 85–7, 89, 136
permits 55, 87, 92–3
place, material 11
place-making 135
police, municipal 58–9, 87, 93, 100
politics, local/municipal 73, 117–18
  and local interactions 81–2, 84, 89, 96–9, 111
politics, national *see* Amal movement; central government; civil war, Lebanon; elections, Lebanon; Future Movement; Hezbollah; local governments; power/influence; sectarianism; Tashnag, political party; vertical relationships
Popular Nasserist Organization (PNO) 50, 51
'Popular Will' list 96, 97
Port of Beirut explosion 33, 44, 50
poverty 44, 63, 76
powerholders, local 11
power/influence
  and local governments 29
    and local interactions 90–1, 92, 96, 97, 98, 99, 105
  and local interactions 22, 105–6
  sectarian 32–3, 38
  and vertical relationships 25–6, 27, 29, 116–17
power-sharing 32, 38, 39, 40, 49
practices, everyday 10
priorities, everyday 8
private sector 35
Project Manager Unit, CDR 113
public-private partnerships 34
public spaces, enhancement of 56–7, 72
puppetry 11, 60

Q
Qada (districts) 33, 34, 35

R
Ramsbotham, O. 26
Randazzo, E. 4
Ras el-Ain landfill site, Tyre 55
reciprocity 57, 115
reconstruction, post-war 34, 40–1, 42
refugees 51
  Armenian 48, 50
  Syrian 43, 48, 50, 58, 63
regulations 92–3, 96, 100, 111, 120, 127, 132

relationships, asymmetric 26, 27, 29–30
religious groups 37–8, 39, 40, 42, 48
  and inclusiveness 66, 67
  and local governments 48, 51, 72–3, 81–2, 90, 102, 137
  and local interactions 81–2, 90, 102
  see also Christians/Christian Maronite community; Muslims
representation, elected 27
resource availability
  and central government 36, 122–3, 127
  financial 35, 36, 122–3, 124–5, 127
  human 35, 36
  and local governments 35, 36, 68, 77, 93, 122–3
  and local interactions 86, 88, 93
  and vertical relationships 111–12, 122–3, 124–5, 127
responsiveness
  and local governments 57–8, 59, 60, 76, 88, 139
  and service delivery 19, 57–8, 59, 76
  and inclusiveness 67, 68
restaurant owners 86
Rigual, C. 3
Roberts, D. 8, 18, 78, 128
Romeo, L. 136
Rosanvallon, P. 6–7, 8

S
Saad, Maarouf 39, 50
Sadr, Musa 45–6, 49
safety, public 58–9
Saida, Lebanon 5, 6, 50–2, 140–2
  and central government 100, 124–6, 127, 130, 133, 140
  Future Movement 50
  and local interactions 96, 97
  and service delivery 73, 75
  and vertical relationships 126, 130, 141
  infrastructural developments 71–3, 130, 140
  legitimacy 70, 72, 75, 100, 140, 141
  local interactions 96–104, 107
    buildings, public 100–1, 104, 106
    civil society 97–8, 99–101, 102–3, 104
    and elections, Lebanon 96–7, 104
    and Future Movement 96, 97
    and Hariri family 96, 97
    and NGOs 98, 99, 100, 101–2, 106
    and participation 98, 99, 105
    and politics 81–2, 96–9
    and power/influence 96, 97, 98, 99, 105
    and trust 98, 100–1, 102, 106
  needs, local/everyday 74, 107, 133, 140, 141
  NGOs 70–1
    and local interactions 98, 99, 100, 101–2, 106

politics, local 73, 81–2, 96–9
  Hariri family 50, 51, 96, 97, 126, 128–9
  Hezbollah 51–2, 96
  Saad family 39, 50
quality of life 69, 128
religious groups 12, 51, 72–3, 102
  Muslims 51, 52, 97, 128–9, 130
resource availability 77, 124–5, 127
sectarianism 70, 128–9, 141–2
service delivery 68–75, 77, 78, 79, 102–4, 140, 141–2
  and capacity 75, 76
  and consumerism 71, 75
  Future Movement 73, 75
  and infrastructural developments 71–3, 140
  and waste disposal 68–70, 74
vertical relationships 14, 124–30, 132, 133
  and capacity 127, 132
  and central government 124–6, 130, 133
  and complementarity 125, 128, 130, 131, 132, 140
  and elites, national 124–5, 126, 128–9, 130
  and financial resources 124–5, 127
  and Future Movement 126, 130, 141
  and Hariri family 126, 128–9
  and international relationships 124–5, 126–7, 140
  and resources, financial 124–5, 127
  and sectarianism 128–9, 141
waste disposal 69–70, 74, 128
Saudi Arabia 41, 42
sectarianism 37–8, 53
  and elites 32–3, 43, 45, 128
  and inclusiveness 77, 138–9
  and local governments 34, 68, 143
    Bourj Hammoud 48, 68, 77, 138–9
    Saida 70, 128–9, 141–2
    Tyre 48, 83, 116, 136, 137
  and local interactions 83, 102
  power-sharing, sectarian 38, 40
  sectarian power/influence 32–3, 38
  and service delivery 36, 65–6, 67, 68, 70, 141–2
  and vertical relationships 116, 123n5, 128–9, 141
service delivery, local 5, 13, 15–20, 31, 54–79
  and autonomy 20, 77
  and capacity 28
    and local governments 55, 58–9, 60, 75, 76, 77, 135
  and central government 17–18, 35–6
  and decentralization 20, 59–60, 75
  and Christians 64, 66–7
  and civil society 35–6
    and local governments 57–8, 64–5, 68, 76–7, 79
  and needs, local/everyday 74, 75
  and waste disposal 53, 95
  and cooperation 77, 78–9
  and development, economic 19–20, 28, 71, 72
  and Future Movement 73, 75
  and gardens, public 55, 69
  and governance, local 20, 63
  and health/medical care 64, 76
  and inclusiveness
    and local governments 19, 57, 64, 65–6, 67, 76–7, 137
    and responsiveness 67, 68
  and infrastructural developments 36, 54, 63
    and local governments 55–8, 60, 71–3, 75, 76, 78, 140
  and interconnectivity 59, 60, 65, 78
  and involvement, external 78, 135
  and legitimacy 17–19, 54, 70, 143
    and local governments 28, 61–3, 65, 68, 72, 75
  and local governments 13, 28, 57–60, 78–9, 89
    and capacity 55, 58–9, 60, 75, 76, 77, 135
    and civil society 57–8, 65, 68, 76–7, 79
    and inclusiveness 19, 28, 57, 64, 65–6, 67, 76–7, 137
    and infrastructural developments 55–8, 60, 71–3, 75, 76, 78, 140
    and legitimacy, local 28, 61–3, 68, 72, 75
    and needs, local/everyday 28, 73, 78
    and responsiveness 57–8, 59, 76
    and waste disposal 69–70, 74–5
  and minority groups 19, 28, 79
    Armenian people 64, 66, 67, 79
  and needs, local/everyday 17, 18, 19, 20, 28, 54–79
  and NGOs 65, 70–1, 74
  and responsiveness 19
    and inclusiveness 67, 68
    and local governments 57–8, 59, 76
  and sectarianism 36, 65–6, 67, 68, 70, 141–2
  and waste disposal 44
    and civil society 53, 95
    and local governments 54, 61–70, 74–5, 128
  see also Bourj Hammoud, Lebanon; Saida, Lebanon; Tyre, Lebanon
service provision see service delivery, local
Shkair, Walid 43
Siniora, Fouad 50, 124, 127, 130
social issues 73
solar panel water heating project, Bourj Hammoud 119–20
South Lebanese Army 46

sovereignty, Lebanese 32, 41
space, imaginary 3, 11
space, public 55, 56, 69, 72
space-making 3, 135
Special Tribunal for Lebanon (STL), UN 42, 43
state building 17–18
Stockholm Conference for Lebanon's Early Recovery 42
subaltern 10
Sukleen, waste disposal company 61
Sykes-Picot agreement 37
Syria 37, 39, 40–2, 47
  civil war 43, 72
  refugees 43, 48, 50, 58, 63

T

Ta'if Peace Agreement 32, 34, 40, 110, 116, 122–3, 143
Tashnag, political party 48–9, 50, 90, 118
taxation 35, 61
terrorists 51
Themnér, A. and Ohlson, T. 8
theoretical approach 12–13, 15–31
top-down approach 135
tourism 71
  Bourj Hammoud 118, 119
  Tyre 48, 56, 78, 86, 134
trade unions 39
transparency 34, 91
trans-scalarity 3, 24–5
Tripoli 35
trust (generally) 83, 98
trust in local government 26, 57, 67
  and local interactions 29
    Bourj Hammoud 93, 94–5, 96, 106
    Saida 98, 100–1, 102, 106
    Tyre 85, 86–7, 88, 89
Tyre, Lebanon 5, 6, 12, 13, 45–8, 134–7
  autonomy 60, 77, 110, 116, 131–2, 135, 136, 137
  buildings, public 55, 84, 85, 136
  civil society 82–4, 86, 135
  civil war, Lebanon 46, 81, 88, 110, 116
  development, local 13, 78, 112–13, 132
  elections, Lebanon 82, 112
  heritage, cultural 47–8, 55–6, 84, 85
  inclusiveness 57, 60, 76–7, 81, 82, 89
  infrastructural developments 85–6
    and service delivery 55–8, 60, 76, 78
    and vertical relationships 116, 132, 134–5
  land availability 55, 111–12, 115
  legitimacy 57, 60–1, 135, 136
  local interactions 81–90, 105
    Beit al-Mamlouk, Tyre 84, 85
    and capacity 85, 86
    and central government 84, 87, 88
    and civil society 82–4, 86
    and heritage, cultural 84, 85
    and inclusiveness 81, 82
    and participation 85, 105
    and pedestrian street 85–7, 89, 136
    and politics, local 81–2, 84, 89
    and resource availability 86, 88
    and trust 83, 85, 86–7, 88, 89
  needs, local/everyday 60, 114, 136
  personal connections 115, 136–7
  police, municipal 58–9, 87
  and politics, local
    Amal movement 45–6, 47, 81–2, 89, 111, 115
    Hezbollah 81–2, 89, 111, 136
    and local interactions 81–2, 84, 89
  reciprocity 57, 115
  religious groups 81–2
    Muslims 45–6, 47, 48, 81, 136, 137
  sectarianism 48, 83, 116, 136, 137
  service delivery 55–61, 89, 134–5
    and capacity 55, 58–9, 60, 77, 135
    and cooperation 77, 83
    and infrastructural developments 55–8, 60, 76, 78
    and interconnectivity 60, 78
    and involvement, external 78, 135
    and resource availability 77, 86, 88
    and responsiveness 60, 76
  tourism 48, 56, 78, 86, 134
  trust 57, 67
    and local interactions 83, 85, 86–7, 88, 89
  vertical relationships 109–17
    and agency, local 132
    and autonomy 131
    and capacity 113, 115, 131
    and clientelism 112, 116
    and complementarity 112, 113, 114, 115, 116, 131, 134–5, 140
    and development, local 112–13, 132
    and infrastructural developments 116, 132, 134–5
    and international relationships 114–15, 132–3, 135–6
  waste disposal 55, 115

U

UNESCO 47–8, 114
UN-Habitat 55, 115
UN Independent Investigative Commission (UNIIC) 42
UN Interim Force in Lebanon (UNIFIL) 42, 46
United Nations Development Programme (UNDP) 43, 118
United States 38, 42
UN Security Council 41, 46
urbanization, Lebanon 34

INDEX

V
vegetable market, Tyre 56–7
vertical relationships 16–17, 108–33
  and agency 30, 108, 132
  and autonomy 26, 108, 131–2, 133
    and local governments 29, 113, 114, 115, 116, 128
  and capacity 113, 115, 127, 131, 132
  and central government
    and complementarity 123, 131, 132, 137, 140
    and local governments 109–11, 116, 117, 119–26, 130, 133
  and clientelism 112, 116, 126
  and conflict resolution 23, 26, 27
  and development, local 112–13, 118–20, 124, 130, 131, 132
  and elites, national 116, 118, 123n5, 124–5, 126, 128–9, 130, 131
  and financial resources 122–3, 124–5, 127
  and governance, local 13, 108–33
  and infrastructural developments 118–19, 120–1, 130
    and central government 112–13, 119–20
    and local governments 112–14, 116, 119–21, 132, 134–5
  and international relationships
    Bourj Hammoud 120–1, 133
    Saida 124–5, 126–7, 140
    Tyre 114–15, 132–3, 135–6
  and local governments 27, 29–30, 109–24, 144–5
    and autonomy 29, 113, 114, 115, 116, 128
    and central government 109–11, 116, 117–26, 130
    and decentralization 122–3, 124
    and infrastructural developments 112–14, 119–21
    Saida 124–6, 140, 141–2
  and needs, local/everyday 114, 124, 133
  and personal connections 115, 118, 124–5, 136–7
  and politics 117, 118, 129, 131
    and Future Movement 126, 130, 141
  and power/influence 25–6, 27, 29, 116–17
  and resource availability 111–12, 122–3, 124–5, 127
  and sectarianism 116, 123n5, 128–9, 141
  and theoretical approach 23–8, 31
  and waste disposal 115, 130
  see also Bourj Hammoud, Lebanon; complementarity in vertical relationships; Saida, Lebanon; Tyre, Lebanon
violence, prevention of 15

W
Walid, Prince 128
waste disposal 44
  and central government 55, 61
  and civil society 53, 95
  and environmental issues 62, 69
  and service delivery 44
    civil society 53, 95
    local governments 54, 55, 61–70, 74–5, 94–5, 128
  and vertical relationships 115, 130
wastewater plant, Bourj Hammoud 120–1
wastewater plant, Tyre 109–10
water supplies 59–60
welfare provision 67
window frames 93
women 20, 21, 83
World Bank 44–5, 112, 114

Y
young people 20

Z
zones of peace, local 24, 27, 131

www.ingramcontent.com/pod-product-compliance
Lightning Source LLC
Chambersburg PA
CBHW071708020426
42333CB00017B/2187